CRITICAL ISSUES IN SOCIAL JUSTICE

Series Editor: **Melvin Lerner**, *University of Waterloo, Waterloo, Ontario, Canada*

Advisory Editors:
Ronald C. Dillehay, *Grant Sawyer Center for Justice Studies, University of Nevada, Reno, Nevada*
Leo Montada, *Center for Justice Research, University of Potsdam, Potsdam, Germany*

A Continuation Order Plan is available for this series. A continuation order will bring delivery of each new volume immediately upon publication. Volumes are billed only upon actual shipment. For further information please contact the publisher.

Values, Achievement, and Justice

Studies in the Psychology of Deservingness

Norman T. Feather

The Flinders University of South Australia
Adelaide, Australia

Kluwer Academic/Plenum Publishers
New York • Boston • Dordrecht • London • Moscow

ISBN: 0-306-46155-2

© 1999 Kluwer Academic / Plenum Publishers
233 Spring Street, New York, N.Y. 10013

10 9 8 7 6 5 4 3 2 1

A C.I.P. record for this book is available from the Library of Congress

For Daryl and Mark again

Preface

When we say that a person deserves a positive or negative outcome, we are making a judgment that is influenced by a number of variables. We would certainly take into account whether the person was responsible for the outcome or whether the outcome could be attributed to other sources. We would also consider whether the actions that led to the positive or negative outcome were actions that we would value or actions that would meet with our disapproval. We might also be influenced by the person's own positive or negative characteristics, by our knowledge of what kinds of groups or social categories the person belonged to, and by whether we like or dislike the person. Information about these different variables has to be considered and integrated in some way, and our judgment of deservingness follows that psychological process, a process that involves the cognitive-affective system.

Values, Achievements, and Justice is about deservingness and about the variables that affect the judgments we make. I use the term "deservingness" although I could equally have referred to "deservedness" or "desert." The terms are all virtually equivalent in meaning, although dictionaries may separate them by using fine distinctions. I assume that the sorts of variables I have just described will affect our judgments of deservingness, and I further assume that a judgment of deservingness is most likely to occur when these variables fit together in a consistent, harmonious, and balanced way.

This book may be seen as forging links between concepts and theoretical approaches that come from social psychology, the psychology of motivation and emotion, cognitive psychology, and the psychology of personality, as well as conceptual analyses that have been presented by legal theorists and philosophers. I make no claim to be an expert as it concerns the latter disciplines. It is clear, however, that legal concepts such as mitigation, justification, responsibility, deservingness, and blameworthiness are relevant to the way we judge outcomes, not only in regard to outcomes that relate to other persons but also for outcomes that relate to ourselves. They have a place in the psychological literature. In an important sense, therefore, this book attempts to span different disciplines, bringing in variables and theoretical ideas that will clarify how judgments of deservingness are determined at the psychological level.

The first part of the book is mainly concerned with clearing some conceptual ground. I consider the meaning of deservingness and responsibility and describe how these concepts have been discussed and differentiated in the relevant literature. I then move on to an analysis of the concept of value, to a description of the content and structure of the domain of values, and to a consideration of how our values affect the way we construe specific actions and outcomes in terms of their attractiveness and aversiveness or, to use more technical terms, their positive and negative valence. Research findings are presented that support the linkage between the general values people hold and the valences of specific actions and outcomes within defined contexts.

I then present a structural model of deservingness that relates a person's judgments of another's deservingness for an outcome to the other's perceived responsibility for the action and its outcome, to the person's positive or negative evaluations of the action and the outcome, and to like/dislike and ingroup/outgroup relations between the person who is judging and the other being judged. I assume that the relations between elements within this structural model tend toward a state of harmony or balance in Heider's sense of this term and that judgments of deservingness or undeservingness will tend to occur when, under conditions of perceived responsibility, a person's evaluations of the other's action and contingent outcome are balanced or unbalanced respectively. Relations between person and other are then assumed to moderate these judgments, with maximum deservingness occurring when all parts of the total structure of relations are balanced.

The second part of the book presents studies from my research program that relate to this model and test its implications in two different types of context—one where positive or negative outcomes (successes or failures) occur in achievement-related situations, the other where negative outcomes (penalties) occur within the context of retributive justice. The latter studies concern how people react to the perpetrators of offenses and the penalties that are imposed on them. They test a social-cognitive process model that includes deservingness as a key variable. I also present the results of studies that investigate the effects of like/dislike relations between person and other, the effects of shared or different social identities, and the effects of differences in the perceived moral character of the other person on reactions to the other's positive or negative outcome.

The final chapter presents a summary of the main contributions made in regard to the theoretical analysis and the research program, bringing out the distinctive features, and it also indicates possible further extensions relating both to theory and future research.

Throughout the book I try to demonstrate how theory generates research and how findings from empirical studies feed back into theory. It will be evident that the theoretical approach I propose explicitly considers both person and situation variables, together with their interaction. In that way my theoretical approach owes a debt to Lewin. It also focuses attention on the important role that values play as influences on the way we evaluate actions and outcomes, whether these actions and outcomes relate to others or to self. I am committed to the view that values and justice variables have an important place in social psychology, influencing the attitudes that we hold and the way that we react both cognitively and affectively to events and outcomes in the social world.

In presenting the results of studies from my research program, I have borrowed liberally from articles that have been published in the *Australian Journal of Psychology*, the *British Journal of Social Psychology*, the *Journal of Personality and Social Psychology*, the *European Journal of Social Psychology*, the *Journal of Applied Social Psychology*, and *Advances in Experimental Social Psychology*. I thank the editors and reviewers for their comments on the initial versions of these articles. This book presents these studies as a coherent and cumulative body of research that is unified by a common set of theoretical ideas.

Many people have contributed to this research, not the least of whom are the participants in each of the studies who were willing to give time to complete the questionnaires. I thank them for their assistance. I also thank my students Leanne Atchison, Sara Dawson, Nick Deverson, Margaret Norman, and Deanna Oberdan, who joined with me in some of the studies. I also wish to thank Ian McKee, my research assistant, for his efforts in data analysis and for his thoughtful contributions in discussions with me. Carol McNally, Joan White, and Kay Douglas have my special thanks for sharing the typing of the manuscript with efficiency and good humor.

Finally, I am indebted to the Australian Research Council for providing funds to support the research that is brought together in this book.

Contents

Values, Achievement, and Justice
Studies in the Psychology of Deservingness

CHAPTER 1

Introduction and Overview

This book is about deservingness—how deservingness is defined, how it can be analyzed in terms of other variables, and how judgments of deservingness affect the way people react both in terms of the way they feel and the actions that they take. It describes a program of studies in which these issues are examined. These studies cover a wide territory and they include both experimental studies and investigations that rely upon specially designed scales and questionnaires. Those who participated in the studies came from many different walks of life, and they include samples of participants drawn from the general population as well as samples of university students.

JUDGMENTS OF DESERVINGNESS

I have focused on deservingness in the belief that it is a key variable not only in justice research but also in social psychology more generally. Our judgments of deservingness are not only involved in the way we perceive the justice of events and outcomes, they also influence many of the attitudes that we hold and how we behave toward others. Beliefs about deservingness are also a part of how we construe self in particular situations, perceiving outcomes that relate to ourselves as either deserved or undeserved.

Thus, in everyday life we might say that a student deserves or does not deserve the grade that he or she obtained on an examination, that a politician deserved or did not deserve to be reelected, that the perpetrator of an offense deserved or did not deserve the penalty imposed by the court, that a business executive deserved or did not deserve the considerable fortune that he or she amassed, or that a high-profile sports identity deserved or did not deserve the victory or defeat that followed a contest.

1

We also extend our reactions to the group and organizational levels. We might say that a political party deserved to be defeated in an election, or that a company deserved its success in the world of commerce, or that a sporting team deserved to fail in view of its poor performance.

Further, in addition to judging the deservingness of others, we also judge ourselves and hold beliefs that we deserve or do not deserve particular outcomes that have occurred in the course of our lives.

POSITIVELY AND NEGATIVELY VALUED ACTIONS AND OUTCOMES

What is noticeable in all of these examples is that the deservingness judgment is applied to some outcome that can either be positive (as with a success or achievement) or negative (as with a failure or defeat). The outcome has positive or negative subjective value in relation to the person making the judgment. It is not a neutral outcome but rather an outcome that engages a person's system of values. Neutral or unimportant outcomes that occur in the flow of behavior and experience without much personal involvement are unlikely to elicit judgments of deservingness. We do not say that a person deserved or did not deserve an outcome in cases where the outcome has no positive or negative value. The outcome has to be sufficiently important so that it engages our values, leading to a judgment that a particular outcome is good or bad, positive or negative.

The examples that were provided also suggest that the outcomes that occur are usually the product of a person's own behavior. The student prepared for the examination and was awarded a particular grade; the politician conducted a campaign and engaged in other election strategies prior to the election; the business executive took a leading role in developing the company and in promoting its products; the sporting team prepared for the contest by engaging in practice sessions. Alternatively, the student might fail to study hard for the examination; the politician might conduct a slack electioneering campaign; the business executive might amass a fortune by shady practices; the sporting team might show little commitment to developing the skills that are necessary to succeed in competition.

These examples imply a further important point, namely, that the behavior that leads to an outcome may also have positive or negative value. We also assign subjective value to the way people behave. Their actions may engage our values, leading to a judgment that a particular · action is good or bad, positive or negative. Thus, an honest action is seen as better than a dishonest action; courage in the face of adversity is preferred to cowardice or negatively valued disengagement from a threatening event.

As we will see in a subsequent chapter, it is important to take account of the subjective values (positive or negative) assigned both to actions and their outcomes because the relation between these separable evaluations has implications for the way we judge deservingness. Positively valued outcomes that follow positively valued actions are generally perceived to be deserved. So are negatively valued outcomes that follow negatively valued actions. A student is seen to deserve a high grade (positively valued) if he or she worked hard for it (positively valued); a business executive is seen to deserve dismissal (negatively valued) if he or she behaved dishonestly (negatively valued).

In contrast, positively valued outcomes that follow negatively valued actions are generally seen to be undeserved. So are negatively valued outcomes that follow positively valued actions. A business executive is seen not to deserve promotion and other benefits (positively valued) if he or she achieved the success by dishonest behavior (negatively valued); a student is seen not to deserve a low grade (negatively valued) if he or she worked hard in preparing for the examination (positively valued).

The way in which positive or negative evaluations of actions and outcomes combine is assumed to be a potent determinant of the way we judge deservingness. The analysis of deservingness will need to take account of actions and their outcomes and how these actions and outcomes are evaluated. This focus acknowledges the intimate connection between values and beliefs about justice. A basic point to be made in this book is that the psychology of deservingness must give careful consideration to how our values influence our judgments of deservingness.

This analysis will lead us into a consideration of the role of personally held values and how they affect the way people construe situations in which actions are instrumental to achieving outcomes. More generally, such an analysis will be relevant to the wider question of what determines whether objects and events are seen as attractive or aversive, or as having positive valence or negative valence, to use Kurt Lewin's (1938) terminology.

CAUSAL ATTRIBUTIONS
AND PERCEIVED RESPONSIBILITY

It would be too simple, however, to restrict the analysis of deservingness to consideration of action-outcome events and the role that values play. Judgments of deservingness also presume that some causal analysis has occurred in regard to what factors produced the outcome. Did the student obtain a high grade in the examination because he or she studied hard or because the examination paper contained very easy questions? Was the business executive successful because of his or her own efforts or because external economic conditions suddenly improved? Did the sporting team fail in competition because its members failed to practice consistently or because it was completely outclassed in terms of its ability? These kinds of questions raise the basic issue of how people attribute causality for events and outcomes. The analysis of deservingness also has to take these causal attributions into account.

In particular, it will be argued that the degree to which a person is seen to be responsible for an action that leads to an outcome is an important variable that affects judgments of deservingness. This perceived responsibility may be related to the nature of the causal attributions that people make for events and outcomes (e.g., Shaver, 1985; Weiner, 1995), and to how they make sense of events and outcomes in terms of their beliefs about causality. A person's responsibility for an event or outcome has been recognized as a key variable in the justice literature (e.g., Hart, 1968), especially in regard to the nature of an offense (e.g., murder versus manslaughter) and its implications for the level of penalty to be imposed. Perceived responsibility has also been subjected to a lot of conceptual analysis as well as empirical investigation by psychologists (e.g., Fincham & Jaspars, 1980; Hamilton & Sanders, 1992; Heider, 1958; Schlenker, Britt, Pennington, Murphy, & Doherty, 1994; Shultz & Schleifer, 1983; Weiner, 1995). We will return to some of the details of these discussions in a later chapter.

For the moment it is sufficient to accept that attributions of responsibility vary and these attributions will affect judgments of deservingness. In some cases a person may be deemed to be not responsible for an outcome. Instead, the outcome is attributed to other causes that are external to the person and beyond his or her control. For example, the success of a company may be attributed to improved economic conditions, and a manager within the company may be seen to bear little responsibility for the company's better performance; a student may be perceived as not responsible for failing an examination when it was clear that he or she could not study because of serious illness. In the latter case we might also say that the student could not be blamed for the failure, raising the question of how judgments of blame relate to attributions of responsibility (Shaver, 1985).

In other cases a person may be held responsible for an action and its outcome. For example, a student whose high grade could be attributed to hard work rather than to an easy examination would be seen as responsible for the achievement; a polician who made serious misjudgments about policy issues and who failed to be reelected would be seen as responsible for the failure. In these cases what happened would be seen as a product of the person's own behavior that was under his or her control. The outcome was contingent or depended upon what the person did. It flowed from the person's actions.

In general, people are seen not to deserve outcomes for which they are not responsible. For example, a sick student would be judged not to deserve the low grade he or she obtained on an examination. The low grade occurred because the student was ill and could not study. However, the obverse is not the case. The situation is more complicated. People can certainly be seen to deserve outcomes for which they are responsible. For example, a hard-working student would be judged to deserve the good grade he or she obtained on the examination. But people can also be seen not to deserve outcomes for which they are responsible. For example, an entrepreneur who made a fortune by shady deals would be judged not to deserve that outcome.

Thus, deservingness and perceived responsibility are not in a one-to-one relation. As we have already seen, other variables that relate to how actions and outcomes are evaluated also affect judgments of deservingness in addition to the effects of perceived responsibility.

OTHER VARIABLES AFFECTING DESERVINGNESS

So far I have argued that judgments of deservingness will be related to evaluative appraisals of actions and outcomes and also to a person's perceived responsibility for the action that led to the outcome. We can add further variables to the list that might be expected to affect whether we judge a person's positive or negative outcome to be deserved or undeserved. One set of variables relates to the quality of the person. Is he or she of good moral character? Is the person arrogant? Can the person be described as having high integrity? These variables that relate to the individual are also evaluative in nature, and generally they may be seen as being derived from knowledge about how the person behaves based on actual observation or some other more indirect information about the person. We might expect that judgments of deservingness will be more favorable when the person being judged is evaluated positively rather than negatively.

A second set of variables relates to possible interpersonal relations between the person who is making the judgment of deservingness and the other person who is being judged. Is the person liked or disliked? We might expect that positive or negative attitudes between one person and another would have some effect on judgments of deservingness so that people will tend to bias their judgments in the direction of favoring or supporting someone whom they like and show an opposite, negative bias toward someone whom they dislike.

A third set of variables relates to the social identity of the person making the judgment and the other who is being judged. Do they share a common social identity? For example, do they both belong to the same ingroup? Or are their social identities quite separate? For example, does the other person belong to an outgroup in relation to the person who is making the judgment of deservingness? As was the case for like/dislike relations, we might expect that shared or disparate social identities would influence judgments of deservingness so that, for example, a member of an ingroup is favored or supported and an opposite, negative bias is shown toward a member of an outgroup.

These different sets of variables (personality or character attributes, interpersonal attitudes, ingroup/outgroup relations) are expected to have effects on judgments of deservingness that combine with and sometimes moderate the effects of action/outcome evaluations and perceived responsibility that have already been described. The relative importance of these different variables will be discussed in the context of studies to be described in a later chapter.

Finally, it is important to recognize that judgments of deservingness occur in a social context that involves social norms and beliefs about rights and obligations and about behaviors that are socially acceptable or unacceptable. There are normative prescriptions and codified systems of laws that define what people are entitled to and what is permitted or not permitted. These prescriptions may be quite general, applying to all members of a society, or they may be associated with social roles, stereotyped beliefs, and assumptions about how people should live their lives (Lerner, 1987). These normative prescriptions may vary from group to group and from culture to culture. They form part of a person's overall belief system that is not only based on experience with the social environment but is also tied in various ways to the values the person holds (Rokeach, 1973).

RELATION TO OTHER APPROACHES

How do the ideas about deservingness that I have presented relate to other discussions in the literature? I begin with a dictionary definition of "deserve" from the *Oxford English Dictionary*.

> To acquire or earn a rightful claim, by virtue of actions or qualities ...
> to become entitled to or worthy of (reward or punishment, esteem or
> disesteem, position, designation, or any specified treatment).

The dictionary also provides a further definition that takes account of
negative actions:

> To have acquired, and thus to have, a rightful claim; to be entitled to,
> in return for services or meritorious actions, or sometimes for ill
> deeds and qualities.

Note that these two definitions relate "deserve" to both actions and
qualities and that they also refer to entitlements.

But how is the concept of deservingness defined and used in psychological discussions and in social and legal theory? In the next two
sections I will review some contributions that come from these two
areas. The review is not meant to be exhaustive. My aim is to describe a
selection of conceptual analyses that includes deservingness or the
related concept of entitlement. We will discover that some theorists
discuss deservingness in relation to the concept of entitlement, framing
it as a particular instance of entitlement. Others prefer to distinguish
between the two concepts. My use of the term falls into the latter camp.
Drawing on distinctions made by legal and social theorists, I will argue
that the two concepts can be distinguished, even though they are often
used in similar ways both in everyday language and in more academic
discussions. But first I turn to a selection of relevant contributions that
have their source in psychological analyses of basic questions that concern social justice.

Some Contributions from Social Justice Research

Belief in a Just World. Lerner (1987) gives entitlement a central
position in his development of a social psychological theory of justice.
Lerner states:

> the experience of entitlement is the essential psychological ingre-
> dient of an entire family of human events associated with social
> justice: issues of equity, deserving, rights, fairness, and the justice of
> procedures, distribution, and retributive acts.... The cognitive com-
> ponent of this generic event is the judgment, often tacit, that some-
> one, or some category of people, is entitled to a particular set of
> outcomes by virtue of who they are or what they have done. The
> "entitled to" is experienced affectively and motivationally as an

imperative, a sense of requiredness between the actor's perceived outcomes and the person's attributes or acts. (pp. 107–108)

Lerner (1987) goes on to distinguish between deserving and fairness, stating that "deserving most often refers to the relations between an actor and his or her fate ... whereas fairness judgments typically imply a comparison of two or more actors' outcomes in that situation" (p. 108).

Lerner (1987) discusses entitlement in relation to information provided by the social structure (normative prescriptions such as the "norm of reciprocity," status-role-based expectations, social concepts and stereotypes, and general assumptions about social motivation and rational decision making). The information that comes from the social world and the way it is structured becomes incorporated into each person's psychological structure so that "people's conceptions of their world, what they are and others want or are entitled to, are to some extent fairly direct representations of that publicly available reality" (p. 109). However, early in life the child develops ideas about what is good and what is bad and what is required in order to operate on the environment, so that one can move from a present condition to a desired end state. Lerner (1987) proposes that:

> although conventional rules of thought and evaluation gradually dominate the maturing child's conscious cognitive processes, the initial constructions of evaluated objects and ways of operating on the environment endure and provide the rather crude templates and scripts for the preconscious organization of all later experiences. (p. 110)

These more primitive constructions are assumed to influence a person's reactions when that person is fully engaged in an encounter and responds with strong affect to outcomes and possible violations of entitlements. Judgments based on more rational thought processes are assumed to occur when the person is less threatened and is involved in fairly routine situations that are further removed from motivational and affective processes.

The more primitive cognitive associations and scripts therefore continue to influence people's reactions when they deal with important events in their lives. Thus, people may assign blame and culpability to others for a bad outcome even when the outcome was unintentional and accidental, reasoning backward and associating a bad outcome with a bad person. The preconscious entitlement view of reality may also be manifested in a general belief that people get what they deserve, a belief in a just world (Lerner, 1980) that accepts that there is an overarching, governing force in the world that delivers justice.

Lerner (1987) argues that on most occasions people will automatically follow the consciously given prescriptions that concern entitlement and the obligations of their status roles, and that they will attempt to employ rational strategies of decision making that promote their self-interest. However, in more motivationally and emotionally charged situations, where norms are violated and the person is threatened, the more primitive and preconscious rules of entitlement may dominate, so that "we become primarily invested in maintaining the belief that we are good people living in a just world" (p. 123). Lerner (1980, 1987, 1997, 1998) describes various types of evidence that are taken to support his assumption of two kinds of cognitive processes—the consciously represented thought forms that reflect the social world, and the more primitive rules of organization that function at an unconscious level.

It will be noted that Lerner's discussion brings in both association and evaluation as important processes that are involved in the formation of the cognitive structures that determine judgments of deservingness. The structures so formed may be conscious representations of the rules of entitlement and social norms that are communicated to the person via the social environment. They may also involve relatively simple associations and evaluations that are laid down early in life and that function at a preconscious level to influence a person's reactions in situations of high involvement. These associations might be simple ones, such as "good people deserve good outcomes" or "bad people deserve bad outcomes."

Lerner (1998) notes that his distinction between two forms of belief in a just world is similar to distinctions made by Epstein, Lipson, Holstein, and Hubb (1992) and by Schweder and Haidt (1993). Epstein et al. (1992) distinguish between two conceptual systems that people are assumed to use in processing the information they receive, namely a rational system and an experiential system. The rational system functions according to conventional rules of inference and logic and operates primarily at a conscious level. The experiential system is more emotionally driven. It is a preconscious system in which "people's personal theories of reality reside—theories that automatically interpret, encode, and organize experience and direct behavior" (p. 328). Epstein et al. (1992) list attributes of the rational and experiential systems that they derived from logical considerations, from comparisons of how people think when they are or are not emotionally involved, from social-cognitive research (e.g., Nisbett & Ross, 1980), and from cognitive research on heuristics and counterfactual thinking (e.g., Kahneman, Slovic, & Tversky, 1982).

In similar fashion, Schweder and Haidt (1993) distinguish between two kinds of moral judgments, those that are arrived at by way of more rational forms of moral reasoning, where there is a considered manipulation of conscious thoughts, and those that are based on moral intuitions where the appraisal process is "introspectively opaque" and more automatic and rapid, leading to reactions that are intuitively valid.

Lerner (1997, 1998) proposes that a lot of the current research on justice is more relevant to the conscious system of judgment that is superimposed on the more simple and primitive cognitive system formed early in life. This latter system comes into play under conditions of high emotion and involvement when there is less opportunity for reflection and rational consideration. For example, when an innocent victim suffers an undeserved, negative event that is very upsetting and emotionally engaging, those who observed the event may be more inclined to derogate the victim when a quick judgment has to be made and when other more rational ways of dealing with the injustice have been closed off (e.g., Simons & Piliavin, 1972). Observers may also be more likely to blame the victim under these conditions and to judge the victim as deserving his or her fate. They use scripts for deserving and justice that are associated with anger and blaming and that were formed early in life. These scripts persist and are accessed automatically under conditions of immediacy and high involvement, even though they do not make sense in terms of more rational considerations of justice based on social norms and other social learning that occurs later. If the observers had time for sober reflection under conditions of low involvement, however, they would probably come to different conclusions based on the conscious system of justice conforming to lay theories and conventional explanations.

A lot of the earlier research on just world beliefs supported the idea that people have a need to believe in a just world where people get what they deserve, and that this belief often overrides motives that relate to maximizing rational self-interest (e.g., Miller, 1977). The concern with justice was also seen to be adaptive in that it enables the individual to perceive the physical and social environments as stable and orderly (Lerner & Miller, 1978). Evidence for these conclusions came from a number of studies (e.g., Lerner, 1965; Miller, 1977; Rubin & Peplau, 1973; Simons & Piliavin, 1972). Reviews of this earlier research have been presented by Lerner and Miller (1978) and by Lerner, Miller, and Holmes (1976).

The more recent discussions by Lerner focus on the emergence of the theoretical distinction between the two forms of belief in a just world that relate to primitive and preconscious associations and to conscious reflection respectively. Lerner (1997, 1998) reviews the evidence that supports this distinction and, as we have seen, he refers to other theoretical approaches that are consistent with it (e.g., Epstein et al., 1992;

Schweder & Haidt, 1993). Other recent evidence about just world beliefs comes from studies of victimizations in a number of different contexts and from studies of how victims themselves react to their negative outcomes (e.g., Montada & Lerner, 1998).

It is clear that Lerner has made seminal contributions to the psychology of justice and deservingness, beginning over 30 years ago and continuing through the present. He notes that it is crucial in future research that investigators recognize the differences between the two systems of belief that he describes, namely the "preconscious experiential and the conscious rational and how they differentially influence people's reactions. The failure to do that in past research has led to seriously mistaken conclusions about how much and in what ways people care about justice" (Lerner, 1998, p. 267). There is also a need in future research to investigate how the two systems interact.

An important implication of Lerner's discussion is that studies of deservingness should include situations where the judge is motivationally and affectively involved as well as situations where judgments can be made under conditions of less involvement (Lerner, 1987, p. 119; 1998, pp. 264–268). Studies in the justice area have more often involved the latter types of condition, as in the case of simulated jury research or in experimental studies that employ specially constructed vignettes. Situations of very high involvement are not always easy to construct in psychological experiments where the emphasis is on manipulating and controlling variables and where there are ethical requirements that concern the welfare of participants. However, it is possible to draw examples from other types of psychological research in which real-life events are the major focus (e.g., important positive or negative events in people's lives). Simulations and other experimental procedures can sometimes be constructed so as to achieve a high degree of realism, leading to relatively high involvement on the part of the judge or observer.

Analysis of the Experience of Injustice. As noted previously, Lerner (1987) assigns the experience of entitlement a key role in considerations about justice, and issues about deservingness are included under this general label. Mikula (1993) also assigns entitlement a key role in his discussion of the experience of injustice. Thus, people claim that injustice has occurred when their entitlements or rights have been violated. In addition, however, the experience of injustice may also be related to causal attributions and justifications. Mikula (1993) draws on a number of sources to argue that the extent to which a situation, event, or treatment is seen to be unjust from the viewpoint of a perceiver will be related to the following variables:

1. *Violation of entitlement*: the extent to which a person's entitlement is perceived to be violated,
2. *Personal causation*: the extent to which the violation of the person's entitlement is causally attributed to an action or omission of some other agent (i.e., a person, group, or an institution) rather than the person affected,
3. *Controllability*: the extent to which the agent is perceived as having had control over the action or omission in question (i.e., he or she could have acted otherwise),
4. *Intention*: the extent to which the action or omission in question is viewed as having been intentionally or purposefully produced by the agent,
5. *Lack of justification*: the extent to which the agent's action or omission is perceived to be insufficiently justified. (pp. 229–230)

These variables may be collapsed into three, namely, a perceived violation of entitlement, the attribution of responsibility to some other agent, and the attribution of blame to the respective agent. Mikula (1993) asserts that conceptually the variables he proposes

> appear to be necessary components of the experience of injustice and the amount of injustice perceived should be larger, the more an entitlement had been violated and the more responsibility and blame is attributed to the causal agent of the incident. (p. 231)

He indicates that his analysis is similar to other analyses that have been described in the justice literature, especially in regard to the sequential arrangement of perceived violation, attribution of responsibility, and perceived blame (e.g., Fincham & Jaspars, 1980; Shaver, 1985).

Mikula's analysis is relevant to the issue of how people react when their outcomes are not in accordance with what they believe they deserve or are entitled to. The focus is on the experience of injustice, especially in situations where people do not get what they believe they are due. The analysis does not speak to the issue of how judgments of deservingness are determined, an issue I have already highlighted, which is a major focus of the research to be described in later chapters of this book. How people react to violations of entitlement is a different question from the question of what determines the degree to which the positive or negative outcomes that occur in relation to others or to self are perceived to be deserved or undeserved.

Social Inequality and Entitlement.   Major (1994) does address the question of what determines judgments of entitlement in her discussion of how people react to social inequality. Her analysis is framed within the context of the disadvantage suffered by women and African-Americans in American society. Her central thesis is that:

> beliefs about *entitlement* are a critical determinant of how members of social groups react affectively, evaluatively, and behaviorally to their socially distributed outcomes (i.e., outcomes in which another person or social system is involved). It is argued that one of the most far-reaching consequences of discrimination and social inequality is that they can alter what people feel they deserve, or are entitled to receive, from their social relationships. The disadvantaged often come to believe they deserve their lesser outcomes, whereas the overprivileged often come to believe that they are entitled to their position of relative advantage. (p. 294)

Major acknowledges that her argument is not new and that the concepts of entitlement and deserving have been central to theories of social justice and relative deprivation and their application to how those who are disadvantaged react to their condition (e.g., Cook, Crosby, & Hennigan, 1977; Crosby, 1976, 1982; Crosby & Gonzalez-Intal, 1984; Davis, 1959; Deutsch, 1985; Gurr, 1970; Martin, 1981, 1986). Her analysis is consistent with this body of literature and it shows how biases that are involved in making social comparisons and causal attributions tend to legitimize disadvantage so that disadvantaged people may come to accept their condition as the way it ought to be. When disadvantage is not perceived to be legitimate, however, they may see their inequality as being undeserved. They may then experience frustration, anger, and resentment that may spill over into active attempts to correct the disadvantage.

In Major's analysis perceptions of entitlement in situations where there is objective disadvantage are determined by the social comparisons that people make and by beliefs about the legitimacy of group differences. The particular forms of social comparison that are made (intragroup, intrapersonal, intergroup) lead to group differences in reference standards. These differences, together with beliefs about legitimacy, then determine group differences in perceived personal entitlements. These differences in personal entitlements then determine the way outcomes are evaluated (e.g., as fair or unfair) as well as how people react affectively and behaviorally.

For example, evidence shows that women are objectively disadvantaged as a group in employment situations, but there is little evidence that they are more dissatisfied than men with their pay or their jobs (e.g., Crosby, 1982; Major, 1994, pp. 295–297). Why? According to Major, they may compare their situation (e.g., pay and conditions) with that of other women (intragroup comparison) or with their own past situation (intrapersonal comparison). These social comparison biases tend to prevent awareness of their disadvantage. They lead to a set of reference standards that would be different had women compared themselves with the male group (intergroup comparison). These reference standards, together with beliefs that legitimize the inequality between women and men in the employment situation, produce a lesser sense of entitlement that may translate into the paradoxical satisfaction with their pay and other conditions of employment.

However, had the disadvantage been perceived as illegitimate and had social comparisons been made at the group level, thereby encouraging awareness of discrepancies between one's own outcomes and those of others, the result would be different. For example, the evidence shows that African-Americans typically score lower than whites on measures of psychological well-being and satisfaction (Major, 1994, p. 297), a difference that can be related to intergroup social comparisons, beliefs that the discrepancy is illegitimate, and a heightened sense that the group is entitled to more in the way of social and economic benefits.

Major (1994) reviews a large amount of research, much of it from her own laboratory, that is consistent with her analysis. She argues that

> Despite the centrality of entitlement in public discourse and theories of social justice ... the psychology of entitlement is still in its infancy.... Given the importance of the construct of entitlement to both personal well-being and collective behavior, it is time for social psychologists to take a broader look at this construct. (p. 346)

Analysis of the Allocation of Scarce Resources. Skitka and Tetlock (1992) include deservingness as a variable that affects the way people allocate resources under conditions of scarcity. Their contingency model of distributive justice builds on previous contributions to the psychology of distributive justice, where the focus is on the principles that people use to judge the fairness or unfairness of distributed outcomes or allocations (e.g., Deutsch, 1985; Leventhal, 1976; Mikula, 1980; Walster, Berscheid, & Walster, 1976). The principles are assumed to form an important basis for judging whether outcomes are deserved or undeserved. For example, high level employees in an organization might judge that they deserve their high salaries because they work hard and demonstrate a high level of qualifications and skill. Their judgments reflect an equity principle, where fairness is related to a match between performance input and contributions and the rewards that follow this input (Adams, 1965; Walster, Walster, & Berscheid, 1978). In other cases, disadvantaged people who are supported by social welfare may be judged to deserve the support they receive because they need the resources in order to survive. These judgments reflect a need principle. In still other cases, resources that are distributed equally among members of a group may be judged to be deserved because such a distribution promotes a sense of harmony and interdependence. These judgments reflect an equality principle of justice.

There is a question here as to whether the words "deserved" or "undeserved" should be used in relation to outcomes that are judged in relation to one or another of these principles or whether it is more accurate to describe the outcomes more generally in terms of being fair or unfair. Should we say that someone in need deserved to be helped, or alternatively that it is fair and just to help them? Should we say that people in a group deserved equal rewards, or alternatively that equal distributions are fair and just in the interests of group harmony and solidarity? I believe there are important differences in the way that terms like entitlement, deservingness, and fairness should be used. Some of these terms (e.g., fairness) are more inclusive than others (e.g., deservingness). I will return to this point subsequently.

Skitka and Tetlock's (1992) contingency model of resource distribution is presented in Figure 1.1. The model proposes that whoever is distributing resources first has to make a judgment about the availability of the resources. Are plenty of resources available or are they in short supply? The decision process ends if everyone can be helped, in which case aid is provided to all claimants. However, if resources are scarce, the allocator moves to the second stage where an attributional analysis is conducted. Are the claimants personally responsible for their predicament (an internal-controllable attribution), or is their predicament due to external factors or other causes that signify that they are not personally responsible? If the claimants are judged to be personally responsible for their predicament, the allocator has to consider whether it is possible to help them given the availability of resources. If there is a match between those who have to be denied help because there are insufficient resources and those who are personally responsible for their predicament, then a decision is made not to allocate aid to the latter but to consider granting aid to the remainder who are not responsible for their predicament. If there is no such match, then we move to the third stage of the model.

At Stage 3 of the model consideration is given to the claimants' deservingness. Skitka and Tetlock propose that the allocator would consider whether some claimants are needier than others and whether providing aid to some claimants would be more effective than providing it to other claimants.

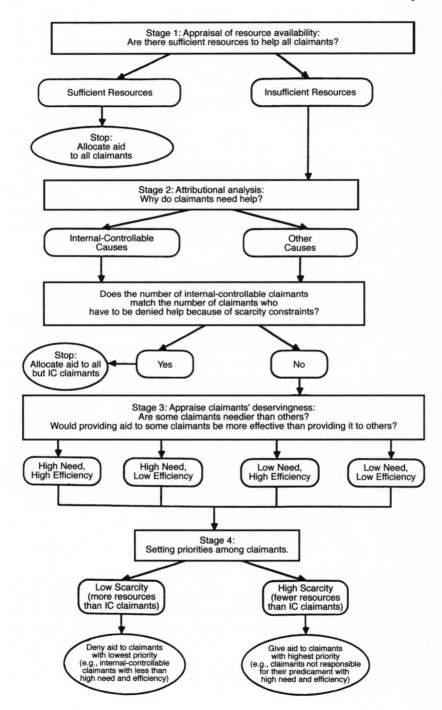

Stage 4 of the model then involves setting priorities among the claimants depending on their level of need and deservingness. According to Skitka and Tetlock (1992):

> When there are more resources than there are personally responsible claimants (low scarcity), people will deny aid to those with the lowest overall priority—internal-controllable claimants with less than high need and efficiency. When there are fewer resources than there are personally responsible claimants (high scarcity), people will deny aid to all personally responsible claimants. However, they will have to deny aid to other claimants as well. Claimants with other causes of need will be denied aid to the extent that they have less than high need and efficiency. (p. 493)

Skitka and Tetlock (1992, 1993) also propose that the allocations that are made will be affected by the personality and ideology of the allocator. They draw on findings by Carroll, Perkowitz, Lurigio, and Weaver (1987) to identify two clusters of personality and ideological variables that they expect to shape allocation preferences. One cluster brings together variables that combine political conservatism, dogmatism, authoritarianism, and internal locus of control. They call this cluster "cognitive conservatism or CC." The other cluster brings together liberal ideals and the principled stage of moral development. They call this cluster "liberal humanism or LH." They expected that:

> High CCs should experience negative affect toward, and withhold resources from, claimants whose needs are due to internal, controllable causes, whereas high LHs should be influenced less by cause of need than by need itself. The moderating effects of personality/ideology should be most evident under no scarcity, when allocators are less constrained by the situation. (p. 496)

The results of their studies show that allocators were much more likely to withhold aid when claimants could be seen as responsible for their predicament. When claimants were not responsible for their predicament, both need and efficiency emerged as joint predictors of allocating aid. Moreover, allocators who were politically conservative were more likely to withhold aid from those who were personally responsible for their plight, regardless of their level of need and whether the aid would be used effectively, even when there were sufficient resources to satisfy all who were claiming. In contrast, allocators with a liberal orientation were more likely to provide aid to all claimants. Skitka and Tetlock (1992, 1993) suggest that conservatives may be more

---

Figure 1.1. A four-stage contingency model of resource allocation. Skitka and Tetlock (1992). Reprinted with permission of the authors and Academic Press.

punitive in their reactions, withholding aid as a punishment. However, this punitiveness toward norm violators can be attenuated under conditions where the personally responsible claimants have reformed (Skitka & Tetlock, 1993).

Analysis of Distributive Justice. In a detailed and insightful discussion of how justice principles operate in the context of distributive justice, Deutsch (1975, 1985) proposes that equity (outcomes should be distributed among individuals in proportion to their inputs or contributions) will be the dominant principle in competitive situations where economic productivity is the primary goal, that equality (an equal distribution of outcomes) will be the dominant principle in cooperative situations where the primary goal is to foster and maintain social relations, and that need (distributing outcomes according to need) will be the dominant principle in cooperative situations where the primary goal is fostering personal development and personal welfare. Thus, different justice principles may be evoked depending on the primary goal of the interaction.

Deutsch (1985) also discusses the conditions under which victims experience a sense of injustice. Central to his analysis is the view that a sense of injustice will be aroused and become more intense with an increase in relative deprivation (see also Crosby, 1982). Deutsch (1985) employs relative deprivation to refer to "the perceived discrepancy between what a person obtains and what he believes he is entitled to obtain in the distribution of goods and harms" (p. 51). Thus, the violation of perceived entitlement is a key determinant of the arousal of a sense of injustice, consistent with the proposals by Lerner, Mikula, and Major that were presented previously.

According to Deutsch (1985, pp. 52–63), a number of conditions can affect people's beliefs about what they are entitled to. These conditions include the influence of official ideologies and myths that legitimize social norms and entitlements; the weakening of official ideologies leading to a breakdown in consensual norms, changes in the legitimacy of entitlements, and possible replacement by new ideologies; social comparisons with comparable others either at the individual or group level; and increases or decreases in bargaining power within a relationship so that people have more or less power to bargain for more, thereby affecting their beliefs about entitlement. Some of these conditions overlap with those that have been described previously in relation to the other theoretical contributions that were discussed.

Deutsch (1985) provides a rich discussion of the strengths and gaps in the social psychology of justice, and he also presents a detailed description of studies from his own research program. Some of the gaps he identifies have been partially filled in the years since the publication of his book, but there is still plenty of scope for developing theory and research to answer the questions that he raised.

The Analysis of Resentment. It will be noted that some of the approaches I have described refer to social comparison processes that give rise to beliefs about entitlement and feelings of injustice (e.g., Major, 1994). The literature concerning social comparison and relative deprivation is extensive and a review of it is beyond the scope of the present book. Tyler, Boeckmann, Smith, and Huo (1997) review those parts of the literature that relate to relative deprivation and social justice. Here I present two examples of this form of analysis in which comparison processes have an important role and in which the focus is on feelings of resentment.

Crosby (1976) proposes a model of egoistical relative deprivation in which she assumes that feelings of resentment experienced by an individual who lacks something (X) depend on five preconditions: (1) The person who lacks X must see that someone else possesses X; (2) must want X; (3) must feel entitled to X; (4) must think that it is feasible to obtain X; and (5) must lack a sense of responsibility for not having X. Note that Crosby's analysis is a model of relative deprivation at the individual level. Various authors have emphasized that it is important to distinguish between individual egoistic deprivation, where comparisons are interpersonal, and group-based fraternal deprivation, where comparisons are at the group level. Thus, a person might feel disadvantaged relative to some other person. Alternatively, people who define themselves in terms of a social category or group (e.g., gender, age, ethnic background) might experience injustice when they compare themselves with other social groups or categories (e.g., Runciman, 1966; Tyler et al., 1997; Walker & Pettigrew, 1984).

Some of Crosby's own research demonstrates the experience of injustice at the group level (e.g., research with working women who recognized that as a group they were unjustly treated) (Crosby, 1982). In discussing this research Crosby gives more prominence to feelings of entitlement when a person lacks something that he or she wants. She uses the terms entitlement and deservingness interchangeably. Prentice and Crosby (1987) note that feelings of entitlement depend in part upon the context, which may or may not provide cues for assessing deservingness. These cues would involve the availability of appropriate targets for social comparison and the existence of some consensus about which principles of social justice are appropriate to the situation.

In his referent cognitions model, Folger (1986, 1987) proposes a more cognitive approach to feelings of justice, which draws upon the analysis of judgmental heuristics, especially the simulation heuristic and its relevance to counterfactual emotions involving such feelings as regret, frustration, indignation, grief, and envy that may arise when "reality is compared with a favored alternative, which one had failed to reach but could easily imagine reaching" (Kahneman & Tversky, 1982). According to Folger (1987), people consider what might have been, constructing their thoughts in a narrative-type way (e.g., Abelson, 1983; Kahneman & Tversky, 1982). These imagined outcomes to which they refer may involve the outcomes of others, or one's past outcomes, or outcomes that are conceivable in theory. The comparison of what actually occurred with more favorable imagined outcomes is assumed to lead to feelings of dissatisfaction. These negative feelings can turn into resentment if the basis or instrumentality that produced the actual outcome is seen to be unfair or unjustified. This resentment can be blunted if a person believes that there are good prospects for amelioration in the future (e.g., the situation might change toward the better).

Folger (1987) compares his referent cognitions model with Crosby's (1976, 1982) earlier and later statements of the preconditions for resentment. He prefers not to use an undifferentiated construct, such as entitlement, but rather to focus on the antecedents to feelings of resentment about undeserved treatment. He proposes that his referent-cognitions model suggests that:

> in order for someone to feel entitled to better outcomes than those currently available, the person must be aware of more acceptable circumstances capable of producing such outcomes (the combination of high referent outcomes and low justification of existing circumstances). Furthermore, even these conditions will fail to yield resentment if there is a good chance that future circumstances may yet produce the desired outcomes within an acceptable period of time (high likelihood of amelioration). (p. 193)

Note that both of the theoretical approaches of Crosby and Folger that I have described involve justice concepts—entitlement or deservingness in the case of Crosby, justification in the case of Folger. Tyler et al. (1997) comment that some theories of relative deprivation are incomplete because they focus on deprivation relative to a standard but leave out consideration of whether the deprivation is linked to justice issues. These kinds of theories may clarify the basis for some emotional experiences, but they fall short of accounting for feelings of justice or injustice.

Some Contributions from Legal and Social Theory

I now turn to a discussion of contributions that have emerged from legal and social theories. These contributions supplement the psychological analyses that were described in the previous section, adding a careful analytic approach to the meaning of different concepts, especially in regard to deservingness and entitlement.

Legal and social theorists have provided discussions of the concept of desert or deservingness, usually in the context of the assignment of a punishment or a penalty for the violation of a law (e.g., Feinberg, 1970; Heath, 1976; von Hirsch, 1986). These discussions involve detailed analysis of the meaning of deservingness and its relation to other concepts such as entitlement. It is difficult to do justice to the richness of some of these discussions in a brief summary. Here I will abstract only some of the main ideas, using the contributions of Feinberg, von Hirsch, and Heath as examples.

Feinberg (1970) argues that "To say that a person deserves something is to say that there is a certain sort of propriety in his having it" (p. 56). But he notes that this general statement would also apply to cases where a person is seen as eligible or qualified for something, or has a right to something, or ought to have it. However, a person might be eligible for selection in a sporting team on the basis of physical fitness yet may not deserve to be selected. A politician may be qualified to be elected by virtue of receiving a majority vote and claim the office as his or her right or entitlement. Yet, for one or another reason, people may say that he or she did not deserve to be elected.

Feinberg (1970) argues that, if a person is to deserve something, it is not sufficient for him or her to satisfy conditions of eligibility and entitlement. The person also has to satisfy conditions that are "not specified in any regulatory or procedural rules" but "whose satisfaction confers worthiness or desert" (p. 58). What are these "desert bases"? According to Feinberg, "If a person is deserving of some sort of treatment, he must, necessarily be so *in virtue of* some possessed characteristic or prior activity" (p. 58). There must be a reason for conferring a judgment of desert that concerns the person and his or her past actions. Feinberg describes various forms of deserved treatment that encompass the awards of prizes; the assignment of grades; rewards and punishments; praise, blame, and other informal responses; and reparation, liability, and other modes of compensation. His discussion involves many fine distinctions, which it would be impossible to capture in a short summary.

It is clear, however, that Feinberg draws a distinction between desert and entitlement. There can be desert without qualification, and qualification without desert. For example, an unemployed person might deserve social welfare benefits but not be entitled to them because he or she has exhausted his or her benefits under the law; alternatively, an unemployed person might be entitled to social welfare benefits because of a badly formulated law but might also be seen not to deserve them (Feinberg, 1970, p. 76). Feinberg also provides examples where situations involve a conflict between desert and entitlement. His general point is summed up in the following statement:

> "Deserve," "fitting," and "appropriate," on the one hand, and "right," "entitlement," and "rule" on the other, are terms from altogether different parts of our ethical vocabularies; they are related in such a way that there is no paradox in saying of a person that he deserves (it would be fitting for him to have) certain modes of treatment which, nevertheless, he cannot claim as his due. (Feinberg, 1970, p. 86)

We also find an emphasis on a person's past actions in von Hirsch's (1986) discussion of deservingness in the context of how one might justify punishments for offenses. According to von Hirsch, "To say someone 'deserves' to be rewarded or punished is to refer to his *past* conduct, and assert that its merit or demerit is reason for according him pleasant or unpleasant treatment. The focus on the past is critical" (p. 46).

Heath (1976) discusses the concept of deservingness in a wide-ranging analysis of theories of rational choice and social exchange. Particularly interesting is his discussion of differences in the concepts of rights, deserts, and need in the context of questions of justice and fairness. Heath begins by noting that we use all three terms "to refer to a general moral entitlement as well as to specific kinds of moral claim ... [that is] as synonyms for 'ought'" (p. 137). Thus, we say that a person has a right to something, or deserves it, or needs it in the sense that he or she has some sort of moral claim to it. But we also use the three terms to indicate different forms of moral claim, distinguishing between claims based on rights, desert, and need.

How are these distinctions made? Heath (1976) proposes that an appeal to rights involves an appeal to an agreed-upon body of law or to formal or informal rules. Someone may have a right to receive social welfare benefits based on formalized laws that concern entitlement, or someone may have a right to receive a gift in a group where the norm of reciprocity prevails. Heath (1976) asserts that, "To discover what the rights are we have to carry out an empirical enquiry to discover what rules are maintained in the society in question. We have to discover where the society stands on the law of contract, the morality of social exchange, and so on" (p. 138).

In the case of desert the question is "more a matter of giving people what their own personal behaviour or personal qualities merit" (Heath, 1976, p. 138). Heath (1976, p.139) refers to a statement by Miller (1974) that "Desert is a matter of fitting forms of treatment to the specific qualities and actions of individuals and in particular good desert (i.e., deserving benefit as opposed to punishment) is a matter of fitting desired forms of treatment to qualities and actions which are generally held in high regard." Heath comments that voluntary actions on another's behalf would meet this criterion of high regard, but there would be a dispute about whether ascribed characteristics of a person, such as birth or status, would deserve returns depending on the person's outcome.

Finally, Heath (1976) notes that need is similar to desert in that it relates to the personal qualities or the situation of the individual who is under consideration. However, "The crucial difference ... is that desert relates to desirable and admirable qualities while need relates to some lack or deprivation" (p. 139).

Heath reminds us that people can subscribe to all three principles of justice at the same time without being inconsistent. For example, in a given instance we might say that a person has a right to a particular outcome given the agreed-upon rules, that he or she deserves the outcome given his or her personal qualities and past actions, and that he or she should be provided with the outcome given his or her needs. However, trade-offs are often the case, given that the three principles may come into conflict in particular situations. Heath (1976) cites an example of this: "I may quite properly hold that a workman deserves to lose his job, since he was caught pilfering from his workmates. But I might also hold that he ought to be allowed to keep his job since he has a large family to support" (p. 140).

These three examples of analyses from legal and social theory are useful in the present context because they help to clarify differences between different kinds of justice principles. With respect to deservingness, they point to aspects of the person and qualities of a person's past actions that are an important basis for forming the judgment of desert. This emphasis is consistent with the line of discussion that I presented at the beginning of this chapter, in which I argued that judgments of deservingness are closely linked to how we evaluate a person's actions and the outcomes that follow from these actions, and to how we perceive the person in terms of liking or disliking, social identity, and moral character.

FAIRNESS, ENTITLEMENT, AND DESERVINGNESS

In the preceding sections I briefly reviewed some theoretical approaches from the psychology of justice and from legal and social theory that include concepts of entitlement or deservingness as central psychological variables. This review was not meant to be exhaustive. It would be possible to refer to many other discussions that refer to these variables or that include these variables along with others in an analysis of how people react to the outcomes of other or of self. I do not propose to present a detailed discussion of this literature in this book, but instead I have tried in the preceding sections to bring out some of the main points, focusing in particular on how different theorists and investigators have discussed concepts of entitlement and deservingness in the justice literature. It should be obvious that, consistent with Lerner's (1987) view, the experience of deservingness or entitlement is an important component of many approaches to the psychological analysis of social justice in its various forms (e.g., Crosby, 1982, 1984; Crosby, Muehrer, & Loewenstein, 1986; Folger, 1987; Olson & Hafer, 1996).

Nor do I propose to present a wide-ranging review of theories and research in the social psychology of justice that covers such topics as relative deprivation, different forms of justice (distributive, procedural, retributive), reactions to justice and injustice, justice as a motive, and social and cultural influences on the perception of justice. Tyler et al. (1997) recently contributed a thorough, analytic review of the justice literature that covers these topics (see also Tyler & Smith, 1998), and there are other compendia that deal with specialized theory and research concerning social justice (e.g., Folger, 1984; Greenberg & Cohen, 1982; Lind & Tyler, 1988; Masters & Smith, 1987; Mellers & Baron, 1993; Messick & Cook, 1983; Vermunt & Steensma, 1991). The Tyler et al. (1997) review shows that the field contains a wealth of interesting ideas that are likely to stimulate new advances in the social psychology of justice in the years to come and to have effects on social psychology more generally.

My focus in this book is on the psychology of deservingness. So my canvas is much more restricted. At the same time, as I have just tried to illustrate, concepts that involve fairness, entitlement, and deservingness are at the heart of the social psychology of justice. Hence, a focus on deservingness is likely to have important implications for the wider justice literature.

Can the terms fairness, entitlement, and deservingness be differentiated at the conceptual level? Fairness seems to be a very general term that can be applied to all areas of justice. We can call a procedure fair or unfair, or a distribution of rewards as fair or unfair, or a penalty imposed on an offender as fair or unfair. The term is very inclusive and we use it in relation to general principles of justice and legitimized values and norms that are part of the social fabric.

As noted previously, Lerner (1987) considers entitlement to be an inclusive term that covers a wide range of human events associated with justice. He includes equity, fairness, deservingness, rights, and the justice of procedures and retributive acts under the general umbrella of entitlement. Major (1994) uses the terms entitlement and deservingness interchangeably in her analysis because she believes that the psychological implications of deserving and entitlement are similar. She notes that many others also use entitlement and deservingness interchangeably rather than distinguishing between them.

We have seen, however, that it is possible to distinguish between entitlement and deservingness (see also Steil, 1994). Entitlement implies that there is a set of agreed-upon rules, norms, and principles at the group or societal level that have legal or quasi-legal status and that can be called upon to determine whether a person is entitled to or not entitled to a positive or negative outcome. This framework may be used to justify a person's claims either on the basis of some ascribed characteristic (e.g., citizenship, gender) or in relation to that person's prescribed conduct in particular situations. The rules and principles refer to a person's rights, and injustice occurs when these rights are violated. Thus, an injured worker may be judged to be entitled to compensation in relation to industrial law; a woman may be seen to be entitled to the same rights and privileges as a man in the same occupation according to equal opportunity legislation.

The term deservingness relates more to outcomes that are earned or achieved as products of a person's actions. We usually say that a positive or negative outcome is deserved or undeserved when it can be related to a person's actions. Thus, it might be said that a person deserved to succeed in his or her career because the success followed a lot of hard work and preparation, or that some people deserve negative outcomes in their lives because they behaved foolishly. We are less likely to say that an outcome is deserved or undeserved when it can be attributed to causes other than the person's actions. Thus, judgments of deservingness and undeservingness presume some contingency between action and outcome. We do not use the language of deservingness to describe outcomes that are clearly independent of a person's actions and that are the result of causes that are beyond the person's control.

Judgments of deservingness may also be related to the ascribed moral character of a person (e.g., Is he or she a person of integrity? Is he or she an arrogant person? Is he or she a "good" or "bad" person?). However, these ascribed characteristics involve evaluations that are usually based on information about the way a person typically behaves or on what others say about a person's conduct. Hence, a person's evaluated actions again become an important component of the way in which the person is judged to deserve or not deserve outcomes.

These are subtle differences, however, and they are certainly open to debate. Do we say, for example, that a disadvantaged person whose negative condition is due to no fault of his or her own deserves to be helped? Do we say that it is fair to help a person who has suffered such misfortune? Do we say that such a person is entitled to aid in relation to accepted social policies? Perhaps we end up running around a semantic circle. Nevertheless, I prefer to discuss deservingness in relation to action-outcome sequences, and much of the research to be discussed in subsequent chapters follows that line. However, I do not ignore the possibility that outcomes may also be attributed to other than personal causes or that judgments of deservingness also occur within a social context that provides sets of rules, norms, values, ideologies, and other social constructions that influence how people respond.

SUMMARY AND OVERVIEW OF CHAPTERS

In this chapter I have focused on the concept of deservingness, which I believe to be a key concept in the psychology of justice. I showed how deservingness and related concepts have been used by others in the justice literature and I distinguish deservingness from similar concepts such as fairness and entitlement.

It should be clear that my analysis of deservingness will involve consideration of outcomes and their relation to a person's actions. As I noted previously, the structure of the action-outcome relation, as determined by the conjunction of consistent or inconsistent evaluations, is considered to be an important cue for judgments of deservingness and undeservingness. Judgments of deservingness are more likely to occur when outcomes are evaluatively consistent with the action that produced them (positive outcome following a positive action, negative outcome following a negative action). Judgments of undeservingness are more likely to occur when outcomes are evaluatively inconsistent with the action that produced them (positive outcome following a negative action, negative outcome following a positive action). Thus, values enter as an important determinant of judgments of deservingness and undeservingness.

Because people differ in their value priorities, it follows that the same action-outcome sequence may lead to different judgments of deservingness and undeservingness depending on the value systems that people hold and their conditions of activation. Actions that are positively valued by some may be negatively valued by others; outcomes that are assigned positive value by some may be negatively valued by others. Hence, evaluations of actions and outcomes and the judgments of deservingness or undeservingness that they imply may differ between people under the same objective conditions. Given the fact that groups and cultures may impart different value priorities to their members, we would also expect to find that judgments of deservingness and undeservingness may differ across groups and cultures for the same objective outcomes.

I also proposed that our judgments of deservingness and undeservingness depend upon the way we assign personal responsibility for actions and their outcomes. We do not usually say that people deserve outcomes for which they are not responsible. However, people can be judged to deserve outcomes for which they are seen to be responsible, and they can also be judged not to deserve outcomes for which they are seen to be responsible. Thus, there is no simple, one-to-one relation between perceived responsibility and judgments of deservingness and undeservingness. Other variables also have to be taken into account, especially the effects of positive or negative evaluations of actions and their outcomes.

Finally, I listed some other variables that I proposed would also influence judgments of deservingness and undeservingness, namely, the perceived moral character of the person being judged, the degree to which the judged person was liked or disliked, and the social identity of the person being judged.

An important question concerns whether these different variables operate independently with summative effects or whether they affect judgments of deservingness and undeservingness according to systemic principles, depending on how well they fit together in a consistent system of relations. I will elaborate on these issues in subsequent chapters of this book.

In Chapter 2, I examine the concept of responsibility in more detail, referring to how the concept has been discussed by others and to research that shows that judgments of responsibility influence both affective and behavioral reactions to an outcome.

In Chapter 3, I examine the concept of value, describing how values have been defined and how they function to influence cognition and action. In particular, I will focus on the way personally held values affect the way people construe actions and outcomes in terms of their attractiveness (or positive valence) and aversiveness (or negative valence).

In Chapter 4, I present a conceptual model of deservingness that relates judgments of deservingness and undeservingness to perceived responsibility, relations between positively or negatively valued actions and outcomes, and to other variables that include attributes of the person being judged, interpersonal relations, and social identity.

In Chapter 5, I apply this conceptual model to the analysis of success and failure in achievement situations, drawing on the results of laboratory studies and other research concerned with attitudes toward high achievers or "tall poppies."

In Chapter 6, I extend the analysis to situations that involve retributive justice. In particular, I present a model that I apply to the analysis of how people react to different types of offenses. This model takes account of values, perceived responsibility, and deservingness. I describe the results of research that investigates the effects of strong versus weak authoritarian values as well as other types of values.

In Chapter 7, I describe the results of research that investigates the effects of like/dislike relations, ingroup/outgroup relations, and perceived moral character on the way people react to different types of offenses.

In Chapter 8, I summarize the main conclusions and relate my conceptual analysis to some other approaches in the literature. I also suggest some possible extensions of the analysis and future directions that might be taken.

CHAPTER 2

Perceived Responsibility

There is a large and complex literature on perceived responsibility that presents philosophical, legal, and psychological analyses of the meaning of the term as well as research findings (e.g., Feinberg, 1970; Fincham & Jaspars, 1980; Hamilton, 1978; Hart, 1968; Hart & Honoré, 1959; Heider, 1958; Robinson & Darley, 1995; Schlenker, Britt, Pennington, Murphy, & Doherty, 1994; Shaver, 1985; Shultz & Darley, 1991; Shultz & Schleifer, 1983; Shultz, Schleifer, & Altman, 1981; Weiner, 1995). These discussions provide distinctions between the different ways in which responsibility has been defined. A perusal of this literature indicates that there is a lot of debate and sometimes confusion about the meaning of the concept and how it is linked to or differentiated from other concepts. The discussions confront us with issues that involve the relation of perceived responsibility for an outcome to causal processes, to a person's capacity to foresee the consequences of events, to role behavior, to legal and moral liability, to intentionality, to mitigating circumstances, to negligence, and to legal and moral justifications.

In this chapter I do not intend to venture into a detailed presentation of this extensive literature. Instead, I will select, by way of example, some treatments of the concept of responsibility that provide insights into its meaning and that are relevant to the model of deservingness that I will present subsequently.

HEIDER'S LEVELS OF RESPONSIBILITY

Because my analysis of deservingness is set within a Heiderian framework, I first describe Heider's discussion of responsibility, as it was presented in his *The Psychology of Interpersonal Relations* (1958). This discussion has been very influential and one can see a direct relation between it and other developments in the conceptual analysis of perceived responsibility (e.g., Weiner, 1995).

Heider refers to personal responsibility in his analysis of how people account for the actions of others and for their own behavior. Consistent with his general approach, he is concerned with identifying the stable structures and processes that underlie the behavior, moving beyond the directly observable facts to uncover underlying dispositional properties of the person's world.

As part of a discussion of the motivational aspects that propel and guide purposive action, Heider makes an important distinction between personal and impersonal causality. According to Heider (1958), "personal causality refers to instances in which p causes x intentionally. That is to say, the action is purposive ... unless intention ties together the cause-effect relations we do not have a true case of personal causality" (p. 100).

Thus, in personal causality, actions are related to a goal and to a person trying to achieve that goal. There is a person-action-outcome sequence tied together by a person's intention. When the effects that occur involve persons but not intentions, then Heider proposes that we are dealing with cases of impersonal causality, and the causal nexus that links the person to the effect is quite different. For example, one can avoid a driverless car that is running downhill by stepping to one side, changing the conditions in order to escape the danger. The car will not change its path in order to find the avoiding person and the avoidance reaction is a simple one. The cause in this case is impersonal, involving a nonpersonal source, namely the driverless car. But the situation would be very different if one were being pursued by another person who intended to inflict harm or injury. The pursued person might act in different ways in order to escape the injury, modifying behavior in order to avoid the pursuer and move to safety. The pursuer might also modify behavior in order to catch the person he or she is pursuing. Causality in this case is personal because the action sequence involves active intentions that relate to the goals of the pursuer and the pursued.

What are the distinctive characteristics of the causal nexus that apply to personal causality? We have already seen that an intention that relates to a goal is a necessary condition. Heider (1958) also proposes that "personal causality is characterized by equifinality, that is, the invariance of the end and variability of the means. Vicarious mediation with respect to an end point is an essential feature of the operational definition of purpose" (p. 101). He refers to Tolman (1932) and Brunswik (1952) who take a similar position. People behaving within some goal structure can adopt different means in their attempts to move toward their goal. If one means is thwarted or blocked, they can then try another. The persistence they show in moving toward an intended goal via one or more means defines their actions as purposive.

In addition, Heider (1958) argues that in personal causality the invariant end or goal is due to the person. He or she is the locus of the effects:

> Because the person controls the causal lines emanating from himself, he not only is the initial source of the produced change, but he remains the persistent cause. Here, if anywhere, one can speak of a local cause, the second characteristic of the causal network in personal causality ... within a wide range of environmental conditions, the person may be thought of as the one necessary and sufficient condition for the effect to occur, for within the wide range the person changes the means to achieve the end, the end itself remaining unaltered. (p. 102)

Thus, the essence of personal causality involves both equifinality and local causality.

How does this distinction relate to the assignment of responsibility? Heider argues that, "if we are convinced that o did x intentionally we generally link the x more intimately with the person than if we think that o did x unintentionally" (p. 112). That is, the other person (o) is seen as more responsible for the action and its outcome (x) in the former instance. We would be less likely to hold a person responsible if the outcome implied that a person lacked ability or if the cause of the outcome could be attributed to variable environmental factors, such as good or bad luck, or to more stable environmental factors, such as the difficulty of the task. Thus, for Heider, the attribution of responsibility implies personal causality when the effects are intended and, "it varies with the relative contribution of environmental factors to the action outcome; in general the more they are felt to influence the action, the less the person is held responsible" (p. 113).

Heider then proposes that there are different levels of responsibility, corresponding to the different ways in which the concept of responsibility has been used and reflecting differences in the degree to which causes are attributed to the person or to the environment. At the most primitive level a person is held responsible for any effect that is associated with him or her, that is, connected with the person in any way.

At the next level, causal processes are involved and a person (p) is held responsible for any effect that he or she caused in the sense that p is seen as a necessary condition for the effect to occur, even though he or she could not have foreseen the outcome and its further consequences.

Heider sees this level as involving impersonal causality rather than personal causality because intentions are not necessarily involved. He compares this level with Piaget's (1932) concept of objective responsibility, assumed by Piaget to occur at an earlier stage of development in contrast to subjective responsibility that involves a consideration of motives.

The next level involves holding p responsible, either directly or indirectly, for any effect that he or she could have foreseen, even though it was not part of his or her goal or intention. Thus, this level also falls outside the framework of personal causality.

At the next level p is held to be responsible for effects that he or she intended and that have their source in p. This level clearly involves personal causality and it corresponds to Piaget's subjective responsibility.

Finally, Heider describes a stage where p's own motives may not be entirely ascribed to p but may have their source in the environment. In this case p acts with intention but there may be coercion from the environment. The behavior still fits within the structure of personal causality but responsibility is shared between the person and the environment. In summary, Heider (1958) reiterates that:

> the issue of responsibility includes the problem of attribution of action. That is, it is important which of the several conditions of action—the intentions of the person, personal power factors, or environmental factors—is to be given primary weight for the action outcome. Once such attribution has been decided upon, the evaluation of responsibility is possible. (p. 114)

There have been detailed analyses of aspects of Heider's levels of responsibility that examine the conceptual status of the levels and the empirical evidence that relates to them and that in some cases revise or reconceptualize Heider's analysis in various ways (e.g., Brewer, 1977; Fincham & Jaspars, 1980; Fishbein & Ajzen, 1973; Shaver, 1985). Are they true developmental stages? Do they form a unidimensional scale? How does perceived responsibility relate to blameworthiness? Shaver (1985) concludes his review by stating that "the levels cannot be regarded as true developmental stages ... the levels cannot be considered to be points along some underlying unidimensional continuum" (p. 95). It should be noted, however, that Heider did not think of his levels as developmental stages but rather as different kinds of attribution (Fincham & Jaspars, 1980, p. 90).

My purpose in describing Heider's analysis of perceived responsibility is to emphasize the following points: (1) The analysis of responsibility can be set within a framework in which a person performs an action that leads to some outcome or consequence. The degree to which there is personal causation involving intentionality is an important condition for assigning responsibility to the person for the outcome; (2) The person acts within an environmental context that contains features that may also affect the attribution of responsibility, reducing a person's responsibility, for example, where there is evidence that the person was coerced by outside forces to perform the act; (3) There are different meanings of responsibility or perhaps, more accurately, different conditions that may underlie a judgment of personal responsibility. These different conditions are to some extent captured in Heider's distinction between different levels.

COMMON SENSE AND LEGAL ASPECTS OF RESPONSIBILITY

Consistent with his general approach, Heider's (1958) discussion of responsibility proceeded from a consideration of the way people explain actions in everyday life. He called his approach "the naive analysis of action," and he drew on the way people try to make sense both of the actions of others and of their own behavior by referring to personal and situational factors such as effort, ability, difficulty, and luck, which are a part of their everyday language.

How is "responsible" used in everyday language? The *Oxford English Dictionary* lists a number of meanings of the word responsible. These meanings include "liable to be called to account" and to be "answerable" to someone else, and "morally accountable for actions" and "capable of rational conduct." The term is also used to refer to a person who is "of good credit or position or repute, respectable, apparently trustworthy."

Fincham and Jaspars (1980) summarize these meanings by stating that:

> the central notion of responsibility in common sense is the idea that a person can be held accountable for something; he is answerable to someone or some social institution for his actions or the outcomes of those actions, although he may be asked to answer for acts not performed but that may have been expected on account of his position. Finally, he may be regarded as someone who is not accountable for some act because he lacks the capability of fulfilling certain obligations. (p. 96)

They also point out that the notion of accountability is a central one that has been used in legal philosophy to express the essential meaning of responsibility (e.g., Hart, 1968; Hart & Honoré, 1959).

Discussions of the ways in which responsibility has been defined by legal experts have been presented by Feinberg (1970), Fincham and Jaspars (1980), Hamilton and Sanders (1992), Shaver (1985), Shultz and Darley (1991), and Shultz and Schleifer (1983), among others. A number of these discussions refer to meanings of the term that were proposed by the legal philosopher, Hart (1968). I do likewise here without much elaboration.

Hart distinguishes between role responsibility, capacity responsibility, causal responsibility, and legal and moral liability responsibility. _Role responsibility_ refers to the demands and obligations made on a person by the role or position that he or she holds. For example, parents are responsible for the welfare of their children; an army officer is responsible for the safety of his soldiers. Responsibility is, therefore, tied to a particular role and the duties that are prescribed by the role. A person in a superior role may also be held responsible for a negative event or consequence produced by a subordinate. In this case the superior is not directly responsible; rather the responsibility is vicarious. As Hamilton and Sanders (1992) note, vicarious responsibility has been most richly developed in military law (see also Kelman & Hamilton, 1989), but it also applies in the civilian realm where "liability may be based on the existence of a role relationship as well as on the employer's actual behavior with respect to role obligations in the relationship" (Hamilton & Sanders, 1992, p. 15).

Capacity responsibility takes account of a person's capacity to respond. The person has to be able to understand the consequences of his or her actions, to be able to reason, and to have control over the actions that he or she takes. For example, a young child may be deemed not to have the capacity to commit an offense in the legal sense; a person suffering from a psychosis may likewise be deemed not to have "a guilty mind" and hence not to be responsible for an offense because of diminished capacity.

Causal responsibility acknowledges that when one is attributing responsibility for an event that has occurred one also looks for a causal relation that links the person with the event. As Hamilton and Sanders (1992) state:

> in most cases where responsibility is assigned there must be, in the language of tort law, a "cause in fact" relationship between the individual's behavior and the consequence. The behavior must be a necessary part of a minimal set of conditions sufficient to produce the consequence. (p. 14)

In _legal and moral liability responsibility_ a person is liable to punishment or other negative consequences if certain criteria are met that include a guilty mind (mens rea), normal capacities, and some connection with the offense that has been committed, either directly by the person or by association with the agent of the offense.

Shaver presents a working definition of responsibility that incorporates these various distinctions. Shaver (1985) proposes that:

> The unmodified term, "responsibility," will be defined as a judgment made about the moral accountability of a person of normal capacities, which judgment usually but not always involves a causal connection between the person being judged and some morally disapproved action or event. (p. 66)

In cases of legal and moral liability a person is liable to sanctions if he or she is unable to provide a satisfactory answer to a charge or complaint. In order to avoid the charge the person has to provide answers that reduce or mitigate the level of responsibility. Recall that the dictionary definition of responsibility refers to answerability and accountability.

What kinds of answers might be given? Hamilton and Sanders (1992) list a number of possibilities (see also Hamilton & Hagiwara, 1992; Shaver, 1985, pp. 83–84). In the case of *denial* an accused person might simply deny any connection with the offense. In the case of a *demurrer* an accused person might claim that there is no rule that is being disobeyed and so he or she is not answerable. In the case of a *collateral defense* a person might challenge another's right to enforce a rule without necessarily denying that a norm has been violated. In the case of a *justification* an accused person might attempt to justify his or her actions by appealing to some rule or order that was obeyed that would make an action acceptable, as would be the case if a soldier was following orders that were handed down by a superior officer, a defense that might be presented in cases of crimes of obedience (e.g., Kelman & Hamilton, 1989).

According to Hamilton and Sanders (1992), "demurrers, collateral defenses, and justifications indicate ways in which responsibility is tied to roles" (pp. 17–18). An accused person might also provide an *excuse*. Excuses are more closely tied to the way we account for human action. For example, an accused person might claim that the action occurred accidentally and was not intended or that he or she was not capable of performing the action. Some excuses might work in a legal defense; others might not completely exculpate the accused person. As Hamilton and Sanders (1992) note, a person's claim that he or she did not intend to inflict harm on a victim might excuse him or her from a charge of first-degree murder but not from a charge of manslaughter.

Hamilton and Sanders (1992) conclude from their discussion of philosophy and jurisprudence that the assignment of responsibility "is contingent upon at least two factors: what the person did, and what the person was obliged to do. General obligations may apply to anyone in a situation; social roles also impose further, more specific obligations" (p. 18). They relate their analysis of legal discussions to Heider's (1958) stages of responsibility attribution, showing that there is some parallel between these stages and the legal concepts. Thus, Heider's first level of association would be evident when a role relationship is present and a person is responsible for another's conduct by association. The second, third, and fourth levels described by Heider refer to conditions where, in legal terms, there would be strict liability, negligence liability, and criminal liability, respectively. The fifth level relates to excuses that might be provided by a person to justify or mitigate an offense.

THE TRIANGLE MODEL OF RESPONSIBILITY

The previous sections presented notions of responsibility that have emerged from common sense, social psychology, and legal philosophy. They show that responsibility has different meanings that relate to the degree of association, causal processes, a person's capacity to foresee the consequences of action, intentionality, and the role that a person occupies. These different meanings have been brought together in a triangle model of responsibility that has been presented by Schlenker et al. (1994). These authors describe the origins of the concept of responsibility and they distinguish between definitions that refer to imputation and causality and definitions that focus on answerability, liability, and sanctions. Like Fincham and Jaspars (1980) and Shaver (1985), they note that causality in the legal sense usually differs from causality in the scientific sense. However, the question about what caused an event remains an important one to be addressed when people attribute responsibility for actions and outcomes, much like the question about answerability and its relation to rules, obligations, and duties that relate to a person's role.

In their triangle model of responsibility Schlenker et al. (1994) propose three key elements that are linked together in a triangle. These elements are the *prescriptions* that should guide the actor's conduct, the *event* that either occurred or is anticipated and that is relevant to the prescriptions, and a set of *identity images* that concern the actor's "roles, qualities, convictions, and aspirations" (p. 634). In order to assign responsibility, a person has to have information about what occurred (the event itself), what the relevant prescriptions are, and what the characteristics are of the actor who is involved. Schlenker et al. propose that the combined strength of the linkages between these three elements determines how much responsibility will be assigned to an actor for an event. The evaluating audience "looks down" on the triangle, and different audiences may reach different conclusions about the actor's responsibility, depending on how they view the linkages in the triangle. Thus, according to Schlenker et al. (1994), responsibility is assigned to an actor in a situation to the extent that:

> (a) a clear, well-defined set of prescriptions is applicable to the event (prescription-event link), (b) the actor is perceived to be bound by the prescriptions by virtue of his or her identity (prescription-identity link), and (c) the actor seems to be connected to the event, especially by seeming to have (or to have had) personal control over the event, such as intentionally producing the consequences (identity-event link). (p. 635)

If we were to apply this analysis to a case where an accused person injured another person, the judgment of responsibility would be influenced by societal and legal prescriptions that relate to the event (e.g., People should not inflict injury on other persons; the prescription-event link), by information about the actor and the prescriptions (e.g., Is the person obliged to follow the prescriptions by virtue of his or her identity in relation to capacity, role, etc.?; the prescription-identity link), and by information about the actor and the event (e.g., Did the actor intend to injure the other person?; the identity-event link).

It will be apparent that the Schlenker et al. triangle model combines the different meanings of responsibility that were described in the previous sections. In order to assign responsibility we have to know something about societal norms and prescriptions and how they apply to the event, something about whether these prescriptions apply to the actor by virtue of his or her role, status, and obligations, and something about the actor and his or her capacities and intentions. Schlenker et al. discuss these different links in detail. They note that the prescription-identity link incorporates many of the aspects of both philosophical and psychological analyses of responsibility, encompassing both the focus on duties, obligations, and roles that make the actor liable for sanctions, and the idea of capacity responsibility that is necessary if the actor is to be held liable for criminal sanctions. They also note that the identity-event link brings in the imputation facet of responsibility and an interest in the causal role played by the actor. In particular, they highlight the importance of answering the question: To what extent did the actor have personal control over his or her conduct and its consequences? Thus, they state:

> If the actor can be seen as having personal control, that is, as intend-
> ing to produce certain foreseeable effects, and doing so under condi-
> tions in which excusing circumstances are absent or minimal, then
> the actor should be regarded as liable for any positive or negative
> sanctions that would be associated with the type of conduct. As
> personal control decreases, so does the actor's responsibility.
> (Schlenker et al., 1994, p. 639)

They go on to say that responsibility is not simply a matter of
internal versus external causality. Some internal causes may be outside
a person's control, such as when a person is depressed and performs
poorly on a task. Some external causes may fail to mitigate or excuse a
person's responsibility when that person was in control of what happened, such as when a criminal is paid to commit murder and carries
out the crime.

Schlenker et al. argue that a judgment of control is important for
assessing responsibility because it makes sense from a societal perspective to sanction people for events that they controlled. Sanctions can
then be used to influence the future decisions that they may make,
perhaps increasing the likelihood that their conduct will be channeled
into prescribed paths that are approved by society. Furthermore, a judgment that a person has personal control over a particular set of actions
or decisions may also have implications for how the person is evaluated
in relation to character. Thus:

> Society cares about people's character and judgment, because char-
> acter and judgment are the stable personal origins of decisions how
> to act. The application of negative sanctions is meant to alter the
> actor's character or judgment so as to obtain "better" conduct in the
> future, just as the application of positive sanctions is meant to rein-
> force the actor's character and judgment. Thus, to say that people are
> autonomous beings who are responsible for their conduct is to say
> that people exercise personal control over the production of events.
> (Schlenker et al., 1994, p. 639)

The three elements within the triangle model may vary in importance. For example, some prescriptions are more important than others
when they involve strongly held values or when they are associated with
greater positive or negative sanctions (e.g., rewards or punishments).
Some events are more important than others, depending on the degree
to which an event leads to positive or negative consequences. The
identity element would become more important the more it involves
central and valued components of self. Schlenker et al. (1994) refer to the
combined importance of the elements as their *potency*, a variable that
will affect evaluative judgments.

These judgments are also assumed to be affected by the combined strength of the connections or links between the elements in the triangle. Responsibility would be especially high if the three links were strong. Under these conditions, transfer of information can occur and "strong responsibility linkages produce compatible associations and categorizations across the elements" (Schlenker et al., 1994, p. 636). In particular, strong responsibility may transfer information from an event to an actor who is behaving according to a set of prescriptions, a transfer that involves both evaluative generalizations and corresponding labeling of the elements (Schlenker et al., 1994, p. 636). For example, a person who is involved in a violent crime may be labeled in a way that fits the crime; a person who succeeds in the world of business may be labeled in a way that is consistent with the achievement. Strong linkages between the elements would also indicate which sanctions are appropriate. Thus:

> responsibility is the adhesive that connects an actor with an event and a set of prescriptions for conduct. It acts as a psychological highway that permits information to flow to the person who is judged to be responsible for a particular event. Ultimately, responsibility permits sanctions to be distributed fairly.... Before a performance, high responsibility provides purpose and direction to behavior; strong linkages are directly rated to determination. After a performance, high responsibility entitles the actor to pertinent rewards or punishments. (Schlenker et al., 1994, p. 640)

These ideas as well as other aspects of the triangle model are summarized in Table 2.1. Schlenker et al. report studies that are based on their conceptualization and that incorporate the various links. The results of these studies show that attributions of responsibility are a direct function of the strength of the three linkages, and when people are asked to judge responsibility, they seek out information that is relevant to the linkages.

JUDGMENTS OF RESPONSIBILITY

The question of how we conceptualize responsibility, its antecedents, and its effects has also been addressed by Weiner (1995, 1996) in an influential analysis. The perspective taken by Weiner is that of an experimental social psychologist concerned with the study of human motivation and influenced by Heider's approach, especially in regard to attribution theory.

Like Heider, Weiner (1995) distinguishes between personal and impersonal causality and argues that judgments of responsibility require evidence of human involvement or personal causality. Not all causality

Table 2.1. Antecedents and Consequences of Responsibility Linkages

Category	Identity-prescription link	Identity-event link	Prescription-event link
State represented by a strong link	Obligation or duty	Personal control	Goal and procedural clarity
Antecedents of a strong link	Actor bound by prescriptions (Examples: clear, unconflicting role requirements; clear personal obligations as a result of the actor's convictions and attributes; being an adult citizen of sound mind and therefore legally responsible)	Actor connected to the event, especially if seen as having personal control over the outcomes (Examples: actor seen as intentionally producing the consequences without coercion or pressure)	Clear prescriptions describe what should occur (Examples: clear goals and rules; obvious scripts for conduct)
Psychological and behavioral consequences of a strong link	Sense of purpose and direction; increased effort and persistence toward goals; lower uncertainty and anxiety	Higher self-efficacy, feelings of internal control, and intrinsic motivation; increased effort and persistence toward goals; lower anxiety	Clarity of purpose and procedure; self-confidence as a result of certainty about goals and rules; lower uncertainty and anxiety
Excuses to weaken the link	Argue prescriptions are not relevant to one's identity or provide conflicting instructions given one's identity (Examples: "I have diplomatic immunity"; "It wasn't my job"; "I was mentally ill"; "I had to miss work because of family duties")	Argue lack of personal control over the event or lack of foreseeable outcomes (Examples: "I failed because I had a bad cold"; "I couldn't help it, I was drunk"; "It was an accident, I didn't mean to do it")	Argue prescriptions are ambiguous or provide conflicting instructions given the situation (Examples: "The requirements were unclear"; "The rules made no sense, they were confusing and contradictory")

Source: Schlenker et al. (1994). Copyright © 1994 by the American Psychological Association. Reprinted with permission.

is personal. One can account for an event, for example, by attributing causality to the situation or environment. Some people may assert that unemployment is caused by unfavorable economic conditions rather than by causes that reside in the unemployed themselves. A judgment of responsibility, however, requires as a first step that the cause of an event be located in the person, that is, that the locus of the cause is internal or personal rather than external or nonpersonal. Weiner (1986) reminds us that causal location has been shown in many studies to be an important dimension of causal thinking.

Assigning the cause of an event to the person, however, does not necessarily result in a judgment that the person is responsible for the event. It may be the case that the cause is uncontrollable, that is, the cause is located in the person but he or she can do little or nothing about it. A person suffering from a severe and debilitating illness may be impeded from finding a job or enjoying an active life. A child who is mentally handicapped may not be able to cope with mastering subjects at school that other children can master. In these cases the cause is within the person, but it is uncontrollable and the person would not be held responsible for its effects. The person cannot change the cause by an act of will. He or she does not have the freedom to make that choice.

In other cases, causes that are located in the person may be seen as controllable, that is, the person has the power to change them. A student whose failure at an important examination can be attributed to lack of effort can change that cause by working harder in the future. Effort is an internal, controllable cause; it can be turned on or off by an act of will or intention. Similarly, a driver who gets a fine for speeding can drive more slowly in the future. The cause is under the person's control; the driver can change it.

Weiner (1995) proposes that assignment of responsibility for an event requires attribution to an internal, controllable cause. However, he does not equate causal controllability and responsibility. Thus, he states that:

> Controllability refers to the characteristics of a cause—causes, such as the absence of effort or lack of aptitude, are or are not subject to volitional alteration. Responsibility, on the other hand, refers to a judgment made about a person—he or she "should" or "ought to have" done otherwise, such as trying harder, eating less, or paying more attention when driving. (p. 8)

Thus, the inference that a person is responsible for an event and its outcome involves a shift from an initial causal analysis to a focus on the person. Weiner proposes that responsibility is not an attribution but a judgment. He reserves the term "attribution" for that part of the process where attention is given to the cause of an event, to a causal analysis that may then lead to a judgment of responsibility.

This distinction becomes clearer when one considers the role of mitigating circumstances. A judgment of responsibility might be softened, alleviated, or eliminated if there are mitigating circumstances. A person might be able to justify his or her behavior in terms of outside pressures or other circumstance, as when a student claims that he or she had to reduce study time in order to care for a sick mother or spouse, or when a police officer intentionally injures a person because others were in danger of being harmed. In other cases, a claim of mitigation might be based on the alleged incapacity of a wrongdoer to foresee the consequences of his or her actions or to distinguish between right and wrong, a defense that might be used for young children or for the insane. Weiner (1995) points out that the circumstances that may absolve a person from responsibility for an alleged offense are hotly debated in the courts and by philosophers.

The main component processes involved in the assignment of responsibility are presented in Figure 2.1. Weiner describes the sequence of events that are represented in Figure 2.1 as conscious and effortful, involving controlled processing, but he also acknowledges that judgments of responsibility may occur automatically and unconsciously. So

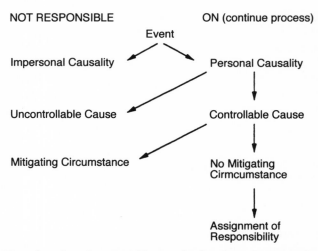

Figure 2.1. Flow chart describing variables involved in the assignment of responsibility for an outcome. Weiner (1995). Reprinted with the permission of the author and Guilford Publishing.

Figure 2.1 presents one particular sequence that is intended to capture the main components and the sequence in which they are assumed to occur. It also represents the judgment process as an on-off process in the interests of simplification.

Where do concepts such as intention and negligence fit into this picture? Weiner acknowledges that the inferences that people make are not all-or-none inferences but vary in their degree. Mitigating circumstances, for example, may reduce the degree to which a person is held to be responsible for an action and its outcome. Whether an action is perceived to be intended or unintended or due to negligence will also affect judgments of the degree of responsibility. A person may commit an offense unintentionally even though he or she should have foreseen the consequences of the action that was taken. In such cases the person may be judged to be negligent but less responsible when compared with the responsibility assigned to the person for an intentionally produced outcome, a difference that is captured in the distinction between manslaughter and murder and between an accidental arithmetical error and tax fraud, or, in everyday life, between accidentally spilling a cup of coffee on someone's carpet and purposely damaging another person's property.

Judgments of responsibility are important for Weiner because they play a key role in social motivation in situations where, for example, the success or failure of others is evaluated, people are stigmatized or not stigmatized, help is given to another person or not given, or anger and aggression are directed toward others. Weiner (1995) proposes that people feel anger toward others who are responsible for negative outcomes, whereas they are more likely to report sympathy toward others who are the victims of negative outcomes. Thus, "anger follows from the perception that others are responsible for a negative plight, whereas sympathy is generated when others are not responsible for their negative condition" (p. 257).

These affective reactions are assumed to be stronger the more important and personally relevant the context is. They follow a cognitive appraisal that takes account of personal causation, controllability, and mitigating circumstances that together lead to the assignment of responsibility (Figure 2.1). These positive and negative affective reactions are also assumed to play a motivating role. For example, we are more likely to help others when we feel sympathetic toward them; we are more likely to want to exact some retribution when we are angry about a person who has harmed us in some way. Weiner (1995, 1996) documents a lot of research that is consistent with this analysis, including many studies from his own laboratory (see also Graham, Weiner, & Zucker, 1997).

It will be noted that the analysis involves a thinking-feeling-acting sequence. Weiner acknowledges that this is not an invariant sequence and is probably most applicable in situations that engage self processes and that involve important goals.

Finally, Weiner (1995) relates his analysis to his earlier attributional analysis of achievement striving (Weiner, 1986), which also involves a sequence in which there is thinking about causes, consequential affect, and subsequent behavior, but where the sequence concerns personal motivation rather than social motivation and the affects involve pride, guilt, and shame rather than anger and sympathy. He proposes that the two analyses can be integrated.

RESPONSIBILITY AND BLAME

Is holding someone responsible for an outcome the same as blaming them for it? In this section I present three approaches to this question, taking as my examples proposals that have been presented by Shaver, Weiner, and Shultz and his coauthors.

Analysis of the Attribution of Blame

Shaver (1985) provides us with a detailed and closely argued analysis of causal processes, responsibility, and blame, to which I have referred in part in previous sections. He distinguishes between responsibility and blame in a sequential analysis that takes account of attributions of causality, knowledge of possible consequences, intentionality, coercion, appreciation of moral responsibility, and justification and excuses. In his model he assumes that a judgment of blameworthiness depends on a prior judgment of responsibility, which in turn rests on a particular attribution of causality. The model is presented as a flow chart and it incorporates the results of a detailed analysis of ideas from social psychology (e.g., Heider), jurisprudence, and philosophy. The flow chart is presented with the caution that it cannot do justice to the complexities involved in attributing causality and assigning responsibility. Furthermore, the model is presented from the point of view of an "ideal" observer and is a simplification in the sense that it excludes the use of heuristics, individual difference variables that might influence the attribution process, and personal needs and motives.

Shaver does emphasize, however, that the attribution of blame involves a process that rests on a causal analysis for morally disapproved consequences (single versus multiple causes) and that takes account of the various dimensions of responsibility (levels of causality, knowledge, intentionality, coercion, and the appreciation of moral wrongfulness) as well as the presence or absence of justifications and excuses. One can use the flow chart that he presents to determine whether there is an absence of blame or blameworthiness. Thus, Shaver (1985) states that:

> When an intentional, voluntary action taken with full knowledge of the consequences and capacity to understand the consequences is the sole cause of a negative occurrence, the actor is justifiably liable for blame.... Once the actor stands accused, he or she may say nothing in defense, simply accepting all the blame that is to come. Or the actor may provide either a justification or an excuse. If either of these replies is accepted by the perceiver, there will be an assignment of substantial moral responsibility, but still no *blame*. Only if the perceiver rejects the justification, or rejects the excuse, will there be the final assignment of blame. (p. 172)

Blame as a Blend Concept

Weiner (1995) also discusses the relation between responsibility and blame but, unlike Shaver, he does not make a clear distinction between the two concepts. According to Weiner, blame is a "blend" concept that is similar to responsibility in its cognitive aspect but that also involves negative affect that is akin to anger. Moreover, it is a concept that is applied to negative actions and outcomes, whereas responsibility is affectively neutral and can be applied to both positive and negative outcomes. We may blame a person for a negative outcome but not for a positive outcome, whereas a person may be seen as responsible for either of these types of outcomes. In addition, we do not blame a person when a negative outcome is trivial or unimportant. Instead, we reserve the term for negative outcomes that are of some magnitude and that may have important consequences. In contrast, a person may be deemed to be responsible for both trivial and more important outcomes. Blame may attach to the latter but not to the former.

Weiner does not see blame as a variable that mediates between responsibility and social behavior. Instead, he proposes that anger and sympathy are the variables that mediate between judgments of responsibility and the sorts of social behaviors with which he is concerned.

Finally, whereas mitigating circumstances reduce perceived responsibility in Weiner's analysis, for Shaver excuses and justifications for a negative event are crucial variables that enable a distinction to be made between responsibility and blame. Thus, the Shaver analysis puts blame at the end of a complex sequence that involves responsibility as a prior variable and that assigns mitigating circumstances a different role when compared with Weiner's analysis.

Information-Processing Model

The question of responsibility and blame is also addressed by Shultz and his colleagues in articles that contain detailed discussion of attribution concepts and legal concepts (e.g, Shultz & Darley, 1991; Shultz & Schleifer, 1983). These discussions take us into complex issues concerned with the nature of causation, the meaning of responsibility, the determination of punishment, and the judgment of benefit. They are especially valuable in drawing attention to the way legal theorists and philosophers have dealt with some of these questions, and in the sorts of examples they provide from actual legal cases.

Here I will refer briefly to an information-processing model that has been applied by Shultz and Darley (1991) to moral judgments made in the context of retributive justice using legal reasoning. The model was developed to deal with cases where a person may have harmed another person. It is a stepwise model that takes account of cause, personal and vicarious responsibility, whether the person should be blamed, and how punishment might be administered. The model is presented in Figure 2.2.

Shultz and Darley (1991) argue that a "judgment of responsibility presupposes a positive prior decision on causation" (p. 254), and that "a judgment of blame presupposes a prior positive judgment of responsibility" (p. 255). Thus, if a person can offer an excuse for the harm, then there is a refusal to accept responsibility for the harm and the issue of blame does not arise. Similarly, if the person can justify the harm by saying that the action and its outcome were not bad on balance, then he or she would successfully avoid blame but still be seen as responsible for the outcome (cf. Shaver, 1985). These two kinds of defense (excuses and justifications) presuppose a positive judgment of causation.

A further presupposition in the model is that "a judgment of punishment presupposes a prior positive decision on blame. Blame is a decision that a person is at fault (given positive decisions on causation and responsibility). If a person is not at fault, then no decision needs to be taken on punishment" (Shultz & Darley, 1991, p. 256).

Shultz and Darley refer to psychological evidence for the relations in the model that come from studies that have used path analysis. In path analysis, relations between variables are examined after controlling

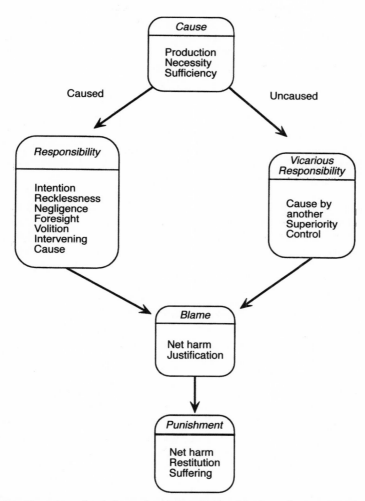

Figure 2.2. Overview of an information-processing model of moral reasoning. Shultz and Darley (1991). Reprinted with the permission of the author and Lawrence Erlbaum Associates, Inc.

statistically for the effects of other variables. In one study Shultz, Schleifer, and Altman (1981) presented participants with hypothetical cases where a passenger in a ship fell overboard and was drowned. The conditions surrounding the event were varied to take account of necessary and sufficient conditions that led to the drowning. Participants provided ratings of cause ("To what extent do you think the [protagonist] was the cause of the [victim's] death"), moral responsibility ("To what extent do you think the [protagonist] is morally responsible for the [victim's] death"), and severity of punishment ("To what extent do you think the [protagonist] should be punished for the [victim's] death"). These concepts were defined on the cover sheet of the questionnaire as follows:

> The question of *cause* concerns the issue of whether or not the harm was *produced* by the protagonist. The question of *moral responsibility* refers to the extent to which the protagonist is *worthy of blame*. And the question of *punishment* deals with the recommended *consequences* for the protagonist. (Shultz et al., 1981, p. 242)

One result obtained from this study was that the relation between the ratings of cause and the ratings of severity of punishment were mediated by participants' ratings of moral responsibility. There were direct positive relations linking cause to responsibility and responsibility to punishment, but the relation from cause to punishment was indirect and mediated by responsibility. Note, however, that the definition of moral responsibility provided to participants by Shultz et al. (1981) imported value considerations ("worthy of blame"). Thus, the concept becomes very similar to what is meant by deservingness, where blame is a negative event that occurs following harm to another person and "worthiness" implies deservingness.

In another study by Shultz and Rose, referred to by Shultz and Darley (1991, p. 257), judgments of blame were obtained separately from judgments of responsibility. Strong relations were found in this study between judgments of responsibility and judgments of blame and between judgments of blame and judgments of severity of punishment. A path analysis showed that the relation between judgments of responsibility and the perceived severity of punishment was much weaker, however, after controlling statistically for differences in judgments of blame, suggesting that this relation was mediated by judgments of blame.

Shultz and Darley also discuss the importance of distinguishing between necessary and sufficient causes when analyzing causation. They refer to variables that affect judgments of personal responsibility and vicarious responsibility, to the role of justification in negating blame, and to variables that might mitigate the severity of punishment. They also describe the development of a computer model to simulate how the ordinary person reasons about harm-doing, incorporating the components that are presented in Figure 2.2.

CONCLUDING COMMENTS

My selective review of the ways in which responsibility has been discussed in the social psychological literature shows that the concept is complex and carries with it more than one meaning. The various treatments of the concept draw upon common sense and philosophical, psychological, and legal discussions and they raise many questions that are still to be answered. For example, does responsibility that is attributed to a person's role have different implications for social judgment when compared with responsibility that is attributed to a person's intentional behavior? What is meant by moral responsibility as distinct from other forms of responsibility? And what does "moral" mean in this context? Are responsibility and blame overlapping terms, or can they be clearly distinguished? To what extent do people move through a clearly defined sequence of cognitive events when judging responsibility, or are these judgments more immediate and automatic? Might the judgments follow affects like anger and sympathy rather than precede these affects, that is, an affect-cognition sequence rather than a cognition-affect sequence? How do individual differences in needs and values and in self-protective mechanisms affect these judgments? Are these judgments also a function of the magnitude of the outcome and its relevance to the perceiver, as those who investigate defensive attribution might claim when the outcome is negative? Are judgments of responsibility affected by interpersonal relations and by ingroup/outgroup relations?

The preceding selection of questions is by no means exhaustive. I will address some of these questions in succeeding chapters in relation to the analysis of deservingness, but I lay no claim to providing complete answers (see also Feather 1996b). Nor do I intend to become involved in a detailed and critical examination of the literature that pertains to some of these questions. My main intention has been to draw out some general ideas about responsibility that give the concept more substance, a necessary aim because, as I indicated in the previous chapter, judgments of responsibility are assumed to affect the way we judge deservingness.

For the moment I will conclude with two general statements: (1) The various treatments of responsibility that I have described assume a framework in which a person or actor performs an action that leads to some outcome. The issue of personal versus impersonal causality is important, especially in regard to the degree to which the causes of actions are perceived to be controllable; (2) There are different meanings of responsibility but each meaning assumes that there is an association between the person and the action that is taken. The person or actor is seen by others to "own" the action, to be bonded to the action, so that together they form a unit.

The strength of this unit, however, will vary depending on the context and the information that is available about the person or actor. For example, a unit that reflects strong intention on the part of the person or actor, and the absence of coercion or other external pressures or constraints that might have forced the action, will be a stronger unit than one where the intention to produce the outcome is absent and where causal attributions can be plausibly made to external forces and to other uncontrollable constraints. The idea of unit formation is one that was developed by Heider (1958), and I will discuss it in more detail in the context of the model of deservingness that I will present in a subsequent chapter.

CHAPTER 3

Values and Valences

The way we judge deservingness depends not only on our beliefs about a person's responsibility or lack of responsibility for an action and its outcome but on other variables as well, especially on how we evaluate both the action and the outcome. I made that point at the beginning of this book, noting that positively valued outcomes that follow positively valued actions and negatively valued outcomes that follow negatively valued actions are both seen to be deserved, whereas negatively valued outcomes that follow positively valued outcomes and positively valued outcomes that follow negatively valued actions are both seen to be undeserved. Thus, judgments of deservingness are associated with actions and outcomes that are congruent in their evaluations; judgments of undeservingness are associated with actions and outcomes that are incongruent in their evaluations.

But what determines whether a particular action or outcome is viewed positively or negatively or as good or bad? Why might some people see another's action as courageous whereas others see it as foolhardy; why might some people see another's success as a positive achievement whereas others evaluate the success less positively?

We are confronted here with the basic issue of how to explain differences in evaluation. In this chapter I will propose that these differences are related to differences among people in the importance they assign to underlying values. For example, those who see another's action as courageous are likely to be individuals who believe courage is an important value relative to other values in their value hierarchy; those who react less positively to another's success are likely to be individuals who believe achievement is a less important value relative to others in their value hierarchy. These statements are not tautologies. They distinguish between the general values that people are assumed to hold and the effects of these values on the way they evaluate particular events and outcomes

Thus, the main focus of this chapter will be on values and their effects on specific evaluations. I will also describe studies from my research program that are relevant to this issue. The emphasis will be on differences among people in regard to the importance they assign to basic values and on how these differences are reflected in the evaluations they make in different situations. It is important to acknowledge that these evaluations will also be influenced by many other variables that include social and group pressures, transient moods, personal needs, and features of the particular situation in which an event occurs. I will note these variables in the course of this chapter, but primary attention will be given to relations between general values and the specific positive or negative evaluations that are assigned by people to actions and outcomes that occur within a defined situation.

THE CONCEPT OF VALUE

Discussions about what values are and how they function at personal and social levels go back over the centuries. These discussions are certainly not exclusive to psychologists. They come from all fields of social science—psychology, sociology, anthropology, economics, political science, education, and religion, as well as being an important concern of philosophers.

In these discussions certain key issues have been considered. These include the questions of how to define and classify values; the assumed "oughtness" quality of values and how they function as superordinate categories; the relation of values to means and ends and to persons and objects; how values influence preferences and choice; how values affect the way people perceive or construe events; the main influences that affect the development of values; how values relate to attitudes and beliefs at the individual and societal levels, and so on. The sociological and social psychological literature contain many thoughtful and useful discussions about values and value systems that are too numerous to summarize here.

Analysis of Values

My approach to values was influenced by the seminal contributions made by Milton Rokeach (1973). Rokeach drew attention to the fact that social psychologists tend to ignore the concept of value, favoring instead to focus on the psychology of attitudes. He saw values as general beliefs that are more abstract than either attitudes or specific beliefs. Attitudes and specific beliefs are associated with particular objects and events, whereas Rokeach proposes that values transcend objects and situations. He conceptualizes values as the general beliefs that people hold about desirable and undesirable modes of conduct and end states of existence. Thus, honesty as a mode of conduct might be preferred to dishonesty; honesty is seen as desirable and dishonesty as undesirable. Equality, as an end state of existence or general goal, might be preferred to inequality; it is seen as more desirable than inequality. Values, therefore, involve general beliefs about what is to be preferred in relation to desirable versus undesirable ways of behaving and desirable versus undesirable general goals. He called the former types of values, *instrumental values*, and the latter types, *terminal values*.

Note, however, that Rokeach does not view values as "cold" beliefs. He argues that people usually feel strongly about their central values and will protect and defend them, as is evident when these values are challenged or frustrated, when people are confronted by difficult moral choices, when they become involved in personal and social conflicts of various kinds, and when their values are satisfied and fulfilled.

Rokeach assumes that values are relatively stable properties of persons but are not unchanging across the lifespan. Some values that are important for an adolescent may not be so important for an older person. Indeed, they may be superseded by other values that become more important as a person takes on new roles and responsibilities, such as moving into the labor force and raising a family. Rokeach proposes that the antecedents of values can be traced to culture, society and its institutions, and to personality. He states they are:

> the joint results of sociological as well as psychological forces acting upon the individual—sociological because society and its institutions socialize the individual for the common good to internalize shared conceptions of the desirable; psychological because individual motivations require cognitive expression, justification, and indeed exhortation in socially desirable terms. (Rokeach, 1973, p. 20)

The consequences of values are many and various. They function as standards and criteria for judgments and preferences in many different ways, providing guidance about what is desirable and what is undesirable (cf. Kluckhohn, 1951). They are central to the self-concept and important features of a person's identity. Rokeach considers them to be determinants of attitudes and behaviors, but fewer in number than the many beliefs and attitudes that people typically hold. The smaller set of values was assumed to influence a person's total belief-attitude system, a system that has a hierarchical form, moving from the specific to the general, but that tends to be integrated and structured in a consistent way. Values are at the core of this system and closely bound with self-conceptions.

According to Rokeach, values become organized into value systems so that some values are seen as more important for self than others. For example, one person might rank equality as a much more important value for self than social recognition; another person might reverse this order of importance. These value systems may then be used by people as a basis for formulating general plans of action that enable them to resolve conflicts and to make decisions. Thus, in Rokeach's analysis, values and value systems are assumed to function as standards or criteria that guide thought and action in many different ways.

Rokeach (1973) also views values as satisfying a variety of motivational functions (value-expressive, adjustment, ego-defensive, and knowledge), but he argues that, in the final analysis, all values are in the service of the self. Thus, "a person's values are conceived to maintain and enhance the master sentiment of self-regard—by helping a person adjust to his society, defend his ego against threat, and test reality" (p. 15).

Rokeach (1973) believes that the consequences of values will be "manifested in virtually all phenomena that social scientists might consider worth investigating and understanding" (p. 3). He sees values as key variables that span the social sciences, different in kind from other related concepts such as attitudes, social norms, traits, interests, and value orientations.

The main aspects of Rokeach's approach to the concepts of value and value systems are summarized in the extended definition that he provides:

> To say that a person has a value is to say that he has an enduring prescriptive or proscriptive belief that a specific mode of behavior or end-state of existence is preferred to an oppositive mode of behavior or end-state. This belief transcends attitudes toward objects and toward situations, it is a standard that guides and determines action, attitudes toward objects and situations, ideology, presentation of self to others, evaluations, judgments, justifications, comparisons of self with others, and attempts to influence others. Values serve adjustive, ego-defensive, knowledge, and self-actualizing functions. Instrumental and terminal values are related yet are separately organized into relatively enduring hierarchical organizations along a continuum of importance. (Rokeach, 1973, p. 25)

The distinction made by Rokeach between modes of conduct and end states of existence is reflected in the sets of instrumental and terminal values that he presents in his Value Survey (Rokeach, 1973). It is a distinction that fits neatly into a motivational analysis that refers to an instrumental behavior sequence that involves actions directed toward proximal and distal goals. The Value Survey lists 18 terminal values and 18 instrumental values that are arranged in alphabetical order, each accompanied by a short descriptive label. Table 3.1 presents Form D, a commonly used version, of the Value Survey. In the usual form of administration the respondent is asked to arrange the values in each set in their order of importance for self, with the most important value at the top of each list and the least important value at the bottom. The rank orders provide information about a person's value system, or the hierarchy of importance that he or she assigns to each set of values. One obtains a value system relating to the terminal values and a value system relating to the instrumental values.

The Value Survey has been used extensively in research (e.g., Ball-Rokeach, Rokeach, & Grube, 1984; Feather, 1975, 1980, 1986; Rokeach,

Table 3.1. Terminal and Instrumental Values from the Rokeach Value Survey

Terminal values	Instrumental values
A comfortable life (a prosperous life)	Ambitious (hardworking, aspiring)
An exciting life (a stimulating, active life)	Broad-minded (open-minded)
A sense of accomplishment (lasting contribution)	Capable (competent, effective)
A world at peace (free of war and conflict)	Cheerful (lighthearted, joyful)
A world of beauty (beauty of nature and the arts)	Clean (neat, tidy)
Equality (brotherhood, equal opportunity for all)	Courageous (standing up for your beliefs)
Family security (taking care of loved ones)	Forgiving (willing to pardon others)
Freedom (independence, free choice)	Helpful (working for the welfare of others)
Happiness (contentedness)	Honest (sincere, truthful)
Inner harmony (freedom from inner conflict)	Imaginative (daring, creative)
Mature love (sexual and spiritual intimacy)	Independent (self-reliant, self-sufficient)
National security (protection from attack)	Intellectual (intelligent, reflective)
Pleasure (an enjoyable, leisurely life)	Logical (consistent, rational)
Salvation (saved, eternal life)	Loving (affectionate, tender)
Self-respect (self-esteem)	Obedient (dutiful, respectful)
Social recognition (respect, admiration)	Polite (courteous, well-mannered)
True friendship (close companionship)	Responsible (dependable, reliable)
Wisdom (a mature understanding of life)	Self-controlled (restrained, self-disciplined)

Source: Feather (1982b). Reprinted by permission of Lawrence Erlbaum Associates, Inc.

1973, 1979), but in recent years it has been superseded by the Schwartz Value Survey (Schwartz, 1992), which I will describe subsequently. There are also other approaches to the measurement of values (Braithwaite, 1998; Braithwaite & Scott, 1991; Feather, 1975, pp. 250–253), but discussion of these alternative approaches is beyond the scope of this book.

Instruments like the Rokeach Value Survey (RVS) can be used in different ways. For example, I have used the RVS to investigate value priorities across generations and across different cultures. I have also requested respondents to rank the values not only for their importance to self but also in relation to their culture and their work environment, asking them to put the values in the order of importance that they perceived their environment as promoting (e.g., the environment of the school that children attend). It then becomes possible to investigate the degree of value fit between self and environment and to relate this "fit" index to other measures such as adjustment and psychological well-being. I have also examined value differences between first- and second-generation immigrants and investigated other differences that relate to gender, age, social class, and political affiliation. Finally, I have investigated relations between the importance of different values from the RVS and measures of general beliefs and attitudes, such as conservatism and the work ethic. I list these topics in order to demonstrate how the RVS has been used to investigate a wide variety of topics. As a measure it has had its critics (e.g., Braithwaite & Law, 1985; Braithwaite & Scott, 1991). The forced ranking procedure has been criticized, as has the reliance of the RVS on a single item for each value rather than on multiitems. However, at the time, the RVS was an important contribution to the literature on values, stimulating a lot of research (e.g., Feather, 1975; Rokeach, 1973). Rokeach's theoretical analysis of the concept of value was also an important contribution.

Values and Value Types

It is important to note that Rokeach saw values as the properties of persons that could be distinguished from the evaluations that are assigned by individuals to specific objects, events, and situations. Schwartz and Bilsky (1987, 1990) built upon the foundations provided by Rokeach by developing ideas about the structure and content of values, ideas that were subsequently developed by Schwartz (1992, 1994a, 1994b, 1996), especially in the context of cross-cultural psychology. Like Rokeach (1973), Kluckhohn (1951), and Williams (1968),

Schwartz (1992) proposes that values are criteria that people use. Thus, he defines values as "desirable, transsituational goals, varying in importance, that serve as guiding principles in people's lives" (Schwartz, 1996, p. 2). He argues that values

> represent, in the form of conscious goals, three universal requirements of human existence: biological needs, requisites of coordinated social interaction, and demands of group survival and functioning. Groups and individuals represent these requirements cognitively as specific values about which they communicate in order to explain, coordinate, and rationalize behavior. (p. 2)

These ideas led Schwartz to a typology of different value types that are distinguished by the different motivational goals that the value types express. This theory of the content of different values according to their motivational goals is summarized in Table 3.2.

Table 3.2 presents ten different motivational goals and the distinct value types that relate to each of these goals. For example, the motivational goal that relates to hedonistic values is pleasure and sensuous gratification for oneself. Representative values are *pleasure* and *enjoying life*. The motivational goal that relates to achievement is personal success through demonstrating competence according to social standards. Representative values are being *successful*, *capable*, *ambitious*, and *influential*. The motivational goal that relates to conformity is the restraint of actions, inclinations, and impulses that are likely to upset or harm others and violate social expectations or norms. Representative values are *politeness*, *obedient*, *self-discipline*, and *honoring parents or elders*.

The representative values listed in parentheses in Table 3.2 come from the Schwartz Value Survey (SVS), which, in the 1992 form (Schwartz, 1992), consists of 56 values based on the analysis of motivational goals. Many of the values in the SVS were selected from the Rokeach (1973) survey, but other values were added to take account of different cultures. The values in the SVS are arranged into two groups, corresponding to terminal and instrumental values, though Schwartz presented evidence that cast strong doubt on the terminal/instrumental distinction. The values in each set are again arranged in alphabetical order, each with a short defining phrase. Instead of ranking these two sets of values, participants are asked to rate each value for importance "as a guiding principle in my life," using a nine-point scale extending from *supreme importance* (7), *very important* (6), (unlabeled; 5, 4); *important* (3), (unlabeled; 2, 1); *not important* (0), to *opposed to my values* (−1). Hence the SVS differs from the RVS by being theoretically

Table 3.2. Definitions of Motivational Types in Terms of Their Goals and the Single Values That Represent Them

Power	Social status and prestige, control or dominance over people and resources. (Social Power, Authority, Wealth) [Preserving my Public Image, Social Recognition]
Achievement	Personal success through demonstrating competence according to social standards. (Successful, Capable, Ambitious, Influential) [Intelligent, Self-Respect]
Hedonism	Pleasure and sensuous gratification for oneself. (Pleasure, Enjoying Life)
Stimulation	Excitement, novelty, and challenge in life. (Daring, a Varied Life, an Exciting Life)
Self-direction	Independent thought and action-choosing, creating, exploring. (Creativity, Freedom, Independent, Curious, Chooosing own Goals) [Self-Respect]
Universalism	Understanding, appreciation, tolerance and protection for the welfare of all people and for nature. (Broadminded, Wisdom, Social Justice, Equality, a World at Peace, a World of Beauty, Unity with Nature, Protecting the Environment)
Benevolence	Preservation and enhancement of the welfare of poeple with whom one is in frequent contact. (Helpful, Honest, Forgiving, Loyal, Responsible) [True Friendship, Mature Love]
Tradition	Respect, commitment and acceptance of the customs and ideas that traditional culture or religion provide the self. (Humble, Accepting my Portion in Life, Devout, Respect for Tradition, Moderate)
Conformity	Restraint of actions, inclinations, and impulses likely to upset or harm others and violate social expectations or norms. (Politeness, Obedient, Self-Discipline, Honoring Parents and Elders)
Security	Safety, harmony and stability of society, of relationships, and of self. (Family Security, National Security, Social Order, Clean, Reciprocation of Favors) [Sense of Belonging, Healthy]

Note: Values in square brackets are not used in computing the standard indexes for value types because their meanings are not consistent across samples and cultures.
Source: Schwartz (1996). Reprinted by permission of the author and Lawrence Erlbaum Associates, Inc.

derived, by presenting participants with larger sets of values, by using rating rather than ranking, and by allowing for "negative" values to which participants may be opposed.

Schwartz theorized about dynamic relations among the value types involving conflicts and compatibilities and reasoned that some value types would tend to come into conflict if they were simultaneously pursued (e.g., self-direction and stimulation versus conformity, tradition, and security; universalism and benevolence versus achievement and power), whereas other value types would be compatible if they were simultaneously pursued. For example, the following pairs of value types would be compatible: power and achievement, stimulation and self-direction, tradition and conformity, and universalism and benevolence.

This consideration of conflicts and compatibilities between value types implies that the value types can be organized into a circular structure, with adjacent value types being compatible and opposite-sided value types likely to cause conflict. This circular structure is presented in Figure 3.1. Adjacent value types are compatible because the values that define the types are assumed to have similar motivational goals. For example, values concerned with achievement and power

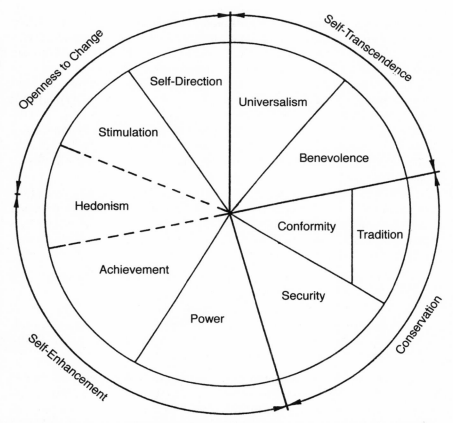

Figure 3.1. The prototypical structure of value systems. Schwartz, 1996. Reprinted by permission of the author and Lawrence Erlbaum Associates, Inc.

express self-centeredness and a desire to enhance self; values concerned with self-direction and stimulation express an intrinsic concern with mastery and openness to change (see Schwartz, 1996, p. 4). In contrast, value types on the opposite side of the circle involve motivational goals that cannot easily be pursued simultaneously. For example, the pursuit of universalism values may involve sacrifices that impede the pursuit of individual achievement values; the pursuit of security values may involve closing off the pursuit of values concerned with stimulation and new directions.

According to Schwartz value conflicts can be classified into two major forms and these conflicts have emerged in 95% of the samples that he has studied. One major conflict opposes value types that involve *openness to change* (combining stimulation and self-direction value types) to value types that involve *conservation* (combining security, conformity, and tradition). This dimension of conflict "reflects a conflict between emphases on own independent thought and action and favoring change versus submissive self-restriction, preservation of traditional practices and protection of stability" (Schwartz, 1996, p. 5).

The second major conflict opposes value types that involve *self-enhancement* (combining power and achievement value types) and *self-transcendence* (combining benevolence and universalism). This dimension "reflects a conflict between acceptance of others as equals and concern for their welfare versus pursuit of one's own relative success and dominance over others. Hedonism shares elements of both Openness and Self-Enhancement" (Schwartz, 1996, p. 5).

The hypothesized circular arrangement of value types has important implications for relations between the value types and external variables. I note these implications here because they were tested in a study that I will describe later in this chapter. Schwartz (1996) summarizes two major implications:

1. Any outside variable tends to be associated similarly with value types that are adjacent in the value structure.
2. Associations with an outside variable decrease monotonically as one moves around the circular structure of value types in both directions from the most positively associated value type to the least positively associated value type. (p. 6)

Hence, one would expect to find a wave pattern in the correlations of an external variable with the value types with movement around the circle. The correlations should decrease to a minimum as one moves from the value type under consideration and approaches the side of the circular structure that contains the opposing value type; they should then increase as one continues around the circle to return to the value type under consideration. Schwartz (1996) notes that whether one finds differences in correlations between an external variable and adjacent value types will depend on the size of the sample. The pattern of change that occurs may also depend on the situational context and the specific characteristics of the behavior in question.

Schwartz (1992, 1994a, 1994b, 1996) has reported the results of studies that relate to his theory of the content and structure of values. He uses the procedure of smallest space analysis (SSA) developed by Guttman (1968; see also Canter, 1985). In this analysis values were represented

> as points in multidimensional space such that the distances between the points reflected the empirical relations among values as measured by the correlations between their importance ratings. The greater the conceptual similarity between two values, the more related they should be empirically, and hence the closer their locations should be in the multidimensional space. (Schwartz, 1992, p. 21)

The results of these studies generally support a circular structure of value types, following the arrangement shown in Figure 3.1. There is also evidence for meaningful changes in correlations between external variables and the value types with movement around the circular structure (Schwartz, 1996), although wave patterns following a regular sine curve were not found. Nor did Schwartz expect to find true sine curves, given the behaviors that he studied (interpersonal cooperation, voting behavior, outgroup social contract) and the context in which they occurred.

As noted previously, Schwartz's research program focused especially on the study of values across many different cultures. He distinguishes between value types that describe differences between individuals and that are based on the analysis of individual-level data, and value types that describe differences between cultures and that are based on the analysis of aggregated culture-level data (Schwartz, 1994b; Smith & Schwartz, 1997). The value types listed in Table 3.2 and presented in Figure 3.1 were based on individual-level data. Discussion of culture-level value types is beyond the scope of the present book.

Values and Abstract Structures

Nearly 30 years ago I presented a distinction between *abstract structures* or organized summaries of experience that capture the focal, abstracted qualities of past experience and that function as criteria or frameworks against which present experience can be tested, and *per-*

ceived structures that represent the information that is immediately present in the environment, structured in some way in an individual's perceptions (Feather, 1971a). I argued that underlying abstract structures are

> residues or summaries of past experience and that they are formed as a person copes with the influx of information that comes from the social and physical environments. They are organized and relatively stable products of information processing and they provide continuity and meaning under changing environmental circumstances. They can change, however, as new and discrepant information is encountered that cannot readily be interpreted in terms of existing schemata. Abstract structures have a normative aspect in that they incorporate the precipitate of modal or most frequent experiences and so represent what ought to be or is usually the case. (Feather, 1980, p. 249)

Abstract structures tend to be organized so that the relations that comprise these structures fit together consistently. Perceived information is tested against the relevant abstract structures, either matching the underlying structures or being discrepant from them. Discrepancies between abstract structures and perceived structures can be resolved by changes in the way the current information is perceived (a form of assimilation), by behavior that produces a fit between the structures or, over time, by accommodation of the abstract structures to consistently appearing discrepant information.

I allowed for individual differences in modes of resolution and in the degree to which people could tolerate inconsistency, and I illustrated these theoretical ideas by referring to my research program concerned with communication effects, causal attribution, and attitudes and selective recall, where I had used a principle of balance or consistency to interpret the findings (Feather, 1967b, 1969a, 1969b). This analysis has since been overtaken by the many advances that have been made in cognitive psychology, involving increasing sophistication in both theorizing and in the development of new methodologies. However, the analysis is still relevant in its basic ideas. Here I relate the analysis to the concept of value.

I have proposed that a value may be conceptualized as an abstract structure that involves an associative network that can take different forms for different individuals. It may involve a general concept or belief about ways of behaving (e.g., being helpful) or about general goals (e.g., freedom). As a structure a value may vary in its degree of differentiation. Some values may be relatively undifferentiated with a limited network of associations; other values may have a high degree of differentiation with a complex network of associations. For example, national security may be an undifferentiated value for some people, a value that is defined in very simple terms without much elaboration; in contrast, equality may have a complex range of associations that extends across different exemplars. The value structure may also have other structural characteristics along such dimensions as integration, isolation, and centrality—to mention just a few (e.g., Zajonc, 1968, pp. 320–338).

Consideration of these various structural characteristics implies that a value may have the same verbal label attached to it (e.g., equality), but individuals may differ in the value, in regard to the content and form of the associative network, despite the presence of a common core of associations that defines the value.

It would be incorrect, however, to conceive of values as "cold" cognitive structures that are remote from affect. They are not affectively neutral abstract structures. They are intimately tied to our feelings. Like Rokeach, I see values as connected to the affective system and as having a normative and prescriptive quality about them, involving what is desirable or undesirable, what ought to be preferred or not preferred.

It should be clear, therefore, that my analysis of the value concept has been influenced by Rokeach's seminal contributions but, as I will indicate in the next section, takes off in some new directions, especially in regard to the way values, as abstract structures, affect the way people construe specific events and outcomes along a dimension of positive or negative subjective value, or attractiveness and aversiveness.

VALUES AND VALENCES

How might we conceive of the attractiveness or aversiveness of objects and events? What leads us to perceive some objects and events as positive and others as negative? These are basic questions in psychology that are often skirted over without much analysis.

My approach to these questions has been influenced by Lewin (1935, 1936, 1938, 1951). He introduced a number of basic concepts in order to account for a person's behavior within a defined situation. His emphasis was on contemporary or immediate causes rather than on historical causes, and he argued that a person's responses should be related to his or her present "life space," which included the person and the psychological environment (or the environment as perceived by the person).

Lewin's dynamic theory is very influential in the psychology of human motivation and discussions of it can be found elsewhere (e.g., Weiner, 1992). Most relevant to the present discussion is his concept of valence, which he uses to represent the positive and negative demand characteristics of objects and events (see also Tolman, 1932, 1955).

In his 1935 book, Lewin describes valences as follows:

> The valence of an object usually derives from the fact that the object is a means to the satisfaction of a need, or has indirectly something to do with the satisfaction of a need. The kind (sign) and strength of the valence of an object or event thus depends directly upon the momentary condition of the needs of the individual concerned.... One may distinguish between two large groups of valences according to the sort of initial behavior they elicit: the positive valences (+), those affecting approach, and the negative (−), or those producing withdrawal or retreat. (pp. 78–81)

Later Lewin developed a more detailed analysis of valence in the context of topological and vector psychology (1936, 1938, 1951). He proposed that:

> The valence Va (G) which an object or activity G possesses for a person at a given time depends upon the character or state of the person P, and upon the perceived nature of the object or activity G. (Lewin, 1938, p. 107)

For example, food in the psychological environment would become more attractive, possessing more positive demand characteristics, as a person becomes more hungry and as the quality of food improves; a threat in the psychological environment would become more aversive, possessing more negative demand characteristics, as a person becomes more concerned with protecting self and as the quality of the threat increases. Positive valences were assumed to be associated with approach behavior (or locomotion toward the region of positive valence, to use Lewin's term); negative valences were assumed to be associated with avoidance behavior (or locomotion away from the region of negative valence). The locomotion that occurred, however, was assumed by Lewin to depend upon the field of psychological forces and the resultant of these forces. Valence was assumed to be a determinant of psychological force, the force toward a positively valent region increasing with the strength of the positive valence and the force away from a negatively valent region increasing with the strength of the negative valence. Force was also assumed to be affected by the psychological distance separating the person from the region of positive or negative valence, the force acting on a person toward a positively valent region or away from a negatively valent region increasing with decreasing psychological distance, and changing more rapidly when a negatively valent region was involved.

These ideas were later applied to the analysis of level of aspiration or goal-setting behavior (Lewin, Dembo, Festinger, & Sears, 1944) in an important theoretical contribution that is an example of a motivational theory of decision making that uses expectancy-value concepts (Feather, 1982b). In this analysis the valences of success and failure relating to a particular level of performance were weighted by the corresponding subjective probabilities, having the effect of moderating the forces toward and away from that level of performance. The level of performance that is chosen as the future goal was then assumed to be associated with the strongest resultant force.

It should be clear, therefore, that in Lewinian theory the concept of valence was bound up with the concept of psychological force. Indeed, Lewin (1936) at one point coordinated valences to force fields, all acting in the same direction, either toward or away from positively or negatively valent regions, regardless of where person (P) was located within the psychological environment. But valence was distinguished from psychological force. It combined with psychological distance to determine the strength and direction of psychological force. Moreover, valence for Lewin was a scalar, varying in strength and sign but having no direction. In contrast, psychological force was a vector, having strength, direction, and point of application (Lewin, 1938).

I want to abstract from this discussion one general point, namely, that needs can induce valences on objects and events. The presence of a need or quasi-need may lead some regions in the psychological environment to become positively or negatively valent, to possess positive or negative demand characteristics. Previously I gave the example of how the presence of hunger will affect the degree to which food is seen as positively attractive. Another example from the theoretical literature can be found in Atkinson and Feather (1966, pp. 328–329). They assumed that valences (in their case, the valences of success and failure) are influenced by underlying needs (in their case, the motive to achieve success and the motive to avoid failure). In presenting a theory of achievement motivation they assumed that the positive valence of success at a task would be positively related to the strength of a person's motive to achieve success, and that the negative valence of failure at a task would be positively related to the strength of a person's motive to avoid failure. These motives multiplied the corresponding positive and negative incentive values of success and failure to determine the level of positive or negative valence. The incentive values depended on the subjective probabilities of success and failure associated with the task. When success at a task was perceived by a person to be unlikely, the positive incentive value of success was assumed to be stronger than when success was perceived to be very probable. When failure at a task was perceived by a person to be very unlikely, the negative incentive value of failure was assumed to be stronger than when failure was perceived to be very probable. Motives, expectancies, and incentive values (or, in reduced form, valences and expectancies) were central concepts in the theory of achievement motivation, which, like the Lewin et al. level of aspiration model, was an example of conceptual analysis set within the expectancy-value framework (Feather, 1982b).

But how do values fit into this picture? Again we can take a lead from Lewin. He had little to say about the concept of value. He saw the concept as a rather unclear one in psychology. However, the short comments that he made reveal that he regarded values as properties of persons that:

> influence behavior but do not have the character of a goal (that is, of a force field). For example, the individual does not try to "reach" the value of fairness but fairness is "guiding" his behavior. It is probably correct to say that values determine which types of activity have a positive and which have a negative valence for an individual in a given situation. In other words, values are not force fields but they "induce" force fields. That means values are constructs which have the same psychological dimension as *power fields*. (Lewin, 1951, p. 41)

It should be clear that the focus in this kind of analysis is on the immediate situation and what it offers, on what Lewin (1936) called the present field that contains both the person and the perceived or psychological environment. Within this situation values like needs were assumed to have motivational functions, inducing valences on objects and events. Although Lewin (1951) did not elaborate on his suggestion that values may induce valences and their associated force fields, it is reasonable to assume that the force fields he coordinated to value-induced valences would combine with the force fields he coordinated to need-induced valences. The former force fields, however, may be more stable over time, given the assumption that values are relatively stable properties of people when compared with the more transient need and tension states that Lewin (1938) was mainly concerned with in his motivational analysis. As I have argued previously (Feather, 1992b), "The forces that correspond to values and norms may ... have a continuing influence on a person's actions because of their greater stability. One would reach a similar conclusion if needs were also conceived to be dispositional in nature" (p. 119).

French and Kahn (1962) follow Lewin in assuming that both needs and values "have the basic property of the ability to motivate goal directed behavior by inducing valences (or incentive values) on certain environmental objects, behaviors, or states of affairs" (pp. 11–12). They consider evaluation and oughtness to be basic properties of values as distinct from needs and they provide examples of cases where values functioned to guide or control the need-induced behavior of an individual.

Consistent with these approaches, I see values as similar to needs in their ability to induce positive or negative valences on objects and events within the immediate situation. They affect the way individuals construe situations in terms of attractive and aversive regions that relate to means and to ends. Thus, a person for whom being logical is an important value will see logical ways of behaving as attractive (or positively valent), and more divergent and illogical ways of behaving as aversive (or negatively valent) in a defined situation. A person for whom power is an important value will see possible outcomes that enable high personal impact as more attractive (or positively valent), and possible outcomes that constrain personal impact as aversive (or negatively valent) in a defined situation. So, just as hunger induces positive valences on food objects, and the need to protect self induces negative valences on possible threats in a situation, values also induce valences on objects and events. The world we perceive is colored by our dominant needs and values, taking on positive and negative characteristics depending on the needs and values that are engaged by the situation and from within the individual.

The controlling aspect of values to which French and Kahn (1962) referred can be conceptualized in terms of this kind of analysis. The positive and negative valences that are induced by needs and values on means-end activities and potential outcomes can be coordinated to forces that may be compatible or in conflict. For example, a person may perceive a possible goal as attractive (or positively valent) because it is linked to strong achievement needs and values, and he or she may pursue the goal by actions that also have positive valence in relation to underlying needs and values (e.g., the value of being honest). In this case the person's actions would be related to forces toward the goal that signifies achievement and toward actions that also have positive demand characteristics, and these forces would be in the same direction because the outcome follows on the action. In Lewin's (1938) terms, it is along the same psychological path. In other cases, conflicts between needs and values may arise, as when harsh actions against another person are controlled in the interest of maintaining group harmony. Here the force relating to a need-induced valence to aggress against the other person is countered by a force relating to a value-induced valence that is expressed by a stronger tendency to maintain the harmony of the group.

VALUES, VALENCES, AND ASSOCIATIVE NETWORKS

I stated previously that values may be conceived of as abstract structures or associative networks that are linked to the affective system. Values have a structure of their own that may vary across persons and groups. The structure of associations captures different shades of meaning. For example, freedom as a value may have a different structure of relations for different persons and groups. In some cases the structure may be complex and highly differentiated; in other cases the structure may be a very simple one without much differentiation at all. Yet the value still concerns freedom because it involves a set of core associations that defines the concept. Once the value is elicited, it affects our cognitive-affective appraisal of situations in terms of demand characteristics.

These effects on appraisal can also be conceptualized in terms of associative networks. I have previously presented a simple structural representation of links between values and attitudes (Feather, 1996e). Valences and attitudes share common characteristics because both refer to objects and events, both may be positive or negative in sign, and both have associations with positive or negative affect. Attitudes, however, are usually seen as being relatively stable, cognitive-affective dispositions that are held by people, and the development of the psychology of attitudes was intimately linked with the emergence of ways of measuring attitudes (Eagly & Chaikin, 1993). Valences, on the other hand, refer to the momentary properties of objects of events in relation to their ability to instigate approach or avoidance behavior, and their emergence was linked to motivational psychology, especially to Lewinian field theory. Yet, as I noted, the two concepts share common features and it would not be too much of an exaggeration to conceive of valences as momentary positive or negative attitudes toward objects and events that are manifestations of underlying needs and values.

From this point of view I present in Figure 3.2 an associative structure that contains two values (Value X, Value Y) and four attitudes (Attitude 1, Attitude 2, Attitude 3, Attitude 4). Value X is linked in the structure to attitudes 1, 2, and 3 and Value Y is linked to attitudes 1, 3, and 4. We can assume that each of these attitudes is linked to a wider set of specific beliefs that are not represented in the diagram. They are part of the person's total belief-attitude-value system.

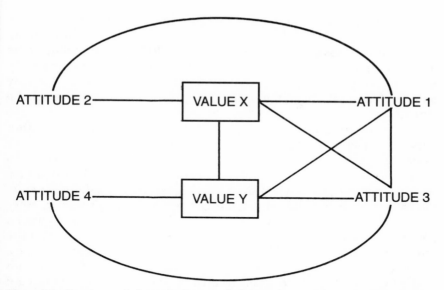

Figure 3.2. Structures relating attitudes to underlying values. Feather, 1996e. Reprinted by permission of the author and Lawrence Erlbaum Associates, Inc.

The structure of relations in Figure 3.2 implies that attitudes 1 and 2 would be related because they are both linked to Value X. Similarly, attitudes 3 and 4 would be related because they are both linked to Value Y. Note also that attitudes 1 and 3 share common values (Value X and Value Y), but attitudes 2 and 4 do not have any values in common.

This form of representation allows for the fact that attitudes may be multidetermined in the sense that a given attitude may express more than one value. When two attitudes have values in common, they would be expected to be related. Thus, attitudes 1 and 3 would be associated because of their common-value base, whereas attitudes 2 and 4 may be unrelated.

The direct link between a value and an attitude provides the basis for the assumption that values may induce valences, where valences may be conceived of as momentary attitudes. Thus, each attitude in Figure 3.2 could also be viewed as a positive or negative valence that is attached to some object or event in the immediate situation.

Consistent with my discussion of values, Figure 3.2 also introduces a vertical arrangement in which Value X is placed above Value Y to signify that it is judged to be a more important value by the person who holds the associative network represented in the diagram. It is not implied by this arrangement that Value X in some ways derives from or is dependent on Value Y, but only that Value X is judged to be more important by a person in his or her value system. A very important value may be closely bound with central beliefs and attitudes, holding a key position in regard to a person's definition of self. Once activated, it may have profound effects on the person's cognitive-affective appraisal of a situation.

But how are values activated? I have assumed that their activation depends on their strength and the presence of situational cues. For example, a person for whom equality is a very important value would be more sensitive to many different forms of equalities and inequalities within situations, even when situational cues are minimal. In this case, the value is more readily activated because it is a strong value. In other cases, situational cues may prime or activate a value. For example, pleasure would be activated as a value when a situation presents the possibility of hedonic fulfillment; freedom would be activated as a value when the situation poses the possibility that basic freedoms are under threat and likely to be obstructed. In these cases, the values are activated because there are clear cues in the situation that elicit them, even though these values may be somewhat less important for the person in relation to other values that may remain latent. Note also that the activation may either occur relatively automatically or following some conscious effort, depending on situational cues and the structure of the associative network. These assumptions are consistent with more detailed discussions of knowledge activation that have been presented by cognitive psychologists (e.g., Higgins, 1996).

I have assumed that the network of relations that involves a value is a learned network that is based on a person's own experience, and that it involves consistent sets of relations that may nevertheless be modified as new discrepant information is processed by the individual (Feather, 1996e). Values that are more strongly held may be the hubs of fairly complex and differentiated networks of attitudes and beliefs (cf. Lusk & Judd, 1988; Tesser & Leone, 1977), in which case the resolution of discrepancies may involve a lot of cognitive work when strongly held values are in conflict (cf. Tetlock, 1986). But one can also argue that some strongly held values are hubs in simply defined structures and that they exert their influence rapidly without much or any conscious effort, enabling a quick and rapid cognitive-affective response to situations and events under conditions where there is no value conflict. We need more theoretical and empirical investigation of the ways in which values are activated or primed and how they exert their effects via networks of association.

Once activated, however, values may prime or activate attitudes and beliefs that are part of its associative network. For example, when freedom as a value is activated in a situation where there is a threat to individual rights, as might occur when a new restrictive law is enacted by a political party, attitudes and beliefs that relate to the political party may also be activated. The activation of the value may spread to other networked attitudes and beliefs. The activation may also have the effect of recruiting new attitudes and beliefs to the network when novel situations are encountered and processed in relation to the cognitive-affective system. These new attitudes and beliefs then become recruited to the associative network involving the value.

The assumptions made in the foregoing rather abstract analysis are consistent with the idea that values, once activated, may induce valences or subjective values on objects and events, influencing the way a person construes a situation in terms of its affective and motivational properties. It is also consistent with the assumption that attitudes may serve value-expressive functions, an assumption that was made by Katz (1960) and by Smith, Bruner, and White (1956) many years ago in the functional theory of attitudes, and that is emerging again in new developments in attitude theory (e.g., Maio & Olson, 1994, 1995, in press a, in press b).

Thus, I assume that values may be conceived as abstract or latent structures that are modifiable by experience and that they exert their effects via associative networks. Our values function as important criteria when we judge possible actions and outcomes within particular situations in terms of their desirability or undesirability. I assume that these links between values and the cognitive-affective construal of particular situations proceed via associative networks that involve structures of values, beliefs, and attitudes that are open to modification. Thus:

> A major function of the values that people hold is to influence the subjective values that they assign to possible actions and outcomes within a situation so that some actions and outcomes are seen as attractive (or positively valent) and some as aversive (or negatively valent).... I therefore distinguish between the general values that people hold and the subjective values they assign to possible actions and outcomes. In an important sense, our general values influence our affective appraisal or evaluation of the different actions and outcomes that are possible within specific situations. (Feather, 1996e, pp. 224–225)

I have given some attention in the preceding sections to value-valence relations and how they might be considered in terms of associative networks. In this analysis I relate valences as demand characteristics to attitudes that have strength as well as sign, but the attitudes (or valences) that I deal with are keyed to the momentary situation and they are not necessarily stable. They may change from time to time and from situation to situation as they are affected by those variables that determine positive and negative valences at any given moment. As I proposed previously, "it is useful to maintain the distinction between attitudes and valences in the language that we employ, with 'attitudes' referring to the more stable orientations and 'valences' to the attractive and aversive features of the momentary situation" (Feather, 1990a, p. 185). But valences are a class of attitudes and they can follow the priming or activation of a value via an associative network, the value inducing positive or negative valences that are attached to particular regions of the psychological environment as it is currently perceived. The associative network forms part of the memory store and the activation of a value that is embedded in an associative network will depend on how strong or important the value is for a person and on the presence of situational cues that may prime the value (e.g., Fazio, 1986, 1995; Feather, 1990a, pp. 192–186).

The determinants of valences extend beyond needs and values to encompass other variables as well. The wider analysis of valences is a neglected area of psychology, though some advances are being made. The positive and negative aspects of valences imply some connection with affect and, in previous discussions (Feather, 1990a, pp. 178–180), I have suggested that valences are often associated with anticipated positive or negative affect so that, for example, the positive valence of food for a hungry person is associated with anticipated pleasure at the thought of eating the food. But it would probably be an oversimplification to identify positive and negative valences as always associated with anticipated pleasure or pain. Anticipation implies learning but there may be some demand characteristics of objects and events that have a built-in biological basis or that develop on the basis of the maturation of the nervous system.

Expectancy-value theory has provided conceptual analyses of valences (e.g., Feather, 1982a, 1982b; Heckhausen, 1977; Mitchell, 1982; Rotter, 1954, 1982; Vroom, 1964), and there have been contributions from other theoretical frameworks as well (e.g., Brendl & Higgins, 1996; Maio & Olson, in press a, in press b; Wright, Contrada, & Patane, 1986). I have suggested that there are other variables in addition to needs and values that have effects on valences (Feather, 1990a, 1992b). These variables would include the objective characteristics of possible events and outcomes as perceived by the person, the difficulty of achieving an outcome, the expected consequences that may follow a particular outcome, the amount of control that one can exert when striving for a particular outcome, the attributed causes of an outcome, and moods and other states of the person. As I noted in an earlier statement:

> Although we can list various factors that influence the subjective attractiveness and aversiveness of events, we are still a long way from having a comprehensive theory of valences. We have progressed, however, beyond Lewin's analysis that linked the valence of an object or activity to the character or state of the person and to the perceived nature of the object or activity.... Further analysis of the interface between cognition and affect should add to our knowledge. (Feather, 1992b, p. 113)

The recent analysis of principles of judging valence by Brendl and Higgins (1996) exemplifies some of the recent developments (see also Tesser & Martin, 1996). Brendl and Higgins discuss four principles that influence judgments of valence. The first principle, *goal supportiveness*, refers to the degree to which some event or activity would facilitate or impede the satisfaction of a goal. Events that facilitate would be judged as positively valent; events that impede as negatively valent. The second principle, *membership status*, refers to the association of an event with some other positively or negatively valenced representation, as when a previously neutral event may acquire positive or negative valence because it has been associated with another positively or negatively valent event. For example, a new product on the market may be judged positively because it costs a lot of money to acquire it. The third principle, *referential status*, involves comparing an event with some reference point, as when a student uses social comparison with classmates to evaluate whether an exam result is good or bad. The fourth principle, *response elicitation*, refers to inferring the positive or negative valence of an event by observation of one's own or other's response to the event. For example, people may be told by others that their performance is good or bad. Brendl and Higgins (1996) discuss these principles in detail and relate their discussion to current cognitive theory and to research on attitudes.

As a further example of recent developments, Maio and Olson (in press a, in press b) have extended the functional theory of attitudes (Katz, 1960; Smith, Bruner, & White, 1956) in discussions of attitude valence, attitude strength, and goal-expressive attitudes. These latter attitudes are assumed to express important and relevant goals that are derived from values.

A detailed discussion of these recent approaches is beyond the scope of this book. My aim has been to present an analysis of relations between values and valences from the perspective of motivational psychology. The analysis has been influenced by Lewinian ideas, but it also draws on ideas from cognitive psychology. In the next sections I turn to studies from my research program that provide evidence about value-valence linkages.

RESEARCH STUDIES

I will refer to three studies that provide evidence about value-valence relations. These studies derive from different areas of inquiry. The first study was part of a research program on the psychological impact of unemployment; the second and third studies presented participants with hypothetical scenarios and obtained ratings of attractiveness and information about choice.

Work Ethic Values and Employment Valence

Feather and O'Brien (1987) used the expectancy-value framework to model relations between values and actions in a study of young people from metropolitan Adelaide, South Australia, who had left school and who were looking for a job. The study was part of a major longitudinal investigation that tracked individuals as they left school and entered the labor market. The participants first answered questionnaires while they were still at school and then subsequently over a two-year period. The main variables included in these questionnaires were measures of the participants' self-concept, values, external control, job need, affect, psychological well-being, job confidence, attributions for unemployment, and the attribution dimensions of internality, stability, globality, personal uncontrollability, and external uncontrollability (Feather, 1990c, 1994b; Feather & O'Brien, 1986a, 1986b).

As part of an investigation of job-seeking behavior among the young unemployed participants, we derived two variables via factor analysis. The first variable was called *control-optimism* because it was defined by confidence about finding a job and feelings of control and self-efficacy. This variable was based upon questionnaire items concerned with the degree to which an unemployed participant felt that he or she had some control over being unemployed, felt confident about finding a job that he or she really wanted in the near future, believed that the cause of his or her present unemployment may not be present in the future, and believed that he or she could change the cause of his or her present unemployment. The control-optimism variable could therefore be taken to reflect each person's general expectation about finding employment. It combined confidence about finding a job with beliefs that one was not helpless but could have some control or impact over the causes of one's present unemployment.

The second variable, *job valence*, is more relevant to the present discussion. It was defined by questionnaire items that were concerned with how much each participant needed a job and how depressed and disappointed each participant felt about being unemployed. Thus, the measure of job valence combined need for a job with negative affect about being unemployed. The stronger the expressed need and the stronger the reported negative affect, the stronger the job valence.

The main dependent variable in this study was job-seeking behavior defined by an item that asked participants how frequently they looked for a job. They could check one of six responses: "Not looking for a job"; "When I feel like it"; "Monthly"; "Weekly"; "Every couple of days"; and "Daily."

We also included a measure of strength of the work ethic, using the Mirels and Garrett's (1971) Protestant Ethic Scale. This scale was modeled on Weber's (1905/1976) classic analysis of protestant ethic values and the involvement of these values in economic development. Items on the scale emphasize the virtues of industriousness, asceticism or the denial of pleasure, and individualism (Feather, 1984).

Most relevant here are the correlations between the work ethic values and the composite measure of job valence. We were able to obtain these correlations for the sample of unemployed participants who were tested in 1981 and again for the sample tested in 1982. The respective correlations were .31 for the 1981 sample and .19 for the 1982 sample, both of which were highly significant ($p < .001$). These are not strong correlations but they do show that values linked to the work ethic were positively associated with job valence. Hence, the assumption that values influence valences was tested directly in a real-life context and it was confirmed.

The valence measure also positively predicted job-seeking behavior, as would be expected. However, job-seeking behavior was unrelated to the control-optimism measure. Possible reasons for this unexpected finding are discussed elsewhere (Feather, 1990c; Feather & O'Brien, 1987). They include the fact that the measure of expectation was a very general one that needs to be refined so that it takes account of specific actions that relate to specific outcomes, and the likelihood that there are external pressures on all unemployed young people to look for a job (e.g., from parents, from government regulations) that would cut across expectation effects. Also, the measure of job-seeking behavior that we used was an amplitude or performance measure (level of activity), and relations between expectations and performance level are difficult to specify. Expectations are better predictors of choice or direction of behavior than they are of level of performance.

Values, Valences, and Choice

A second study (Feather, 1995b) involved a differentiated measure of values, the Schwartz Value Survey (SVS; Schwartz, 1992), enabling measures to be obtained on ten value types. (I described the SVS and the ten value types in a previous section.) The value types are arranged in a circular structure (see Figure 3.1) with some value types adjacent to each other in the circle (e.g., power, and achievement), whereas others are on opposite sides of the circular map (e.g., self-direction and security). The structure has an explicit motivational basis, given the assumption made by Schwartz (1992, 1996) that values express motivational goals that are more similar for adjacent value types.

Recall also that the total value structure can be viewed as being composed of four higher-order value types that form two basic, bipolar dimensions that can also be justified on conceptual and theoretical grounds. These higher-order value types comprise *openness to change* versus *conservation*, setting stimulation and self-direction in opposition to security, conformity, and tradition values, and *self-enhancement* versus *self-transcendence*, setting power, achievement, and hedonism values in opposition to universalism and benevolence values.

Furthermore, the circular arrangement of value types has implications for dynamic relations. Some value types would tend to conflict if they were simultaneously pursued because they involve conflicting motivational goals (e.g., self-direction and conformity). Other value types would tend to be compatible if they were simultaneously pursued because they involve motivational goals that are compatible (e.g., power and achievement).

Given the circular arrangement of value types, I expected that measures of valence and choice for a particular event would be similarly associated with adjacent value types on the circle but that these associations would decrease as one moved toward the opposite side of the circle, becoming less positive and changing to negative, depending on the situational context and the consequences of behavior for the expression or attainment of the motivational goals of the value types. That is, I expected that relations with the value types would follow a wave pattern, as described previously.

The study involved 239 students who were sampled from the introductory classes in psychology at Flinders University, Adelaide, South Australia, in 1992 and 1993. They completed a questionnaire that contained the 56-item version of the Schwartz Value Survey (Schwartz, 1992), ten scenarios that described situations that could be assumed to engage particular sets of values, and standard demographic items (see Feather, 1995b). Participants used the −1 to 7 rating scale described previously to rate each of the 56 values with respect to their importance for self.

Following Schwartz (1992), participants' ratings of importance for subsets of values were combined so as to obtain scores for each of the value types. For example, each person's score for the achievement value type was based on that person's ratings for the following specific values: successful, ambitious, capable, influential; each person's score for the conformity value type was based on that person's ratings for the following specific values: self-discipline, obedience, politeness, and honor of parents and elders; and each person's score for the benevolence value type was based on that person's ratings for the following specific values: being honest, loyal, helpful, forgiving, and responsible. The selection of values defining each value type were those recommended by Schwartz (1992, p. 52) on the basis of smallest space analyses of the ratings of the 56 values obtained from teachers and students in 20 countries. They were values that emerged empirically in a region representing that value type in at least 75% of his samples. An updated version of the values comprising each value type, based on a wider selection of countries, is presented in Table 3.2.

A distinctive feature of the study was the careful design of ten hypothetical scenarios. Each scenario described a situation in which two alternatives were specified. Participants were asked to read each scenario, to put themselves in the role of the specified stimulus person in the scenario, and to respond to the two alternatives that were offered. These alternatives were derived so that they related to different value types. Participants first used a 7-point scale to rate "how attractive or desirable you would personally find it, i.e., in relation to how much it would attract you." They were then asked, "Now if you had to choose between (a) and (b) in reality, which alternative would you choose?" They checked either alternative (a) or (b) to signify their choice.

The complete set of scenarios is presented in the original publication. Here I present a summary of their content (Feather, 1995b, p. 1140):

Exam scenario. A student preparing for an exam has to decide whether to study with another student the night before the exam in order to help each other, or to study alone in the hope of improving his or her chances of getting a good grade. These alternatives were assumed to involve benevolence values versus achievement values, respectively.

Camp scenario. A student at a weekend camp in the mountains has to decide whether to go off on his or her own to explore a path leading from the camp, or to stay with the group in the camp and follow the leader's directions. These alternatives were assumed to involve stimulation and self-direction values versus conformity values, respectively.

Organization scenario. A student has to decide whether to join an organization that has as its aim the protection of the environment, even at the cost of economic sacrifice, or to join an organization that promotes economic development and the achievement of wealth and power. These alternatives were assumed to involve universalism versus power values, respectively.

Job scenario. A student who has just graduated from a university has to decide between choosing a job with a predictable career path and a lot of security but not much opportunity for freedom, independence, or creativity, and a job that offers these features but with less security in the long term. These alternatives were assumed to involve security versus self-direction values, respectively.

Essay scenario. A student preparing to write an essay has to decide whether to lend his or her notes on the essay topic to another student, or to hold on to the notes in the hope that he or she could write an essay reflecting individual effort and originality and thereby enhance the chances of getting a high grade. These alternatives were assumed to involve benevolence and achievement values, respectively.

Graduation scenario. A student who has just finished high school has to decide between taking a year off and traveling around Australia, enjoying a relaxed lifestyle and life's pleasures, or to begin university studies, following a traditional path that may lead to a secure job. These alternatives were assumed to involve hedonism and stimulation values versus tradition and security values, respectively.

Club scenario. A student has to decide between running for political office in a student organization, thereby gaining some social recognition, influence, and authority, or joining an organization that respects equality and open-mindedness and that tries to work out solutions to universal problems concerned with peace, social justice, and the environment. These alternatives were assumed to involve power versus universalism values, respectively.

Research scenario. A research scientist has to decide between joining a team that is working on an ongoing project using traditional procedures with the possibility of finding useful results, or working individually on a project that explores a new area and that could lead either to a new discovery or to failure to find any useful results. These alternatives were assumed to involve tradition values versus self-direction values, respectively.

Party scenario. A student in the week before final exams has to decide between going to a party where he or she will have a good time and find a lot to enjoy, or staying at home and working hard in order to do well on the exam. These alternatives were assumed to involve hedonism and stimulation values and security and achievement values, respectively.

Warmth scenario. A university graduate has to decide whether to take a job that involves helping others within a warm and caring relationship, or working in an organization that is developing policies that may lead to a better society in the general sense. These alternatives were assumed to involve benevolence values versus universalism values, respectively.

Note that some of these scenarios were constructed so as to present participants with alternatives that involved value types that were on opposite sides of the circular structure proposed by Schwartz (1992, 1996). These were the exam scenario, the camp scenario, the organization scenario, the job scenario, the essay scenario, the graduation scenario, the club scenario, and the research scenario. For example, the alternatives for the exam scenario pitted the achievement value type against the benevolence value type. Other scenarios presented participants with alternatives that involved value types that were more adjacent on the circular structure. These were the party scenario and the warmth scenario. For example, the alternatives for the party scenario were designed to engage the hedonism and stimulation value types for one alternative and the achievement and security value types for the other.

I focus here on the relations between value types and participants' judgments of valence for the alternatives for each scenario. The correlations are presented in Table 3.3. These correlations show that most of the valence measures were positively correlated with the value types that each alternative was assumed to engage. Note also that statistically significant positive correlations were obtained with value types that were adjacent to those that were assumed to be involved in a particular alternative. The camp scenario provides a good example. In this case the

Table 3.3. Correlations between Value Types and Valence Measures for Each Scenario, with Mean Value Held Constant

Scenario and alternative	Assumed scenario values	Value type-valence correlations									
		Power	Achieve-ment	Hedon-ism	Stimu-lation	Self-direction	Univer-salism	Benev-olence	Tradi-tion	Conform-ity	Security
Exam											
(a)	Benevolence	-.13*	-.16**	-.11	.02	.03	.19**	.07	-.04	.05	-.06
(b)	Achievement	.15**	.12*	.08	-.06	.02	-.12*	-.06	.01	-.06	.02
Camp											
(a)	Stimulation/self-direction	-.09	-.08	.06	.30***	.18**	.29***	-.09	-.24***	-.28***	-.22***
(b)	Conformity	.04	-.02	-.16**	-.33***	-.29***	-.21***	.18**	.26***	.24***	.28***
Organization											
(a)	Universalism	-.29***	-.23***	-.06	.04	.11*	.59***	.01	-.13*	-.27***	-.15*
(b)	Power	.34***	.19**	-.03	-.07	-.14*	-.30***	-.07	.15*	.13*	.14*
Job											
(a)	Security	.20***	.04	.13*	-.16**	-.27***	-.22***	-.02	.07	.23***	.18**
(b)	Self-direction	-.21***	-.10	-.12*	.14*	.30***	.35***	.01	-.14*	-.26***	-.27***
Essay											
(a)	Benevolence	-.10	-.13*	.04	.06	-.05	.14*	.00	-.12*	.08	.07
(b)	Achievement	.24***	.14*	.07	.01	-.02	-.15*	-.08	.08	-.12*	-.07

Graduation										
(a) Hedonism/stimulation	−.12*	−.06	.17**	.24***	.17**	.22***	−.01	−.22***	−.26***	−.23***
(b) Tradition/security	.17***	.05	−.01	−.22***	−.27***	−.19**	.10	.29***	.20***	.14*
Club										
(a) Power	.41***	.38***	.14*	.12*	−.03	−.29***	−.19**	.00	−.07	−.07
(b) Universalism	−.31***	−.17**	−.14*	.00	.16**	.55***	−.01	−.11*	−.26***	−.17**
Research										
(a) Tradition	.18**	.00	.20***	−.01	−.24***	−.04	−.06	.07	.00	.09
(b) Self-direction	−.26***	.08	−.13*	−.02	.31***	.21***	.07	−.18**	−.08	−.13*
Party										
(a) Hedonism/stimulation	.04	−.02	.30***	.34***	.02	.09	.07	−.20***	−.22***	−.24***
(b) Achievement/security	−.02	.10	−.18**	−.29***	.01	−.05	−.01	.08	.10	.21***
Warmth										
(a) Benevolence	−.24***	−.07	−.08	−.20***	−.09	.07	.33***	−.03	.06	−.02
(b) Universalism	.01	−.03	−.05	−.02	.05	.16**	−.04	−.02	−.11*	−.04
Mean score	2.20	4.34	4.70	3.95	4.88	4.61	4.85	2.28	3.67	3.83
SD	1.35	1.17	1.36	1.34	0.87	1.00	0.87	1.19	1.19	1.12

Note: $N = 228$ for the partial correlations.

*$p < .05$, two-tailed test   **$p < .01$, two-tailed test   ***$p < .001$, two-tailed test

Source: Feather (1995b). Copyright © 1995 by the American Psychological Association. Reprinted with permission.

valence or attractiveness of exploring a path leading from the camp was positively associated with the importance assigned by participants to stimulation, self-direction, and universalism values, and the valence of staying in the camp with the group was positively associated with the importance participants assigned to benevolence, tradition, conformity, and security values. I had assumed that the valence of exploring the path would be associated with stimulation and self-direction values and that staying with the group would be associated with conformity values (Table 3.3). Clearly, however, other value types that were adjacent to those predicted were also implicated.

As another example, consider the results for the graduation scenario. In this case, the valence or attractiveness of taking a year off from studies and traveling around Australia was positively related to the importance assigned by participants to hedonism, stimulation, self-direction, and universalism values, and the valence of beginning university studies immediately after high school graduation was positively related to the importance assigned by participants to tradition, conformity, security, and power values. Here, again, the valence of each alternative was associated with the predicted value types (Table 3.3), but these valences were also positively associated with value types that were adjacent to the value types that were predicted to be engaged by each alternative. However, the correlations for these adjacent value types were not consistently weaker than the correlations for the value types that were specified. In some cases they were stronger.

In general, the results provided strong evidence for the predicted positive relations between value types and valences, consistent with the assumption that an important function of values is to induce valences on objects and events. Eighty-five percent of the 25 assumed scenario values in Table 3.3 were involved in statistically significant relations with the valence measures as predicted. Additionally, adjacent value types were also involved in significant positive relations with the valence measures for some of the scenarios.

Table 3.3 also provides information about relations between value types and valences as we move toward the opposite side of the circular map. These correlations shifted to negative for value types that were on opposite sides of the circular map to the value types that an alternative was assumed to reflect. Again, let us take the camp scenario as an example. In this case, the valence of exploring a path away from the camp was negatively related to the importance assigned by participants to tradition, conformity, and security values. The valence of staying with the group was negatively related to the importance assigned by participants to hedonism, stimulation, self-direction, and universalism values. These values were adjacent on the circular map but they were on the opposite side to the predicted value types for each alternative (see Figure 3.1).

With the graduation scenario, the valence of taking a year off from studies with the aim of having a good time and enjoying life's pleasures was negatively related to the importance assigned by participants to tradition, conformity, security, and power values. The valence of starting university studies and following a traditional career path was negatively related to the importance assigned by participants to stimulation, self-direction, and universalism values.

Note that for both of these examples, the value types that were negatively related to the valence of each alternative would be those that would imply actions that would conflict with the given alternative. These results are consistent with the hypothesis that relations between value types and valences depend upon where the value types are located in the circular map. They also support Schwartz's (1992, 1996) assumption that there is a dynamic structure to the value types. Some value types that are adjacent are compatible when they are pursued simultaneously; other value types that are opposite imply conflict when they are pursued simultaneously. This general statement is also consistent with the Brendl and Higgins (1996) analysis of the principles involved in judging valence. In terms of their principle of goal supportiveness, alternatives that would facilitate the expression or attainment of the goals relating to a value type tended to be judged positively; alternatives that would impede the expression or attainment of the goals relating to a value type tended to be judged negatively.

These differences in relations were also evident when the analysis involved the higher-order value dimensions rather than the specific value types. For example, in the case of the job scenario, the valence of taking a job that offered security without much opportunity for freedom, independence, and creativity in the workplace was negatively related to a composite measure of openness to change and positively related to a composite measure of conservation; the valence of the alternative of taking a job that offered opportunities for a lot of independence, freedom, and creativity in the workplace but less security was positively related to openness to change and negatively related to conservation. Thus, these results supported the hypothesis that the valence of alternatives would be related to the higher-order value dimensions (Feather, 1995b).

I do not present here the detailed results of the analysis of the choices participants made between the alternatives for each scenario because they were largely consistent with the results already presented

(Feather, 1995b, pp. 1143–1144). For example, for the organization scenario, choosing to join an organization that promoted economic development and the achievement of national wealth and power rather than choosing to join an organization that promoted protection of the environment and community effort was positively related to the importance assigned by participants to power, achievement, and conformity values but negatively related to the importance assigned by participants to universalism and benevolence values. As a further example, for the essay scenario, choosing not to share one's essay notes with another student in the hope of enhancing personal success by getting a high grade rather than choosing to help another student by lending him or her the essay notes was positively related to the importance assigned by participants to power and achievement values and negatively related to the importance assigned by participants to universalism and benevolence values.

As would be expected, the choices made by participants followed the alternative with higher judged valence. For the most part the effects of values on choice were mediated by the valences (Feather, 1995b, pp. 1144–1145). The study that I described was not designed to vary other factors that would affect choice. The focus was on value-valence and value-choice relations. However, as I have argued previously (Feather, 1990a) in discussing the general framework of expectancy-value theory,

> whether a person has a tendency to act in a particular direction will depend on that person's expectation about whether he or she can perform the action to the required standard, on a further set of expectations about the potential consequences of the action, and on the valences (or subjective values) associated with the activity and with the anticipated outcome. Those actions will be preferred that can be coordinated to the dominant motivational or action tendencies that relate to a combination of these expectations and valences. (p. 163)

Thus, valences are only one set of variables that affect the choices a person makes and the direction behavior takes.

It is clear, however, that the results of this study with hypothetical scenarios provided strong support for the hypothesis that the valences or attractiveness of alternative courses of action would be related to the value types, and that the choice between alternatives would be mediated by the valences. The results were obtained over a range of scenarios that sampled different types of values from the Schwartz circular map. I consider them to be robust findings "that support the assumption that values have an important role as variables that affect our cognitive-

appraisal of situations and the choices that follow that appraisal"
(Feather, 1995b, p. 1145).

Values, Valences, and Food-Related Behavior

A third study (Feather, Norman, & Worsley, 1998) was similar in
design to the study that has just been described but it focused on the
valences and choice of foods that were presented or consumed under
different conditions. Hence, it was more restricted in focus when compared with the previous study, dealing with a situation of applied
relevance—the presentation and consumption of food.

We again used a scenario methodology but, in this case, we presented participants with scenarios that could be assumed to vary in the
degree to which they would engage values. For example, one scenario
that we used provided participants with a fairly bland choice between
either sweet pastries or a savory plate of salad, fruit, or nuts that might
be assumed to be more beneficial to health. Another scenario presented
alternatives that could be assumed to involve different motivational
goals relating to value types that may come into conflict when pursued
simultaneously. In this scenario values concerned with tradition were
set against values concerned with stimulation. Specifically, participants
had to choose between going to a traditional Christmas dinner with
family or going on a surprise Christmas trip with friends, sampling lots
of different food, and having an exciting time. In contrast to the first
example, we assumed that this scenario would be more engaging as far
as the elicitation of values was concerned because it clearly involved an
opposition of motivational goals that related to value types on the opposite side of Schwartz's (1992, 1996) circular structure.

Our participants again completed the 56-item version of the
Schwartz Value Survey and, as in the previous study, we followed
Schwartz's recommendations (Schwartz, 1992, p. 52) when selecting
values to define each value type. For example, the values defining the
stimulation value type were excitement, novelty, and challenge in life;
the values defining the *tradition* value type were showing respect for
tradition, being humble, accepting my portion in life, being devout, and
being moderate; the values defining the *hedonism* value type were
pleasure and enjoying life; and the values defining the *universalism*
value type were broadmindedness, wisdom, a world of beauty, equality,
unity with nature, a world at peace, social justice, and protecting the
environment. As in the previous study, participants rated each of the 56
values with respect to importance for self ("as a guiding principle in

your life"), using the −1 to 7 rating scale that was described previously. These ratings were combined for each participant for the subsets of values that defined each value type.

We presented participants with five different scenarios, each with two alternatives describing food that was presented or consumed under different conditions. These scenarios involved:

- a wedding reception where the alternatives consisted of either sweet pastries or a savory plate of salad, fruit, and nuts.
- two brands of salmon with one brand using environmentally friendly fishing methods and another brand that did not use these methods but had a better taste.
- Christmas celebrations with one alternative involving a traditional dinner with family and the other a surprise Christmas trip with the details a "mystery" but where different foods would be sampled and where there would be a lot of excitement.
- going with a group to a fashionable restaurant where the food was not particularly healthy or going alone to a restaurant that served healthier foods but one that the group might find too boring.
- selecting either a healthy and hygienically packaged food from a snack bar or a less healthy food that was packaged in an environmentally friendly manner using a biodegradable wrapper.

Which value types were these alternatives assumed to elicit? In terms of Schwartz's (1992) classification, alternatives in which taste was a salient feature were assumed to prime hedonistic values concerned with pleasure and comfort; alternatives specifying environmentally friendly products were assumed to elicit universalism values concerned with general social welfare; alternatives involving surprise and excitement were assumed to elicit stimulation values concerned with excitement and novelty; alternatives involving traditional foods were assumed to elicit tradition values concerned with respect for tradition or religion; alternatives involving conformity to group pressure were assumed to elicit conformity values concerned with restraining actions and impulses that might violate social expectations or norms; and alternatives in which health was the salient feature were assumed to elicit security values concerned with safety, harmony, and stability. We based this last linkage (healthy foods/security values) on the assumption that health is an important contributor to personal welfare. It should be noted, however, that Schwartz (1992) found that the value "healthy" tended to vary in its location on his circular map, though in most cases it was classified as a security value.

Note that our approach in constructing these scenarios was to devise alternatives that could reasonably be assumed to be linked to particular value types. Our scenarios have face validity in that respect. A detailed derivation and justification would involve "a close analysis of the consequences of a behavior or attitude for the expression or attainment of the motivational goals of the value type, leading to the identification of the most relevant type" (Schwartz, 1996, p. 22). This kind of analysis was conducted by Sagiv and Schwartz (1995) in their study of readiness for outgroup contact in a realistic context where different motivational goals could be assumed.

Participants responded to each of the five scenarios by rating each alternative for its attractiveness, using a 5-point rating scale. They then indicated which alternative they would choose (see Feather et al., 1998).

The five scenarios and the Schwartz Value Survey were presented, along with other items about age, gender, and so forth, in a booklet that was distributed to 593 shoppers in 12 supermarkets in four geographic regions of metropolitan Adelaide, South Australia, representing low, low medium, high medium, and high socioeconomic status groups. Thus, the sampling took place in a realistic setting and it involved members of the public rather than student groups. The shoppers were asked to return the booklet by mail, using a postage-paid envelope. We obtained completed booklets without missing data from 464 participants, a very high response rate (78%).

As in the previous study, we expected that the valence or perceived attractiveness of each alternative would be related to the value type that was assumed to be engaged by that alternative. Specifically, we predicted that perceived attractiveness would be positively related to hedonistic and security values for the wedding scenario; to universalism and hedonistic values for the salmon scenario; to tradition and stimulation values for the Christmas celebrations scenario; to conformity and security values for the restaurant scenario; and to security and universalism values for the snack bar scenario. These predicted value types are presented in Table 3.4. We also predicted that the value-induced valences would mediate the effects of values on choice.

As noted previously, however, we assumed that the five scenarios would vary in the degree to which they would activate the predicted values we have listed in Table 3.4 for each alternative. Schwartz (1996) recommended that researchers "take competition between the relatively enduring systems of individual's value priorities into account" (p. 22), and, in line with that recommendation, we expected to find strong evidence for value elicitation and value-valence-choice relations for the

Table 3.4. **Statistically Significant Correlations (rs) Relating Value Types to Valence Measures, with Mean Value Held Constant**

Scenario and alternative	Predicted value type	Value types significantly associated with valence
Wedding		
Sweet food	Hedonism	No value types
Healthy food	Security	Hedonism (−.15**)
Salmon		
Environment	Universalism	Power (−.10*), universalism (.35***), tradition (−.16***), conformity (−.15**)
Taste	Hedonism	Universalism (−.14**), security (.11*)
Christmas		
Traditional	Tradition	Achievement (−.12*), hedonism (−.15**), self-direction (−.14**), stimulation (−.15**), security (.20***), tradition (.12*)
Mystery trip	Stimulation	Hedonism (.22***), stimulation (.32***), benevolence (−.15**), tradition (−.18***), conformity (−.26***), security (−.13**)
Restaurant		
Group	Conformity	Power (.10*), hedonism (.12*), security (.10*)
Alone	Security	Universalism (.10*), security (−.15**)
Snack bar		
Health	Security	No value types
Environment	Universalism	No value types

Note: N = 401 for partial correlations involving valence measures.
*p < .05, two-tailed test   **p < .01, two-tailed test   ***p < .001, two-tailed test
Source: Feather et al. (1998). Reprinted by permission from the *Journal of Applied Social Psychology, 7,* p. 648, Table 2. V. H. Winston & Sons, Inc., 360 South Ocean Boulevard, Palm Springs, FL 33480. All rights reserved.

Christmas celebrations scenario where the two alternatives provided clearly different motivational goals, relating to value types that were on opposite sides of Schwartz's circular value structure.

The results in Table 3.4 show that there was mixed support for the value-valence hypothesis for the set of scenarios that we used in the study. The best support came from the salmon and Christmas celebrations scenarios. The latter scenario provided the strongest results and the greatest contrast in correlations. In the case of the salmon scenario, participants' ratings of the importance of universalism values were positively related to the perceived attractiveness of the environmentally friendly salmon and negatively related to the perceived attractiveness of the tastier but less environmentally friendly brand. For the Christmas celebrations scenario, participants who gave higher ratings to tradition values tended to rate the traditional Christmas dinner as more attractive and the mystery Christmas trip as less attractive, when compared with participants who rated tradition values as less important. Participants who rated stimulation values as more important tended to rate the traditional Christmas dinner as less important and the mystery trip as more important, when compared with participants who rated stimulation values as less important.

Table 3.4 also shows that there were other values, in addition to the predicted ones, that were associated with the valence measures. For both the salmon and the Christmas celebrations scenarios, the direction of relations involving these other value types was consistent with the assumption of adjacent (or compatible) value types and opposing (or incompatible) value types (Feather, 1995b; Sagiv & Schwartz, 1995; Schwartz, 1992, 1996). For example, security and tradition value types are adjacent on Schwartz's circular map, and they are opposite to stimulation and hedonism value types. The correlations of these value types with the attractiveness or valence ratings were consistent with this structural arrangement in the case of the Christmas celebrations scenario. For the traditional Christmas alternative, these ratings were positively related to the importance assigned to security and tradition values and negatively related to the importance assigned to stimulation and hedonism values. In contrast, relations involving these value types were in the reverse direction for attractiveness ratings for the mystery trip alternative, again consistent with the location of these value types on the circular structure.

I do not present details here concerning the choices made by participants between the alternatives that were presented for each scenario. They can be found in the original report (Feather et al., 1998). By way of summary, however, the choices made for the salmon and for the Christmas celebrations scenarios were consistent with the valence results that have just been presented. Thus, in the case of the salmon scenario, choice of the tasty brand of salmon rather than the environmentally friendly brand was negatively related to the importance assigned by participants to universalism values. In the case of the Christmas celebrations scenario, the choice of going on a mystery trip rather than partaking in the traditional Christmas dinner was positively related to the importance participants assigned to stimulation values and negatively related to the importance they assigned to tradition values.

As was the case in the previous study (Feather, 1995b), the choices made by participants followed the alternative with the higher judged valence. More detailed multiple regression analyses showed that the effects of values on choice were mediated by the valences (see Feather et al., 1998).

The results of this third study are of interest because they showed that value-valence relations were not consistently obtained across all five scenarios. Their emergence depended on the scenario. The results were strongest for the Christmas celebrations scenario; they provided some support for the salmon scenario; and they were weakest for the other three scenarios. Note that the former two scenarios provided more information about context. These two scenarios set the context in which food was either presented or consumed, adding information beyond that conveyed by the food itself. This additional information probably enabled a more ready engagement of the value types that the scenarios were designed to elicit. The remaining three scenarios provided less information about extrinsic variables that would produce sharp contrasts in the context and symbolic significance of food. The emphasis was more on the intrinsic properties of the food such as its taste or health-giving properties.

In general, therefore, the results of the third study suggest that it is important to allow for the context in which food is presented when predicting value-valence relations associated with different alternatives. As we noted in the original report of this study, "At a social gathering red wine may be perceived as attractive because of its taste; at a communion service its attractiveness may also be related to deeply held religious values" (Feather et al., 1998, p. 653).

A further point to be made is that the effects of values may become more evident when a person has to choose between alternatives that involve conflicting values and where trade-offs between important values have to be negotiated and resolved (Schwartz, 1996; Tetlock, 1986; Tetlock, Peterson, & Lerner, 1996). Alternative courses of action that are in conflict as far as basic values are concerned set problems for the decision maker, especially when the alternatives are equally attractive. The values may be more readily engaged, leading to clearer value-valence relations. The differential effects of values may be less apparent when the choice between alternatives involves compatible values that do not involve important trade-offs and where the choice is somewhat bland.

Other interpretations of the results of this study of food-related behavior have been presented in the original report (Feather et al., 1998). Note that, in contrast to the study that was described in the previous section (Feather, 1995b), we restricted our scenarios to a defined area, the presentation and consumption of food. It is possible that the valence of different types of food may be more closely related to their intrinsic properties than to individual differences in needs and values. These intrinsic properties may dominate other variables, as when one food is preferred to another because of its flavor, despite the context. In the wedding scenario, for example, healthy but flavorsome foods may have been preferred to sweet tasting foods and that preference may not alter even when the context of consumption is varied. The intrinsic properties of the food may have much greater weight as variables that influence the valence of each alternative when compared with individual differences in needs and values.

THE ENGAGEMENT OF VALUES

In order to examine value-valence relations we need to be able to specify the conditions under which values are aroused and the processes by which activated values induce valences on specific objects and events. I have considered these issues in various parts of this chapter, especially when discussing values, valences, and associative networks and also when discussing the results of the two studies that used hypothetical scenarios. Now it is time to examine the engagement of values in more detail.

It is important to recognize that not all situations engage our values. Some behavior runs relatively automatically without much conscious control or planning (e.g., Bargh, 1996; Uleman & Bargh, 1989; Feather, 1982a, pp. 403–405). We do not attempt to explain pushing the brake pedal of a car at a stop light, or other forms of habitual or "mindless" activities, in terms of values that are engaged by the situation. We use different forms of explanation to account for these kinds of events.

The engagement of values is more likely to occur in situations where there is a means-end structure that involves possible actions that may lead to goals (i.e., the situation must provide the possibility for a goal structure to emerge). Such situations may engage needs as well as values. The athlete who is trying to win at competition by superior performance may be motivated in part by a need to achieve that functions as an implicit motive (Weinberger & McClelland, 1990). The competitive situation may also elicit general values that relate to achievement, values that are closely tied to the self-concept and that are consciously experienced. How then do needs and values differ? Weinberger and McClelland propose that implicit motives such as the need to achieve are acquired early in life; are best measured by indirect means, such as fantasy productions; and are built largely on nonverbal experiences that involve affect. They propose that implicit motives have long-term effects on behavior and are predictive of behavior in free-response situations. In contrast, according to Weinberger and McClelland (1990), self-attributed motives such as values are closely tied to the self-concept and are built on "more highly symbolic representational capacities, such as linguistically coded communications and instructions" (p. 587). They are better able to predict short-term behavior in more constrained and structured situations where conscious choices have to be made.

I believe that this distinction between the functions of needs and values is too limiting and that values "also have long-term effects on a person's behavior, functioning to influence both the short-term and long-term goals that become salient for a person and the selection of plans and actions that relate to these goals" (Feather, 1995b, p. 1136). Thus, they have a motivational role, exerting their effects by way of the valences that become attached to objects and events within a person's psychological environment. As argued previously, in this sense they are like needs, inducing valences on objects and events.

However, that is not to say that values are identical to needs. Values have a normative base involving a dimension of goodness-badness. Needs are not necessarily defined in relation to an evaluative dimension. Moreover, in agreement with Weinberger and McClelland (1990), values are more verbalizable and closer to conscious awareness than many underlying needs, and they are intimately bound with a person's sense of self (Rokeach, 1973). A person can usually describe the important values that he or she holds, such as being honest or valuing freedom or family security. Indeed, that assumption is basic to the value measures that have been developed (e.g., Rokeach, 1973; Schwartz, 1992, 1996). These measures, such as the Rokeach Value Survey and the Schwartz Value Survey, assume that a person can report on the importance of values in regard to self.

Needs can be conceived either as momentary states of the person (e.g., an immediate need for food or water) or as relatively stable dispositional properties of persons that are acquired early in life (e.g., a general need to achieve, or a need for power) (Atkinson & Feather, 1966; McClelland, 1985). Values are usually conceived to be relatively stable in nature when compared to more transient states of the person, although their relative importance to the individual may alter as a result of socialization and other life experiences. Thus, needs and values share similarities in their ability to induce valences on objects and events once they are activated, but they also differ in kind.

The eliciting conditions for needs and values overlap to some extent, although, in the case of transient needs like the need for food or water, physiological conditions are also important. Situational cues play an important role for the engagement of both needs and values. For example, the elicitation of the need to achieve depends on the presence of cues in the situation that hold out the promise of possible achievement, where outcomes can be measured against standards of excellence (Atkinson & Feather, 1966). The engagement of values is more likely to occur in situations that can be structured in terms of paths or actions that can lead to short-term or long-term goals.

I now focus on the role of the situation in relation to the engagement of values. One obvious point is that the situation has to be relevant to particular values. For example, situations that may either provide or obstruct opportunities for power or achievement would be relevant to power and achievement values; situations that may either enable or block the seeking of new experiences would be relevant to stimulation values; situations that may either foster or frustrate independence and freedom of action would be relevant to self-direction values. In these cases the situation provides information about the possibility of fulfilling the value, or about barriers and threats that may prevent some degree of fulfillment. The situation would be viewed positively where pursuit of the value is facilitated by the opportunities that are afforded, and negatively where the situation constrains or blocks the possibility of realizing the value. Thus, the content of the situation has to be relevant to underlying values, in terms of what it offers and in terms of what it constrains or frustrates, if these values are to be engaged. In terms of an earlier analysis (Feather, 1971a), there has to be some match or connection between the perceived situation and the way it is defined, and the latent abstract structures or values that could possibly be engaged.

Recently, Schwartz (1996) has also drawn attention to the importance of context when relating single behaviors to general values that are transsituational in nature. He reported studies of interpersonal cooperation, voting behavior, and readiness for outgroup contact where these behaviors were hypothesized to relate to particular value types defined by the circular structure of values. Careful consideration was given to the consequences of each behavior for the expression or attainment of the motivational goals of the value types. In the study of outgroup social contact (Sagiv & Schwartz, 1995), hypotheses for the majority group (Jews) differed from those of the minority group (Arabs) because social contact would have different potential meanings and consequences depending on whether Jews or Arabs were the main focus, implying different sets of value-behavior relations.

Schwartz (1996) also argues that the usual order of conflicts and compatibilities among values that is implied by the circular structure of value types may sometimes be distorted by externally imposed social constraints. Within Israel, for example, the sociopolitical context for Arab minorities would affect the degree to which the motivational goals relating to values can be attained.

Schwartz (1996) notes that value-behavior relations for the three examples that he discusses tended to follow the wave or sinusoid pattern implied by the structure of value systems, but true sine curve patterns were not found. Nor did I find true sinusoid patterns in the two studies of value-valence relations described in the preceding sections. There were irregularities and sometimes reversals in the pattern of correlations between the value types and the valence measures (see Table 3.3). Note that a regular order may be difficult to obtain in practice because of the varying reliabilities of the measures. Also, as Schwartz (1996) proposed, deviations from the sinusoid order and departures from symmetry and smoothness may occur because of the specific nature of the situational context and the constraints that are imposed.

I have argued that we need more research on how the context of the situation may affect value-valence relations (Feather, 1995b, p. 1148). For example, does conflict always occur when values on opposite sides of the circular structure are pursued simultaneously? In some cultures that emphasize interdependence and communal effort, it may be possible to pursue conformity and achievement values simultaneously without the conflicts that are implied by the circular structure. In these cultures the achievements that are valued are those that follow team effort and conformity rather than individual effort and self-direction. They are the outcome of team effort, group harmony, and loyalty to the organization (e.g., Feather & McKee, 1993; Markus & Kitayama, 1991; Triandis, 1995). Similarly, one can imagine cases where values that are adjacent on the circular structure may be in conflict when pursued simultaneously rather than being compatible. A person may simultaneously pursue a life of pleasure and also place high value on achievement. These values may come into conflict. For example, the pursuit of pleasure may be at the expense of high achievement; the pursuit of achievement may set limits on a hedonistic lifestyle.

Achievement and hedonism would also be in conflict in some religious or ethical ideologies. For example, Weber (1904–1905/1976) describes the Protestant work ethic as one that involves hard work and the denial of pleasure. In terms of this ethic, achievement and hedonism would be incompatible.

Also, in the case of political ideology, Rokeach (1973) proposes that political ideologies may vary depending on the importance assigned to freedom and equality. These two values may be compatible or in conflict depending on the degree to which both are emphasized or deemphasized in the ideology, or the degree to which one is emphasized or the other is deemphasized (see also Braithwaite, 1998).

The situation itself also defines whether actions and their associated values are compatible or incompatible. For example, values that are adjacent on Schwartz's circular structure may come into conflict in a choice situation where only one alternative can be selected. Thus, a person may have to choose between voting for a political party that emphasizes traditional values as part of its political platform and a party where the major emphasis is on social welfare and promoting prosocial values. Conversely, a situation may allow values that are on opposite sides of the circular structure to be pursued simultaneously. For example, a person may embark on a course of action that may satisfy self-direction values and that may, at the same time, be judged to be likely to lead to security in later life. Compatibilities and incompatibilities in courses of action and the values that may be associated with them therefore depend crucially on the affordances and constraints that the situation provides. The content and structure of the situation determine what values are likely to be engaged and what trade-offs are possible.

More generally, situations may be structured in such a way as to facilitate or impede the realization and fulfillment of values. Values may be engaged when the situation provides opportunities for their satisfaction, as when outcomes that are relevant to particular values are clearly available and possible of attainment. Values may also be engaged when the situation challenges or obstructs actions that would lead to their satisfaction, as when a political regime frustrates or denies the fulfillment of important social values. Thus, "The structure of what is possible in a particular situation, in terms of the perceived connectedness of activities, barriers, and goals, has to be considered in relation to conflicts and compatibilities as well as the way value types are organized and relate to one another" (Feather, 1995b, p. 1148).

Moreover, the structure and content of the situation not only affects the engagement of needs and values and an individual's subsequent construal of possible actions and outcomes as positive or negative, but the situation also influences a person's efficacy and outcome expectations that, together with the valences, are important determinants of the final behavior that occurs (Feather, 1982a, 1990a, 1992b).

The points that I have raised in this discussion and the examples that I have provided imply that "the conflicts and compatibilities that occur between values may not always follow the sort of Platonic form expressed in the Schwartz model" (Feather, 1995b, p. 1148). They are closely bound with the context of possible courses of action within a situation and with the motivational goals whose attainment the situation either facilitates or prevents.

This discussion of the role of the situation should not divert attention from one further important point, namely, that the engagement of specific values also depends on each person's own value structure. Values that are very important for a person are more likely to be engaged when compared with values that are less important. For example, a person for whom equality is an important value is likely to be especially sensitive to all specific forms of equality and inequality, much more so than a person for whom equality is further down the value hierarchy.

CONCLUDING COMMENT

The main aim of this chapter has been to develop the idea that values, as properties of persons, have the ability to confer positive or negative valences on actions and outcomes, once the relevant values are engaged. This idea that what we value and hold to be important affects the way we construe situations plays an important role in the structural model of deservingness that is the subject of the next chapter.

CHAPTER 4

The Deservingness Model

The variables that were discussed in the preceding chapters, namely, perceived responsibility, values, and valences, are basic variables in the structural model of deservingness that will be the focus of this chapter. Here we are concerned with how these variables combine to affect a person's judgments of deservingness. As I indicated in the first chapter, these judgments are assumed to depend upon the degree to which the other person who is being judged is perceived to be responsible for the positive or negative outcome that occurred. People are usually judged not to deserve outcomes for which they are perceived not to be responsible. But when they are seen to be responsible for an outcome they are not necessarily seen to deserve it. This is because judgments of deservingness also depend on the structure of the subjective values (or valences) that a person assigns to both the action and the outcome that follows it.

I propose that positive outcomes that follow positive actions will tend to be seen as deserved, as will negative outcomes that follow negative actions. Likewise, positive outcomes that follow negative actions will tend to be seen as undeserved, as will negative outcomes that follow positive actions. The review of theory and research that I presented in the preceding chapter showed that whether objects and events are seen as attractive (positively valent) or aversive (negatively valent) will depend upon a number of variables that include a person's needs and values. In the present context, actions and outcomes are assumed to derive their positivity or negativity from the general values that people hold and the degree to which they are engaged within a situation. Thus, I assume that there is a connection between the general values that a person holds and the way that person perceives particular actions and outcomes as positive or negative. This assumption is consistent with the theory and research that I reviewed in the preceding chapter.

The emphasis on the way actions and outcomes are structured in terms of their subjective values (or valences) implies that we should seek some way of representing relations in a structural or configural form and that we also need to develop some theoretical ideas about how the structure might be organized. My development of a structural model has been influenced by Heider's (1958) contributions, especially his principle of structural balance, and by the subsequent use of signed digraphs to represent structures that involve elements and relations (Cartwright & Harary, 1956; Harary, Norman, & Cartwright, 1965). I will describe the principle of structural balance and its subsequent developments in a later section before introducing the structural model of deservingness.

We should, however, recall that, in the first chapter, I drew attention to some other variables that might be expected to influence judgments of deservingness, in addition to perceived responsibility and evaluative appraisals of actions and outcomes in terms of their positivity and negativity. These other variables were the quality of the person as revealed in judgments of moral character; interpersonal relations, or like/dislike relations, between the person who is making the judgment of deservingness and the other person who is being judged; and the social identity of both the person who is making the judgment and the other who is being judged, especially in relation to whether the other person belongs to the same ingroup as the judge or is a member of an outgroup.

In the next two sections I will briefly consider these other variables, focusing in particular on relations between person (p) and other (o) but also commenting on the question of perceived moral character.

SOCIAL IDENTITY AND INTERPERSONAL RELATIONS

Questions of interpersonal relations and social identity are central concerns of social identity theory and self-categorization theory (Tajfel & Turner, 1986; Turner, Hogg, Oakes, Reicher, & Wetherall, 1987). In these approaches a distinction is made between personal and social identity. These two forms of identity are assumed to involve different ways in which a person can categorize self. Tajfel (1978) defined social identity as "that *part* of an individual's self-concept which derives from his knowledge of his membership of a social group (or groups) together with the value and emotional significance attached to that membership" (p. 63). I might say, for example, that I am an Australian or on the academic staff of Flinders University. On the other hand, personal identity involves self-categorization in terms of personal characteristics that enable individuals to distinguish themselves from other individuals in the social context. I might say, for example, that I enjoy a game of tennis or that I like visiting art museums. Thus, a person might categorize self in relation to the groups to which he or she belongs, or in terms of personal characteristics that distinguish self from others at the individual level.

The literature on social identity and self-categorization is now extensive and a review of it is well beyond the scope of the present book (e.g., see Abrams & Hogg, 1990; Brewer, 1991, 1993; Brewer & Brown, 1998; Hogg & Abrams, 1988, 1993; Oakes, Haslam, & Turner, 1994; Turner et al., 1987). An important assumption in the approach is that people attempt to maintain favorable self-concepts and that these self-concepts derive not only from their own personal experiences but also from the way they define themselves in terms of their group memberships. People are assumed to seek social identities that will maintain or enhance their self-esteem. One important way of maintaining a positive self-image at the social identity level is for a person to engage in intergroup comparisons that enable the person's ingroup to be viewed in a favorable light in comparison with outgroups.

Thus, the selective differentiation that occurs between ingroups and outgroups is assumed to accomplish "a relatively positive self-evaluation that endows the individual with a sense of well-being, enhanced self-worth and esteem" (Hogg & Abrams, 1988, p. 23). Or, as Brewer (1993) puts it, "Just as self-esteem may be enhanced by positive comparisons between the personal self and other individuals, self-esteem may also be achieved through *positive distinctiveness* of the ingroup from relevant outgroups" (p. 2). The tendency to favor the ingroup over the outgroup may therefore be interpreted in terms of esteem-related processes that are assumed to accompany reinforcement of a person's positive social identity.

One can question the assumption that the motivational basis for differentiating in favor of the ingroup lies in a person's desire to maintain and enhance self-esteem (e.g., Crocker, Blaine, & Luhtanen, 1993; Feather, 1994c, 1995a, 1996d; Hogg & Abrams, 1990, 1993; van Knippenberg & Ellemers, 1993). This assumption is probably too simplistic and fails to take account of the variety of other motives that may operate to affect group members' attitudes and behaviors toward ingroups and outgroups (Feather, 1996d). For example, I have reported evidence that relations between the degree to which people favor the products and achievements of their own nation and their level of identification with their nation are moderated by the value priorities that they hold (Feather, 1994c). There is also evidence that the psychological processes that are assumed to be central to social identity theory are more evident in groups or individuals who are collectivist and relational in their orienta-

tions when compared with groups or individuals who are more individualistic and autonomous in their orientations (Brown, Hinkle, Ely, Fox-
Cardamone, Maras, & Taylor, 1992; Hinkle & Brown, 1990).

Moreover, the research evidence does not always show that ingroup
favoritism occurs, nor that when it occurs, it tends to be much stronger
the more a person is identified with his or her ingroup. Brewer (1993)
indicates that "positive distinctiveness motives cannot account for why
members of socially disadvantaged and stigmatized minorities maintain
positive self-esteem in the face of negative intergroup comparisons"
(p. 3). Hinkle and Brown (1990) note that "a commonly obtained finding
in the literature is that the intergroup comparisons of low status groups
frequently takes the form of out-group favoritism, mirroring the reality of
such groups' lower relative position" (pp. 50–51). Nor does the evidence
show that people spontaneously engage in intergroup comparisons even
when requested to do so (Hinkle & Brown, 1990).

Clearly, there are a number of variables that affect the tendency for
people to favor their ingroup at the expense of the outgroup and many of
these are still being investigated (e.g., Brewer, 1991, 1993; Brewer &
Brown, 1998). Oakes et al. (1994) note that the early studies and subsequent studies that were guided by social identity theory recognized

> that ingroup bias was by no means an automatic consequence of min-
> imal social categorization ... it was a function, *inter alia*, of (1) the
> degree to which subjects identified with the relevant ingroup and
> (2) the salience of the relevant social categorization in the setting,
> (3) the importance and relevance of the comparative dimension to
> ingroup identity, (4) the degree to which the groups were comparable
> on that dimension (similar, close, ambiguously different), including,
> in particular, (5) the ingroup's relative status and the character of the
> perceived status differences between groups. (p. 83)

These studies also showed that outgroup favoritism would occur
where the outgroup was perceived to be superior to the ingroup on the
dimension on which comparison was made. Oakes et al. (1994) state that:

> Tajfel and his colleagues argued that, in addition to categorization, a
> process of social identification, accompanied by motives for positive
> self-evaluation and intergroup distinctiveness, underlay intergroup
> discrimination and this psychological sequence itself interacted
> with conflicts of interest and the larger social context. (p. 84)

In their analysis of stereotyping, Oakes et al. emphasize categorization
but they also underline the importance of other variables such as the
comparative context and the dimensions along which comparison occurs. Other researchers have drawn attention to the effects of group

norms, group identification, group status, and group variability on self-stereotyping, discrimination in favor of the ingroup, and intergroup perceptions, in relation to both experimental and naturally occurring groups (e.g., Branscombe, 1998; Doosje, Ellemers, & Spears, 1995; Ellemers, Van Rijswijk, Roefs, & Simons, 1997; Jetten, Spears, & Manstead, 1996; Spears, Doosje, & Ellemers, 1997). As noted previously, we also need to take account of the general values that those within a group hold (e.g., collectivist versus individualistic; power and achievement versus universalism and benevolence) because these value differences would also be expected to affect how a group reacts to its own members and also to those who belong to defined outgroups. The effects of these value differences may become more apparent in naturally occurring groups than in artificial groups that are studied in laboratory settings.

It is reasonable to assume, however, that a person's social identity will have some effect on how that person judges the degree to which another person deserves or does not deserve a particular outcome. There are a number of studies that have documented relations between social categorization and variables such as intergroup attributions, the allocation of resources, and ingroup versus outgroup favoritism (see Abrams & Hogg, 1990; Brewer, 1979; Brewer & Brown, 1998; Brewer & Kramer, 1985; Hewstone, 1989; Hogg & Abrams, 1988; Messick & Mackie, 1989, for some reviews). Many of these studies do provide evidence that group members tend to discriminate in favor of their own group, that is, these members show a degree of ingroup bias. This bias might also be expected to occur when a person judges deservingness. In this case, an ingroup member may be favored when compared with an outgroup member. Specifically, an ingroup member may be judged as more deserving of a positive outcome and as less deserving of a negative outcome when compared with an outgroup member. But, as noted above, these kinds of effects may also be affected by a range of other variables, such as the status of the group, a person's degree of identification with the ingroup, the comparative context, the norms and values that the group holds, the dimension of comparison, the degree to which the ingroup is homogenous in regard to the dimension, the cohesiveness of the ingroup, whether it is a minority or a majority group, whether it is an artificial or natural group, and a person's own needs and values. My prediction about the effects of ingroup/outgroup membership on judgments of deservingness is therefore only a first approximation. The research on groups tells us that the situation is likely to be much more complicated and that favoring the ingroup may be moderated by a host of variables.

The same sort of general prediction can be made when the focus is not on social identity and group membership but on interpersonal attraction. Here the interest would be in interpersonal relations and whether person (*p*) likes or dislikes other (*o*). The liking or disliking may be grounded in personal experience with the other person or it may be influenced by group membership or other variables, but it is a relation between individuals rather than between groups. We might expect on the basis of social influence theory that a liked other person will be favored in various ways when compared with a disliked other person (Eagly & Chaikin, 1993, pp. 638–642). In the present context, a liked person may be judged as more deserving of a positive outcome and as less deserving of a negative outcome when compared with a disliked person. Our perceptions of deservingness may, therefore, be influenced by how much we like or dislike the person who is being judged. Again, this general prediction may be moderated by a number of variables, which would include the situational context and whether the other person who is liked or disliked is or has been involved in a close relationship with the perceiver or judge or has a more distant relationship with less personal involvement.

The structural model of deservingness to be presented in the chapter explicitly allows for the representation of both social identity, in terms of ingroup versus outgroup, and interpersonal relations between person (*p*) and other (*o*) as they are reflected in *p*'s liking or disliking of *o*.

PERCEIVED MORAL CHARACTER

A further variable that might affect judgments of deservingness concerns the perceived qualities of the person who is being judged. I noted in the first chapter that dictionary definitions of deservingness refer to a person's earning a rightful claim by virtue of his or her actions or qualities. For example, in relation to qualities, people who are perceived to have integrity may be seen to deserve positive outcomes and not to deserve negative outcomes.

The reference to "quality" implies evaluation, in particular an evaluation of a person's moral character. The concept of moral character has tended to be ignored in psychology, although it was a focus of research in the 1920s and 1930s (e.g., Hartshorne & May, 1928; Hartshorne, May, & Maller, 1929; Hartshorne, May, & Shuttleworth, 1930). Allport (1937) argued that one impediment to the study of moral character was the difficulty in defining the concept. He noted that the term was defined in many different ways and that, in any case, character was an unnecessary concept because it could be subsumed within the study of personality. Thus, according to Allport (1937), "Character is personality evaluated; and personality is character devaluated" (p. 52).

Personality variables, however, may convey evaluative information. Even the personality variables described in the "big five" or five factor model (neuroticism, extraversion, openness to experience, agreeableness, and conscientiousness) have evaluative overtones depending on how they are construed (e.g., Costa & McCrae, 1992; McCrae & Costa, 1987; Wiggins & Trapnell, 1997). For example, a person who scores high on conscientiousness may be seen as having a stronger character than one who scores low on conscientiousness, depending on how much conscientiousness is valued by whoever makes the judgment. As Feather and Atchison (1998) note, "Personality characteristics are often described in a value laden way, making it difficult to separate them from judgments of character where values are central to the description" (p. 126).

Judgments that take account of moral character are an important part of everyday life. The interest among psychologists in such topics as values, moral development, and justice is testimony to the importance of considering the fundamental role of evaluations that involves criteria of desirability and undesirability, goodness and badness, and fairness and unfairness. However, the study of moral character as a variable in its own right, and one that involves the global evaluation of persons, has continued to remain in the background, although there are some exceptions to this statement (e.g., Hogan, 1973, 1975).

The definition of moral character remains a difficult issue. It raises the questions of not only what we mean by "character" but also what we mean by "moral." Are there aspects of character that do not require qualification as moral aspects? Perhaps the meaning of moral character implies some connection with particular types of values. We might take a lead from Rokeach (1973) who distinguished between two kinds of values: terminal values that are concerned with general goals or end-states of existence, and instrumental values that are concerned with modes of conduct or ways of behaving. He further divided the instrumental values into two classes: moral values and competence values. Moral values were described as those having an interpersonal focus and which, when violated, arouse feelings of guilt and pangs of conscience for any wrongdoing. Competence values were described as having more of a personal focus and, according to Rokeach, these values are not especially concerned with morality. When competence values are violated a person may experience feelings of shame about personal inadequacy rather than feelings of guilt about wrongdoing. Thus, according to Rokeach (1973), "behaving honestly and responsibly leads one to feel that he is behaving morally, whereas behaving logically, intelligently, or imaginatively leads one to feel that he is behaving competently" (p. 8).

Furthermore, Rokeach proposed that the "oughtness" quality of values described by Heider is more an attribute of instrumental values than of terminal values and more an attribute of moral values than of competence values. According to Heider (1958) the experience of "ought" can be "represented as a cognized wish or requirement of a suprapersonal order which has an invariant reality, and whose validity therefore transcends the point of view of any one person" (p. 222). Rokeach (1973) assumed that the "oughtness" of certain values originates in society, "which demands that all of us behave in certain ways that benefit and do not harm others. It is an objective demand ... in order to ensure that all people can live out their lives in a social milieu within which people can trust and depend upon one another" (p. 9). This form of analysis implies that individuals who are judged to have high moral character will be those who are seen to strongly endorse moral values such as being honest, responsible, helpful, and loving in what they say and in how they behave. The global appraisal may see them as persons of integrity who show care and consideration for others.

This global evaluation would be based on direct observations of a person's controllable and voluntary behavior (e.g., Harcum, Rosen, Pilkington, & Petty, 1995), and also on information from others about a person's character. These sources of information would be relevant not only to one's character assessment of another person but also to how one judges one's own character. The information that is assembled would be coded in terms of important values that are part of how one defines whether someone is a "good" or "bad" person. So the judgment of moral character would involve processing information in relation to value categories and integrating the products of this assessment into an overall assessment.

In the structural model of deservingness that I present in this chapter, moral character can be conceptualized in relation to the consistency of a person's good or bad actions that affect the way that person is perceived either positively or negatively. However, that is not to deny that our judgments about the moral character of others are also influenced by social information and appraisals that come from others and via the mass media.

BALANCE THEORY

How might the variables that I have discussed combine to affect a person's judgments of deservingness? Would they combine additively so that these judgments are related to a summation of perceived responsibility, evaluative appraisals of actions and outcomes, ingroup/outgroup relations, like/dislike relations, and perceived moral character? Would the combination be more complex and take account of the interactive effects of evaluated actions and evaluated outcomes? For example, one could represent the interaction of these variables by a product term that multiplies the signs (positive or negative) of the subjective values (valences) assigned to the actions and their contingent outcomes, and add this product into the set of variables. Positive products would be expected to be associated with deservingness; negative products with undeservingness. Clearly, there are different kinds of models that one could propose.

In the model that I propose it is assumed that the variables may be combined into a structure that follows the principle of consistency or balance (Heider, 1958). My interest in this form of organization is consistent with previous use of this principle when modeling communication effects, attitude-consistent recall, and causal attributions for success and failure in terms of balanced and unbalanced structures (Feather, 1967b, 1969a, 1969b, 1971a).

What do we mean by balance? Heider (1958) used the term to describe the organization of relations between entities or elements of a structure. He considered two types of relations, namely, sentiment relations and unit relations, which correspond respectively to evaluation and association. Sentiment or attitudinal relations involve any two elements of a structure, one of which must refer to a personal entity. A positive sentiment relation implies positive evaluation as reflected in liking, favoring, and agreeing with; a negative sentiment relation is taken to imply negative evaluation as reflected in disliking, opposing, and disagreeing.

The other type of relation is a unit relation. A unit relation is taken to imply positive association or linking together of elements; a negative unit relation is harder to define but it may be taken to imply dissociation—not just a null relation or a neutral lack of association, but an active pushing apart or resistance to unit formation between elements. It may be difficult to realize a negative unit relation empirically, especially when a person has some association with another personal or impersonal entity, as when he or she performs an action or belongs to the same group as another person.

In Heider's (1958) analysis, a positive unit relation was applied to dyads where entities in the structure were related through similarity, causality, ownership, or other unit-forming characteristics. He gave scant attention to the possibility of negative unit relations. Indeed, he did not make a clear distinction between a negative unit relation and the absence of a relation between entities (i.e., negative versus null).

These two types of relation, sentiment and unit, embody the central ideas of evaluation and association within structures. I use both types of relation in the structural model of deservingness. I view the processes of association and evaluation as basic in the formation of the structures that I will describe. My position has remained the same as when I first proposed that the person could be seen as "an active processor of information, associating separate units of information on the basis of similarity, causality, contiguity, ownership, etc., and evaluating information along a good-bad dimension" (Feather, 1971a, p. 357).

Following Heider (1958), I assume that the sentiment, or attitudinal relations, and the unit relations within a structure may tend toward a consistent form of organization that follows a principle of balance. Heider defines his principle of balance in terms of a tendency for unit (U and not U) relations and sentiment (L or DL) relations to fit together harmoniously.

> A dyad is balanced if the relations between the two entities are all positive (L and U) or all negative (DL and not U). Disharmony results when relations of different sign character exist. A triad is balanced when all three of the relations are positive or when two of the relations are negative and one is positive. Imbalance occurs when two of the relations are positive and one is negative. The case of three negative relations is somewhat ambiguous. (pp. 202–203)

We can illustrate this principle by considering person (p), other person (o), and impersonal object (x) as entities. The following are examples of balanced states: p likes something he or she made (pLx, pUx), and p likes what his or her friend likes (pLo, pLx, oLx). Some examples of unbalanced states are as follows: p likes someone who does not reciprocate the liking but is negative toward p (pLo, $oDLp$), and p likes what his or her friend dislikes (pLo, pLx, $oDLx$).

Heider assumed that states of balance would be preferred over disharmony and that new relations may be induced so as to produce a balanced state. He also assumed that where relations are not in balance there would be a tendency for them to change in the direction of achieving a balanced set of relations. If such a change could not be achieved, the state of tension associated with the imbalance would persist, motivating further attempts at resolution.

Heider's principle of balance and the assumptions that are associated with it may be set beside other theories, such as dissonance theory and congruity theory, which also assume that individuals have a preference for consistent states of affairs (Abelson, Aronson, McGuire, Newcomb, Rosenberg, & Tannenbaum, 1968). The Heiderian view is of structures containing relations that are dynamically interdependent, moving toward harmonious organization.

GRAPH THEORY

How can balanced and unbalanced structures be represented? One possible way of representing structures is to use the mathematics of linear graphs (Cartwright & Harary, 1956; Harary, Norman, & Cartwright, 1965), though other representations using sets of propositions can also be employed. I will use graph theory to represent elements and relations in the structural model of deservingness. A brief explication of this form of representation is necessary before I describe the deservingness model.

The use of graph theory involves the mapping of elements and relations into points and lines of a linear graph. It then becomes possible to compare different structures and to define the overall balance within the system. For example, Figure 4.1 presents a number of structures, half of which are balanced and half of which are unbalanced according to Heider's principle. In these structures I represent a positive sentiment or attitudinal relation by a solid line and a negative sentiment or attitudinal relation by a dashed line. A positive unit relation is represented by a solid bracket and a negative unit relation by a dashed bracket. An arrow on a line indicates the direction of a sentiment or attitudinal relation. Thus, Figure 4.1a represents a situation in which person (p) likes other person (o), and both like impersonal object (x). This is a balanced triad in which a person likes what his or her friend likes.

The structures in Figure 4.1 are called signed digraphs because the lines in each structure may have both sign (positive or negative) and direction. Structures a, b, c, d, e, and f are balanced, and structures g, h, i, j, k, and l are unbalanced. Also in Figure 4.1, structures a, c, f, g, h, and l involve only one type of relation, in each case a sentiment or attitudinal relation. The remaining structures involve both sentiment and unit relations.

Each of the signed digraphs in Figure 4.1 involves one semicycle, which is defined by Cartwright and Harary (1956) as "a collection of lines obtained by taking exactly one from each pair $\overrightarrow{AB}$ or $\overrightarrow{BA}$, $\overrightarrow{BC}$ or $\overrightarrow{CB}$, ..., $\overrightarrow{DE}$ or $\overrightarrow{ED}$, and $\overrightarrow{EA}$ or $\overrightarrow{AE}$" (p. 283). Each of these semicycles has a sign that is defined as the product of the signs of its lines. For example, the semicycle $\overrightarrow{PO}$, $\overrightarrow{OX}$, $\overrightarrow{XP}$ is positive in Figure 4.1a but negative in Figure 4.1g.

We can use the sign of a semicycle to define balance and imbalance. Cartwright and Harary (1956) generalized Heider's principle by defining a signed digraph as completely balanced when the signs of all the semicycles it contains are positive (see also Harary et al., 1965). In Figure 4.1, all of the semicycles on the left-hand side of the figure are positive in

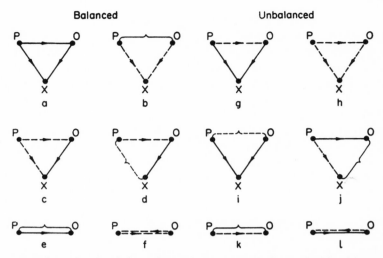

Figure 4.1. Balanced and unbalanced signed structures involving attitudinal (sentiment) and unit relations. Feather, 1971a. Copyright © 1971 by the American Psychological Association. Reprinted with permission.

sign and are balanced. They either contain two positive relations or two negative relations in the case of the dyads; or two negative relations and one positive relation in the case of the triads. In contrast, all of the semicycles on the right-hand side of Figure 4.1 are negative in sign and unbalanced. They either contain one positive relation and one negative relation in the case of the dyads, or two positive relations and one negative relation or three negative relations, in the case of the triads.

Larger structures that involve more than three elements can also be represented by using signed digraphs. The structural model of deservingness is a case in point. As we will see subsequently, it contains four elements that are linked via sentiment or unit relations.

These larger structures may contain a number of semicycles, all of which must be positive if the entire structure is to be completely balanced. If some of the semicycles within a complex structure are unbalanced, then the structure cannot be completely balanced but balanced only to some degree. One can compute the degree of balance in a complex structure by taking the ratio of the number of balanced semicycles within the structure to the total number of semicycles (Harary et al., 1965, p. 346).

Harary et al. (1965, pp. 340–359) discuss other aspects of balance in structures. These include *local balance* (where a structure is balanced only for those semicycles that contain a particular element or point), and *limited balance* (where negative semicycles beyond a certain length are ignored on the assumption that they may be empirically unimportant). Harary et al. illustrate local balance by considering a structure in which some positive semicycles included person (*p*) while another negative semicycle in the structure did not include person (*p*). The structure would not be completely balanced. However, it may be in equilibrium as far as *p* is concerned because it is locally balanced for *p*, and *p* is indifferent to the negative semicycle of which *p* is not a part. Limited balance allows for the possibility that semicycles beyond a certain length may be empirically unimportant as far as balance is concerned. In a large group of people it may make little difference to the affective structure if long semicycles are negative, as would occur, for example, if a pair of individuals in the large group dislike each other.

I will note some further developments of balance theory after I have presented the structural model of deservingness but only insofar as they have some relevance to further elaboration of the model.

THE STRUCTURAL MODEL OF DESERVINGNESS

The Deservingness Triad

I begin the presentation of the structural model by first considering the triad of relations that incorporates a person's positive or negative evaluations of another person's action and its contingent outcome. I proposed previously that an outcome would be perceived as deserved if a positive outcome followed positively valued instrumental behavior, or if a negatively valued outcome followed negatively valued instrumental behavior. In contrast, an outcome would be seen to be undeserved if a negatively valued outcome followed positively valued instrumental behavior, or if a positively valued outcome followed negatively valued instrumental behavior.

We can represent these four possibilities in the four signed digraphs in Figure 4.2. In each of these structures the person is represented as a judge who is evaluating actions and outcomes as they relate to some actor who could be self or other. Following convention, a positive sentiment or attitudinal relation is represented by a solid line and a negative sentiment or attitudinal relation by a dashed line. For example, in Figure 4.2a the person positively evaluates both the action and its outcome; in Figure 4.2c the action is positively valued but the outcome is negatively valued.

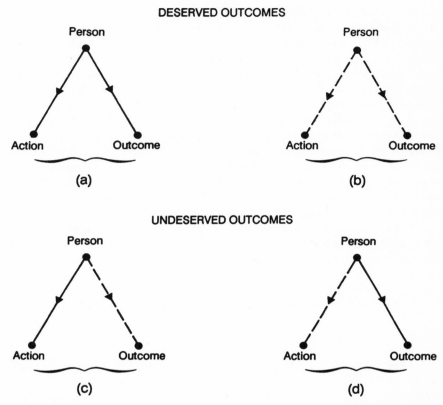

Figure 4.2. Balanced and unbalanced structures representing deserved and undeserved outcomes. Feather, 1996e. Reprinted by permission of Lawrence Erlbaum Associates, Inc.

In all four structures, I connect action and outcome by a positive unit relation that is represented by a solid bracket. This positive unit relation represents the fact that the outcome follows the action or is contingent on it, that is, the outcome is produced by the action and, in this sense, is bound to it.

The top two structures in Figure 4.2 are balanced according to Heider's (1958) principle. The signs of the semicycles, obtained by multiplying the signs of the relations, are positive in each case. The semicycles involve either three positive relations as in Figure 4.2a or two negative relations and a positive relation as in Figure 4.2b. The relations in each structure are in balance, fitting together in a consistent manner, and there would be no pressure to change them.

In contrast, the bottom two structures in Figure 4.2 are unbalanced according to Heider's principle. The signs of the semicycles, obtained by multiplying the signs of the relations, are negative in each case. Each semicycle involves two positive relations and a negative relation. These relations form an inconsistent set. They are unbalanced and they would be associated with a certain amount of tension or pressure to change, which may not be easy to resolve.

The two top structures in Figure 4.2 are assumed to represent situations where the outcome is judged to be deserved. For example, Figure 4.2a could represent a situation where a student obtains a high grade in an examination (positively valued) following a lot of hard work (positively valued). Figure 4.2b could represent a situation where a dishonest business entrepreneur is dismissed from an organization (negatively valued) because of unethical behavior (negatively valued). The student would be judged to deserve the high grade; the business entrepreneur would be judged to deserve his or her dismissal. In both of the two structures that represent these situations the two sentiment or attitudinal relations have the same sign (both positive or both negative).

The bottom two structures in Figure 4.2 are assumed to represent situations where the outcome is judged to be undeserved. For example, Figure 4.2c could represent a situation where hard work on the part of a student (positively valued) is followed by a low grade on the exam (negatively valued). Figure 4.2d could represent a situation where dishonest behavior on the part of a business entrepreneur (negatively valued) is followed by promotion to high levels of management in the firm (positively valued). The student would be judged not to deserve the low grade; the business entrepreneur would be judged not to deserve his or her success. In the two structures that represent these situations one of the sentiment or attitudinal relations is positive and other is negative.

Note that the behaviors that I have used to illustrate each of the structures in Figure 4.2 are controllable actions for which the actor could be seen to be responsible. For the balanced structures these actions are followed by outcomes that are seen to be deserved; for the unbalanced structures they are followed by actions that are seen to be undeserved. Thus, the analysis recognizes that an actor may be seen to be responsible for an outcome that he or she deserves and also responsible for an outcome that he or she does not deserve. The analysis therefore separates responsibility and deservingness. An action for which an actor is deemed to be responsible would be associated with judgments of deservingness in the balanced triads but with judgments of undeservingness in the unbalanced triads.

Following the discussion of values and valences in the previous chapter, I assume that the positively and negatively valued actions and

outcomes in Figure 4.2 can be related to the underlying general values
that are held by the person or judge. That is, the general values that the
person holds would affect the way particular actions and outcomes are
evaluated via the associative networks that are primed within the situation. For example, honest actions would be viewed positively and dishonest actions would be viewed negatively by a person for whom honesty is an important value; successful outcomes would be viewed
positively and unsuccessful outcomes would be viewed negatively by a
person for whom achievement is an important value. Consistent with my
previous discussion, these subjective evaluations (or valences) would
also be influenced by other variables, but a person's general values are
assumed to play an important role. Thus:

> Whether an outcome is seen to be deserved or not deserved depends
> on the values of the person who makes the judgment, but the effects
> of these values are assumed to be mediated via their effects on the
> way specific actions and outcomes are evaluated. (Feather, 1996e,
> pp. 230–231)

Extended Structures

The balanced and unbalanced triads in Figure 4.2 are simple representations that can be extended so as to take account of the perceived
responsibility of the other (o) for the action that leads to the outcome, as
well as representing different forms of relations that can occur between
the person (p) who is judging the outcome and the other (o). As I have
argued, I would expect that these other variables would affect judgments
of deservingness and undeservingness in addition to the positive and
negative evaluations assigned by p to o's action and its contingent
outcome.

The extended structures in Figure 4.3 and Figure 4.4 include other
(o) as an additional entity within each signed digraph in addition to
person (p) who takes the role of the judge with the task of determining
whether o deserves the outcome. This extension enables the representation of different kinds of relation between person and other and between other and action. All of the relations in Figures 4.3 and 4.4 are
from the point of view of the person or judge. Each of the signed digraphs
in these figures contain three semicycles (person-other-action; person-
action-outcome; person-other-action-outcome).

In Figures 4.3 and 4.4 I use a positive unit relation to link other to
the action. As before, the positive unit relation is represented by a solid
bracket and it denotes that other is perceived to own the action, to pro-

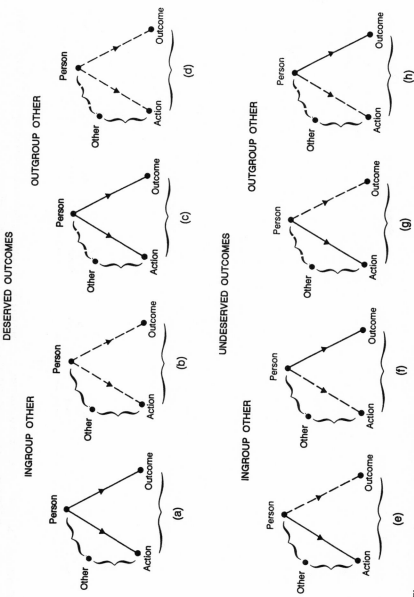

Figure 4.3. Balanced and unbalanced structures representing deserved and undeserved outcomes for ingroup other and outgroup other. Feather, 1996e. Reprinted by permission of Lawrence Erlbaum Associates, Inc.

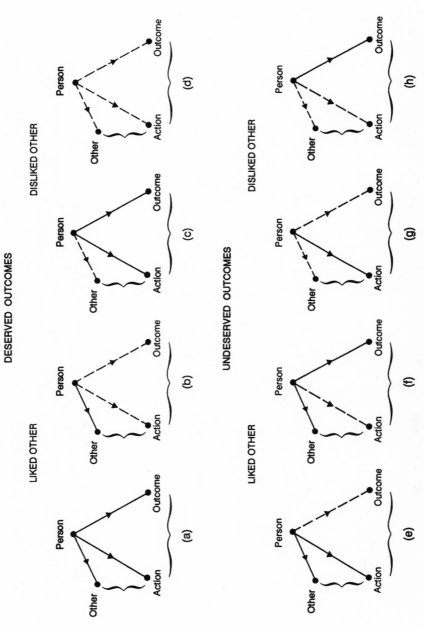

Figure 4.4. Balanced and unbalanced structures representing deserved and undeserved outcomes for liked other and disliked other. Feather, 1996e. Reprinted by permission of Lawrence Erlbaum Associates, Inc.

duce it, and to be responsible for it. A negative unit relation between other and action, represented by a dashed bracket, could be used to represent cases where other is perceived to be not responsible for the action and as disowning it. But, as I noted previously, such a negative unit relation may be difficult to realize if, in fact, other (*o*) actually performed the action. Situations where *o* acted under duress, or was coerced by powerful forces to perform the action against *o*'s wishes, may imply a negative unit relation between other and action. However, even in these cases, the actor produced the action. Therefore, there is an association between the actor and the action that he or she performs, and this association may prevent the perception of complete disownership.

In Figure 4.3 the other new relations are positive or negative unit relations that link person with other. These relations are represented by solid or dashed brackets, respectively. We can use these positive and negative unit relations to model cases where other belongs either to the person's ingroup (positive unit relation) or to a perceived outgroup (negative unit relation). Figure 4.3 classifies the structures on that basis.

The relations that link person to other in Figure 4.4 are positive or negative sentiment or attitudinal relations. These relations are represented by solid and dashed lines, respectively. These positive and negative sentiment relations can be used to model interpersonal situations where person or judge likes the other (positive sentiment or attitudinal relation) or dislikes the other (negative sentiment or attitudinal relation). Figure 4.4 classifies the structures on that basis.

The remaining relations in Figures 4.3 and 4.4 have the same meaning as before and, as was the case in Figure 4.2, the structures are partitioned into those relating to deserved outcomes and those relating to undeserved outcomes, using the deservingness triads as the criterion.

It should be evident that the structures in Figures 4.3 and 4.4 extend the simple triads in Figure 4.2 and enable us to develop hypotheses about the effects of ingroup versus outgroup membership and interpersonal liking and disliking. One interesting fact about the eight structures in each set is that, in each case, only two signed digraphs are completely balanced, with all three semicycles within them having a positive sign. These are the structures in Figure 4.3a and 4.4a, and in Figure 4.3d and 4.4d. The structures in Figure 4.3a and 4.4a respectively would represent situations where a member of a person's ingroup performs a positive action that leads to a positive outcome (Figure 4.3a), or where a liked other performs a positive action that leads to a positive outcome (Figure 4.4a). The structures in Figures 4.3d and 4.4d respectively would represent situations where a member of a person's outgroup performs a negative action that leads to a negative outcome, or where a disliked other performs a negative action that leads to a negative outcome. In all of these cases the outcome would be perceived to be deserved.

The remaining six structures in Figures 4.3 and 4.4 are unbalanced. Only one semicycle out of the three semicycles within each structure is balanced according to Heider's (1958) principle. All of the other semicycles are negative in sign and are unbalanced. For example, Figures 4.3b and 4.4b both contain a balanced deservingness triad (person-action-outcome) but the other two semicycles (person-other-action; person-other-action-outcome) are negative in sign and are unbalanced. These two structures would represent situations where an ingroup other (Figure 4.3b) or a liked other (Figure 4.4b) performs a negative action that leads to a negative outcome. As another example, Figures 4.3g and 4.4g both contain a balanced semicycle (person-other-action-outcome), but the other two semicycles (person-other-action; person-action-outcome) are negative in sign and are unbalanced. These two structures would represent situations where an outgroup other (Figure 4.3g) or a disliked other (Figure 4.4g) performs a positive action that leads to a negative outcome. One can sense the imbalance or disharmony in these different examples.

MODES OF RESOLUTION

When structures are unbalanced we would expect that the perceiver or judge would experience some tension or discomfort and that there would be pressure to change one or more relations so as to achieve a balanced state of affairs (Feather, 1971a; Heider, 1958). The extensive review of consistency theories by Abelson et al. (1968) includes discussion of how inconsistencies might be resolved.

I assume that the unbalanced structures in Figure 4.3 and 4.4 may vary in the ease with which there can be change in the direction of achieving a consistent set of relations. Balance could be restored if one or more of the relations were to change in sign. Whether a relation changes would depend on its strength or resistance and the degree to which it is embedded in a tightly structured network that would be thrown out of balance if a particular relation were to change (Feather, 1971a, pp. 366–367).

It would be difficult for a person or judge to modify the positive or negative evaluations of other's action and other's outcome if these evaluations are consistent with reality and are based on the stable and important values that the person holds. One cannot easily distort actual events when the evidence is there for all to see. A negative evaluation assigned to a clearly dishonest course of action cannot be readily changed to a positive evaluation; a positive achievement cannot be readily changed to a negatively valued outcome. The reality constraints prohibit such changes. Thus, unless there is ambiguity in regard to either the action or the outcome so that either could be interpreted in different ways, relations in the person-action-outcome triad in most cases would probably retain their formal structure. That means that the four bottom structures in Figures 4.3 and 4.4 would remain unbalanced even if changes in other relations were possible. Relations may change in the direction of balancing the triad if reality constraints are weak (as would occur if the situation is fluid or ambiguous enough to enable different interpretations of action and outcome) and if they are weak relations that are based on values that are not strongly held. In such cases, for example, a person might revise his or her evaluation of a negative action so that it is seen as justified given the circumstances (i.e., the action is now seen as positive), or the evaluation of what might be seen as a positive outcome is revised so that it is seen as not so positive after all. Conversely, the evaluation of a positive action might shift to negative, or the evaluation of a negative outcome might shift to positive.

The situation is different for the four top structures in Figures 4.3 and 4.4. In these cases the person-action-outcome triad is balanced. Complete balance could be achieved in these structures by changing either the person-to-other relation or the other-to-action relation. For example, the imbalance in Figure 4.3b would be resolved if other (o) was excluded from the ingroup and was now perceived to be an outgroup member (the positive unit relation between p and o changes to negative) or if the person (p) assumed that there were mitigating circumstances that were the prime cause of the negative action so that other's (o) perceived responsibility for the negatively valued action was reduced and possibly reversed in sign (the positive unit relation between o and action changes to negative). As another example, in Figure 4.4c, person (p) may change his or her view of other (o) so that the other who performed the positively valued action is now seen as a likable person (the negative sentiment or attitudinal relation between p and o changes to positive) or person (p) may perceive other (o) as not responsible for the positively valued action, assuming, for example, that it was the result of other factors that diminished or reversed other's ownership (the positive unit relation between o and action changes to negative). Either change in each structure would resolve the imbalance. Note, however, that these changes are also subject to reality constraints. The ingroup member may be a key player in the group and difficult to relegate to the outgroup; the other person may be so unpleasant that it may be difficult to change one's negative attitude to a positive one. Also, as noted previously, the fact that other performed the action may make it difficult for a person to see other as disowning the action and actively distancing self from it.

I assume that judgments about deservingness that relate to the balanced structures in Figures 4.3 and 4.4 should tend to occur more automatically when compared with those that relate to the unbalanced structures. The balanced structures that are laid down in memory may be accessed more easily and responses that relate to these structures are likely to occur more rapidly without a great deal of cognitive effort. However, when structures are unbalanced the person has to engage in cognitive work in order to resolve the inconsistencies that are present. In these cases, responses to the unbalanced structures should take longer to process, and it is likely that judgments would be less automatic and more variable, depending on how difficult it is to resolve the imbalance.

It will be noted that in presenting the structures in Figures 4.3 and 4.4 I have assigned relations in the person-action-outcome triad a key role in classifying the structures as they might relate to judgments that outcomes are deserved or undeserved. This is consistent with the previous discussion of the balanced and unbalanced deservingness triads in Figure 4.2. But, in the extended analysis, a person's judgments about deservingness and undeservingness are also assumed to be modified by the nature of the unit and sentiment or attitudinal relations between person and other and by whether other is perceived to own or be responsible for the action. This extension broadens the analysis of deservingness and it enables predictions to be made about the effects of social identity (ingroup versus outgroup) and interpersonal relations (liking versus disliking). So it connects two important areas of social psychology within the same form of analysis. For example, the extended model implies that the decision made by a jury in a case where a crime has been committed may be influenced by whether some members of the jury share a common social identity with the accused (e.g., in terms of gender, class, race, or social background), by whether the defendant presents self in such a way as to evoke feelings of like or dislike, and by judgments about the defendant's degree of responsibility or the offense. These variables may interact with evidence about the defendant's actions and the nature of the outcome, perhaps having more weight when the evidence is weaker or ambiguous.

SOME POSSIBLE EXTENSIONS

Note also that further extensions of the model are possible. Here are some possibilities:

1. We could add sentiment and unit relations that link other elements within the structure, providing these additions make psychological sense. For example, the addition of a sentiment or attitudinal relation between other and action would represent whether o is seen by p to like or dislike, or to favor or disfavor, the action that o takes. For example, there may be cases where o is seen to act against his or her wishes, behaving in a way that is at odds with what o would really prefer to do.
2. The addition of unit and sentiment relations between other and outcome would represent cases whether o is seen to own or be responsible for the outcome, or is seen to like or dislike the outcome. There would be cases, for example, where o is seen not to favor the outcome that occurs, as might happen when o's positive action leads to a negative outcome.
3. The removal of the unit relation between action and outcome would signify that the outcome is unrelated to the action, that is, that there is a null relation. This form of representation could be used when it is clear that the outcome is not contingent on o's action but can be attributed to other causes, such as the intervention of others, changes in the nature of the situation, or accidental circumstances. Similarly, the removal of the positive unit relation between other and action so that there is a null relation would imply that o is not associated with the action and that judgments of deservingness or undeservingness therefore do not apply to o.
4. Self could be included as an element in the model in place of (o). This extension would enable representation of how (p) or judge evaluates self, enabling an analysis of the effects of different levels of self-esteem on how person judges the degree to which self deserves or does not deserve outcomes that follow from his or her actions. The sentiment or attitudinal relation between p and self would signify whether p evaluates self positively or negatively.

At a more general level it is clear that the structures presented in Figure 4.3 and 4.4 are set within the traditional framework of balance theory that links entities by sentiment and unit relations and that considers relations only with respect to their positive or negative sign. These structures present the skeleton of what are, in fact, cognitive representations of complex situations. But it is useful to know what the skeleton might look like before putting flesh on the bones.

An important limitation of the structures is that they do not provide for the representation of the strength of relations. The focus on positive and negative relations has led some critics to argue that traditional balance theory resembles a two-valued logic (e.g., Feather, 1971a, p. 367; Insko, 1984, p. 136; Runkel & Peizer, 1968), and that, by implication, it would require much more development if it is to capture the full range of human thought and motivation. Clearly it would be a major contribution if one could develop structural models that deal with the strength of relations as well as their sign. We could then represent differences in such variables as the degree to which a person or judge favors or disfavors other's action and the outcome to which it leads, or likes or dislikes the other person who is being judged, or assigns high or low responsibility to the other for the action that he or she takes.

There have been attempts to extend balance theory to take account of the problem of strength of relations and the complexity of belief systems. I discussed the question of strength of relations in an earlier article (Feather, 1971a, pp. 367–369), drawing on the results of a study of interpersonal attraction in which I varied the sign and the strength of relations (Feather, 1966). I proposed two possible principles, a similarity principle and a discrepancy principle, that might be applied to relations of different strength within dyads and triads respectively. Others have also addressed this question in various ways (e.g., Insko, 1984; McGuire, 1960; Wellens & Thistlethwaite, 1971a, 1971b; Wyer, 1974; Wyer & Goldberg, 1970). Discussion of these different approaches is beyond the scope of this book. However, I will briefly refer to two recent contributions.

Insko (1984) described theory and empirical research that followed from Wiest's (1965) extension of Heider's (1958) theory of cognitive balance. Wiest conceptualized Heider's triad, involving person, other, and impersonal object, as a cube with four balanced corners. When these corners were connected a tetrahedron or three-sided pyramid was formed within the cube. Triads lying either on the surface of or within the tetrahedron were assumed to be balanced. Insko proposed that one could use linear extrapolation in relation to the tetrahedron to take account of different quantitative values.

A different approach has recently been proposed by Read and Miller (1994). They draw upon developments in cognitive science, especially work on knowledge structures (e.g., Schank & Abelson, 1977) and on parallel constraint satisfaction processes in connectionist systems (e.g., McClelland, Rumelhart, & PDP Research Group, 1986), arguing that "parallel constraint satisfaction processes seem to provide an explicit, computational implementation of the gestalt ideas that underlie much of the work on cognitive consistency" (p. 211). In their analysis the relations are causal relations and they connect propositions that take account of knowledge structures. Following Thagard (1989, 1992), they develop a model of explanatory coherence that enables one to "evaluate the explanatory coherence of the entire system, as well as the strength or acceptance of each explanatory hypothesis" (Read & Miller, 1994, p. 216). In their approach they allow for the flow of activation between nodes of a structure, for local rather than global coherence, and for the importance of propositions in terms of their functional relevance.

The Read and Miller analysis is too complex to present in detail here but it does provide a new approach to the modeling of balanced and unbalanced structures that uses ideas from connectionist theory. The analysis is applied to sets of relations that have presented some problems for balance theory (e.g., the romantic love triangle, where two people who love the same third person dislike each other), to the classic Festinger and Carlsmith (1959) study of counter attitudinal advocacy, and to a consideration of different modes of resolving inconsistency that include such modes as denial, bolstering, transcendence, rationalization, and differentiation.

CONCLUDING COMMENTS

The developments that have occurred in cognitive science since the earlier statements of balance theory imply that the structures I have presented in Figures 4.3 and 4.4 should be considered in relation to the relevant knowledge structures possessed by those who make the judgments of deservingness or undeservingness. The context of judgment and the knowledge structures that a person brings to the situation are obviously important frames for judgment that have to be taken into account. For example, how one reacts to a penalty for an offense would depend not only on perceived deservingness but also on one's knowledge about the law, on how serious the offense is seen to be, and on the social norms that are salient at the time.

It may well be the case that a detailed propositional analysis that allows for the content of belief systems using connectionist principles and associative networks will be a promising future direction to take in modeling judgments of deservingness. However, I have kept to a much simpler analysis that is consistent with my own interests and with my own knowledge structure. Returning to Heider (1958), it is interesting to note that he made the connection between balance and deservingness when discussing reactions to the lot of another person (Feather, 1994a). Thus, he stated that "the situation is balanced if the experiences of another are in accord with what he deserves" (Heider, 1958, p. 284).

I have taken this idea further in the present analysis by relating perceptions of deservingness (and undeservingness) "not only to balanced or unbalanced structures but also to other variables that centrally include perceptions of responsibility and underlying values that influence a person's evaluative reactions to actions and their outcomes" (Feather, 1996d, p. 234). My analysis also implies that there may be a tendency for people to move toward the balanced deservingness structures when they make their judgments, though reality constraints and the wider belief systems they possess may render harmony impossible.

In the next chapter I will describe some research studies concerned with success or failure in achievement situations, the results of which may be interpreted in terms of the structural model of deservingness that I have presented.

CHAPTER 5

Achievement and Deservingness

In this chapter I will describe some studies that have included deserv-ingness as a variable in situations involving success and failure. The successful achievement or failure to achieve varied in its significance in these studies from success or failure at an examination at one extreme to achieving high public status or falling from a high status position at the other extreme. Some of the studies to be described used the experimental method with manipulation and control of variables; other studies in-volved actual public figures who either currently occupied high posi-tions in their chosen vocations or who had recently suffered a reverse and fallen from their high status positions.

TALL POPPY RESEARCH

My interest in studying high achievers developed from a past record of involvement in the analysis of behavior in achievement contexts (e.g., Atkinson & Feather, 1966; Feather, 1982a), but it was especially influ-enced by a desire to investigate the truth or otherwise of an observation commonly made within my own culture. It is often said that Australians like to see those in high positions experience a fall, as when a high profile politician commits a foolish act, or a well-known person in the entertain-ment industry suddenly experiences a decline in popularity, or a busi-ness executive who heads a major company is removed from office. These people are called *tall poppies* and a common claim by journalists and other social commentators who reflect on Australian attitudes is that Australians like to see tall poppies fall and be brought down to size. This belief about tall poppies is promulgated in the mass media and it tends to be accepted without much critical analysis. I decided to initiate a detailed investigation of this belief about tall poppy attitudes partly to check on its validity as a distinctive characteristic of the Australian culture but also more generally to come to some understanding of why such an attitude might occur and the variables that might influence it.

The term "tall poppy" is defined by the *Oxford English Dictionary* as "an especially well-paid, privileged, or distinguished person" and by the *Australian National Dictionary* as "a person who is conspicuously successful" and (frequently) as, "one whose distinction, rank, or wealth attracts envious notice or hostility." The term is not a recent invention but has a history that goes back to Roman times. Livy, the Roman historian, referred to the symbolic decapitation of the heads of the tallest poppies by the elder Tarquinius when this Roman ruler was walking in his garden. The symbolic act by Tarquinius of cutting down the tall poppies was then conveyed by a messenger to his son, Sextus Tarquinius, who understood the meaning of the message and then disposed of the chief men in the state of Gabii. Thus, he was able to deliver the state without resistance to the Roman king. In this case the destruction of the tall poppies was an exercise in power aimed at bringing about the downfall of high status rivals, thereby securing the prize for oneself.

My research on tall poppies was not concerned with situations where a person was actively engaged in trying to surpass others and win in some competition. There is already a large literature that concerns the way motives for achievement and power, as well as other personality characteristics and situational variables, interact to influence choice, performance, and persistence in contexts where people can evaluate their outcomes in relation to standards of excellence or in terms of their impact on other people (e.g., Atkinson & Feather, 1966; McClelland, 1985; Spence, 1983; Winter, 1973; Winter, John, Stewart, Klohnen, & Duncan, 1998). My interest was in investigating tall poppies who were not involved in some competitive struggle but who were viewed at a distance by an observer or judge. The tall poppies could be presidents or prime ministers; sporting personalities; high profile entertainers; high-status people in science, literature, or the arts; business leaders of important companies; or students or academics who had excelled in their chosen pursuits. These are tall poppies who are viewed at a distance without direct contact. Information about their high status and achievement is communicated via the press, radio, television, or other media, where they become a focus of attention. Their actions and outcomes are assumed to interest segments of the population or even the public at large. They are tall poppies in a more distant field and we become involved in their successes and failures in a more impersonal way.

I have reviewed the research program on tall poppy attitudes in earlier publications (Feather, 1994a, 1996e). At the theoretical level the analysis of these attitudes can appeal to different theoretical perspectives, depending on what kinds of questions are being asked. I described a number of theoretical approaches that provided ideas about the conditions under which we might want to see tall poppies fall or remain where they are. These approaches were Heider's (1958) discussion of how a person reacts to the lot of another person, attribution theory as related to motivation and emotion, the conceptual analysis of personal and cultural values, theoretical approaches to the analysis of justice and deservingness, and social comparison approaches to the analysis of envy. There are probably additional ideas that can be gleaned from other theoretical perspectives, but the approaches that I mentioned appeared to be especially relevant.

These various approaches would lead one to expect that negative attitudes toward high achievers or tall poppies may relate to a high value placed on equality as reflected in the reduction of status differences within a group or within society; that where there is a lot of envy people may experience a certain amount of *Schadenfreude* or malicious joy when a high status person falls from the top of the ladder; that a tall poppy may be viewed negatively and his or her fall may be viewed positively if the high achiever is seen not to deserve the high status; conversely, that a tall poppy may be viewed positively and his or her fall may be viewed negatively if the high achiever is seen to deserve the high status; that people who occupy low status positions or who have low self-esteem may compare themselves unfavorably on relevant dimensions with those who have moved high up the ladder of achievement, and that they may be more likely to want to see tall poppies reduced in status when compared with people who have higher status and higher self-esteem; that tall poppies who are generally liked and who conform to group or wider social norms may be protected against negative tall poppy attitudes and their high status and achievement may be approved and reinforced; and that a person might bask in the reflected glory of another's high achievement. These sorts of predictions can be derived from the theoretical approaches that I mentioned and many of them were tested and confirmed in the research program (Feather, 1994a, pp. 65–66).

The tall poppy research is significant in relation to the present discussion because it shows that an important variable that affects the way people react to the success or failure of a tall poppy is the degree to which the tall poppy is seen to deserve his or her high status or any subsequent fall that might occur. It became clear in the course of this research program that values, responsibility, and deservingness were closely involved as variables that affect the way people react to the rise and fall of tall poppies. This insight led me to a closer consideration of the meaning of deservingness and to the conceptual model that I presented in the preceding chapter. I now turn to a consideration of some of the relevant tall poppy studies in which deservingness was included as a variable.

TWO EARLY STUDIES

Two early studies used hypothetical scenarios or vignettes to vary the status of a stimulus person and the conditions under which the stimulus person suffered a fall.

A Fall in Examination Performance

The first study involved 531 male and female students who were enrolled in Grade 11 classes in high schools in metropolitan Adelaide. Grade 11 is the penultimate grade before students complete their high school studies. At the end of Grade 12 students present themselves for a final public examination and their results are crucial in determining which courses they can enter at any one of the three universities in Adelaide. The scenarios that were devised for the study focused on examination performance and referred to the final important examination. Hence, they had a degree of realism for the students who participated in the study.

These scenarios described a student who either had a consistently high level of performance at high school (a tall poppy who was usually at or near the top of the class) or had a level of performance that was consistently about average (Feather, 1989). I manipulated the extent to which this stimulus person fell from his or her previous high position in the final important examination that would qualify the student for entry into university studies. I was interested in finding out whether the participants in the study would experience some degree of pleasure or *Schadenfreude* when the stimulus person fell, or whether the fall for both the high status performer and the average performer would elicit similar reactions of sympathy or unhappiness. Would these affective reactions depend on the status of the stimulus person and on the extent of the fall? Would they also depend on how much the stimulus person was liked or disliked?

The participants answered a questionnaire in which they were presented with a scenario in which a high school student was described as either a high or average achiever at school. Subsequently, they were informed that the student suffered a fall in the final public examination at the end of Grade 12 (the matriculation examination). The fall could take one of three forms depending on the initial status of the stimulus person in the scenario: from high performance to middle performance, from high performance to low performance, or from middle performance to low performance.

Before information about the fall was presented the participants rated the high or average performer on a variety of scales. These 7-point scales concerned causal attributions for the stimulus person's performance that referred to ability, effort, ease of task, good luck, and friendly teachers; personality characteristics assessed by composite measures based on semantic differential, bipolar adjective scales; and degree of attraction for the stimulus person, assessed by a composite scale that involved items that referred to social interaction, perceived similarity, and liking. The composite scales were derived via factor analysis.

The results from this first set of ratings showed that participants attributed the high achiever's success more to ability, effort, and friendly teachers and less to good luck when compared with the average achiever's performance. The personality picture of the high achiever that emerged was that of a person who was ambitious and who possessed positive qualities but who was also more reserved and less sociable than the average achiever. The mean attraction ratings were almost identical for the high achiever and the average achiever. So neither stimulus person was initially liked more than the other. There was no evidence that the stimulus person who was the high performer or tall poppy was perceived as less attractive.

After participants received information about the fall of the high achiever or the average achiever in the final examination, they again used 7-point scales to rate the stimulus person with respect to causal attributions, but in this case the causes referred to lack of ability, lack of effort, a difficult task, bad luck, and unfriendly teachers. They also used 7-point scales to rate the degree to which they believed that the stimulus person deserved to fall, whether they would feel privately pleased about the stimulus person's fall, and how they thought the stimulus person would feel about the fall. In addition, they indicated whether they thought that they would feel more friendly toward the stimulus person (scored 3), about the same as before (scored 2), or less friendly (scored 1), now that the stimulus person had obtained a lower grade.

The results of this study are presented in Table 5.1. These results show that there were no statistically significant differences across the three fall conditions in the causal attributions and deservingness ratings that the student participants provided. Table 5.1 also shows that the mean ratings of participants' pleasure about the fall were below the

**Table 5.1. Mean Scores for Causal Attributions
and Other Post-Fall Variables in Relation to Type of Fall**

Variable	Midpoint of scale	Mean scores			df	F
		High to middle status	High to low status	Middle to low status		
Causal attributions						
Lack of ability	4	3.48	3.49	3.72	2,512	1.40
Lack of effort	4	5.10	5.04	5.01	2,514	.06
Difficult task	4	4.57	4.77	4.42	2,514	1.87
Bad luck	4	2.62	2.73	2.85	2,513	.86
Unfriendly teacher	4	3.02	2.88	3.18	2,513	.94
Deserve to fall	4	4.34	4.05	4.31	2,509	1.91
Respondent pleasure about fall	4	3.57	3.16	2.78	2,511	11.38***
Stimulus person pleasure about fall	4	1.72	1.33	1.66	2,513	6.49**
More friendly attitude	2	2.16	2.12	2.04	2,506	3.40*

Note: $N = 175$ for high to middle fall; $N = 173$ for high to bottom fall; $N = 183$ for middle to bottom fall. Minor variations from these Ns occurred because of missing cases.

$*p < .05$ $**p < .01$ $***p < .001$

Source: Feather (1989). Copyright 1989 by the Australian Psychological Society. Reproduced by permission.

midpoint of the scale, that is, generally they were unhappy about the fall. Thus, there was no evidence to show that these participants experienced *Schadenfreude* or feelings of satisfaction about the stimulus person's diminished performance, although it is possible that feelings about the fall could have involved a certain amount of unexpressed pleasure combined with a greater degree of sympathy. It may not be easy to discover *Schadenfreude* because people may not want to admit to it. Foster (1972) observed that people fear the consequences of envy, for example, and that envy is often denied, appearing in muted or disguised forms.

Examination of the means shows that participants reported least displeasure when the stimulus person fell from being a high performer to being a middle or average performer ("with a mark that is similar to the marks obtained by a lot of others in his [or her] class"), and most displeasure when the stimulus person fell from being a middle or average performer to being a low performer ("with a mark that is much lower than the marks obtained by most others in his [her] class"). Similarly, they reported feeling more friendly toward the stimulus person when the stimulus person was the high achiever who fell to the middle of the class and least friendly toward the stimulus person when the stimulus person was the average performer who fell to near the bottom of the class.

Further, more specific comparisons involving pair-wise statistical tests showed that the student participants reported less displeasure when the stimulus person fell from the high to the middle position than from the high to low position, less displeasure when the fall in the final examination took the stimulus person from the high to the low position than from the middle to the low position, and less displeasure when the fall was from high to middle than from middle to low. All of these differences were statistically significant. The difference in reported friendly attitude was statistically significant when the comparison was between a fall from the high to the middle status position and a fall from the middle to the low status position. But the other comparisons that involved the more friendly attitude variable were not statistically significant. Falling below the average performance of the rest of the class would denote a failure on the scale of performance. So it is not surprising that the participants in this study, who were students themselves, would report feeling especially displeased about this outcome and that they would also report that the stimulus person would be unhappy about it (see Table 5.1).

These findings could be interpreted as demonstrating the importance of underlying values. The participants seemed to show a preference for the average position in the classroom, a preference where the stimulus person would become more similar and equal to most of the other students. Such a preference might reflect the influence of equalitarian values on the part of the participants in the study. The high achiever who fell to the middle of the class would become closer and more equal to the group, reducing the difference in status. The average achiever who fell from the middle of the class to a very low position would become more deviant in regard to the group's average position that defined the normal range of accomplishment. The middle of the class in regard to performance may be seen as the normative position of the group, and a preference for that position would reflect collectivist, equalitarian values. There is evidence from other studies in the research program on tall poppies that favoring the fall of tall poppies in general is related to equalitarian values (Feather, 1994a, 1996e) and also from cross-cultural research that shows that Australians tend to be relatively high in equalitarianism (Feather, 1998a). The preference for the middle position might also have been related to a fear of rejection by the peer group. Being "too different," a "brain," or a "nerd" in terms of one's high achievements may have some negative consequences in the classroom, given the conformity pressures that influence adolescent attitudes.

Related evidence comes from research on the effects of pratfalls or blunders. In a study by Helmreich, Aronson, and Le Fan (1970), it was found that male participants with average levels of self-esteem reported liking a competent person more after that person suffered a pratfall or blunder (clumsily spilling a cup of coffee). They explained this increased liking as probably due to the humanizing of the competent individual. The foolish blunder made him closer and more similar to participants who were average in self-esteem and therefore more approachable (see also, Deaux, 1972).

How does deservingness fit into this picture? In this study I did not manipulate the stimulus person's responsibility for the outcome. Nor did I manipulate the actions of the stimulus person that led to the outcome. So the results of this study do not speak directly to the structural model of deservingness that was described in the preceding chapter. However, the results are relevant in two ways. First, as I have noted, they suggest that participants' values influenced the way they reacted to the stimulus person's fall. As we have seen, values have an important role in the deservingness model, influencing the way actions and outcomes are evaluated.

Second, further correlational analyses provided information about some of the correlates of the degree to which the stimulus person was perceived to deserve the lower grade or mark that he or she obtained on the final matriculation examination. In particular, deservingness ratings concerning the fall in performance were positively correlated with participants' ratings of lack of ability as a cause of the fall, $r(522) = .16$, $p < .001$; positively related to the importance assigned to lack of effort or hard work, $r(523) = .16$, $p < .001$; negatively related to the importance assigned to the difficulty of the exam, $r(523) = -.10$, $p < .05$; and negatively related to the importance assigned to bad luck $r(522) = -.12$, $p < .01$. Although these correlations were statistically significant, they were not strong correlations (Feather, 1996e, p. 237). They do show, however, that deservingness was related to participants' judgments about the causes of the stimulus person's lower performance and, by implication, to the stimulus person's responsibility for the lower grade or mark. For example, one would expect that a person who was judged not to try hard would be seen as more responsible for a fall in performance than a person who exerted a lot of effort, and that a person who was confronted with a very difficult task would be seen as less responsible for a fall in performance than a person for whom the task was very easy.

The correlational analysis also showed that there was a positive relation between how pleased participants reported they would feel about the fall and their ratings of the stimulus person's deservingness, $r(519) = .12$, $p < .01$; and a negative relation between the degree to which they reported more friendly attitudes toward the stimulus person and their ratings of the stimulus person's deservingness $r(514) = -.13$, $p < .01$. Again these correlations were low but statistically significant (Feather, 1996e, p. 237). They indicate that participants' reported affective reactions were related to their judgments about the degree to which the stimulus person deserved to fall.

Finally, the correlational analysis also showed that there were negative correlations between the composite measure of attraction to the stimulus person and reported pleasure about the stimulus person's fall, that is, the more participants reported liking the stimulus person, the less pleased they were about the fall. These negative correlations were consistently negative and statistically significant for all three types of fall.

A Study of Cheating

A second study (Feather, 1989) also varied the status of the student achiever (high, average), but in this study explicit information was provided about the cause of the fall (cheating at an examination). This kind of information was not provided in the study outlined in the above section. Participants in that study were left to make their own interpretations about the causes of the stimulus person's fall. As is evident in

Table 5.1, they saw lack of effort and a difficult task as the most important causes of the fall and their judgments about possible causes were similar for the three types of fall.

There were 361 male and female participants in the second study. They were students who were sampled from the introductory psychology class at Flinders University. They responded to a hypothetical scenario that introduced a male or female university student who was either a high achiever ("receives As or distinctions in his [her] coursework and exams and he [she] is usually either top of the class or very close to top") or an average achiever ("receives Cs or passes in most of his [her] coursework and exams and his [her] results are like those of most others in his [her] class").

As in the first study they first rated the stimulus person on semantic differential, bipolar adjective scales that were used to assess personality characteristics, and they responded to items that were used to assess attraction to the stimulus person. Factor analysis was again used to derive composite measures for these variables. Measures of causal attributions were not included in the questionnaire. Analysis of these data again showed that the high achiever was seen as more achievement oriented and assertive and less sociable and less of a good mixer when compared with the average achiever. Attraction scores were very similar for both types of stimulus person. So, as was the case in the first study, whether the stimulus person was a high achiever or an average achiever made no difference to participants' composite ratings of attraction toward the stimulus person. They were not less attracted to the high achiever or tall poppy.

Instructions then asked participants to imagine that they were taking a major examination with the stimulus person and that they became aware during the examination that the stimulus person was cheating. They were then asked three questions about how they would react to the discovery that the stimulus person had cheated. They used 7-point scales to rate how likely it was that they would report the stimulus person to the authorities, how likely it was that they would discuss the cheating with their fellow students, and how they would privately feel if the stimulus person was caught cheating by someone in authority.

Participants were then asked to assume that they were members of a disciplinary committee that had the task of presenting recommendations about what disciplinary actions should be taken in regard to the stimulus person's cheating. They were asked to recommend one course of action from a list of six possible actions ranging from no penalty (1) to expulsion from the university (6). They were also asked to what extent the stimulus person deserved to be expelled from the university, and how pleased they would be if the stimulus person was expelled.

Table 5.2. **Mean Scores on Post-Cheating Dependent Variables for High Achiever and Average Achiever**

| Variable | Midpoint of scale | Mean scores | | df | F |
		High achiever	Average achiever		
Report to authorities	4	2.86	2.09	1,351	16.06**
Discuss with others	4	4.64	4.42	1,353	1.20
Pleased about discovery	4	4.81	4.33	1,353	7.96*
Penalty for cheating	3.5	3.32	3.04	1,352	9.41*
Deserve penalty	4	4.17	3.46	1,352	15.98**
Pleased about expulsion	4	3.52	2.93	1,351	19.40**

Note: $N = 361$. Minor variations from this N occurred because of missing cases.
*$p < .01$ **$p < .001$
Source: Feather (1989). Copyright 1989 by the Australian Psychological Society. Reproduced by permission.

The main results, presented in Table 5.2, show that participants reported feeling more pleased when the high achiever was caught cheating than when the average achiever was caught. They were also more pleased when the high achiever was expelled from the university than when the average achiever was expelled, though in neither case were participants happy about expulsion (mean scores for this variable were below the midpoint of the scale). Participants also reported that they would be more likely to report the high achiever to the authorities, to exact a harsher penalty for the high achiever if they were on the disciplinary committee, and to judge the high achiever to deserve the penalty more when compared with the average achiever. Table 5.2 shows that all of these differences were statistically significant.

A further analysis relating to the deservingness variable showed that participants' ratings of how much they believed the stimulus person deserved to be expelled from the university for cheating was positively related to their ratings of how pleased they would feel that the offender had been caught, $r(358) = .27$, $p < .001$, and how pleased they would feel about the expulsion of the stimulus person, $r(357) = .57$, $p < .001$; positively related to the severity of the penalty for the cheating offense, $r(358) = .34$, $p < .001$, and positively related to whether it would be likely that they would report the offender to the authorities $r(356) = .31$, $p < .001$ (Feather, 1996e, p. 238). All of these correlations were statistically significant.

Finally, as was the case in the previous study, reported feelings of pleasure about the fall were again negatively correlated with the composite ratings of attraction. Thus, the more that participants were initially attracted to the stimulus person, the less pleased they were that the stimulus person was caught cheating or expelled from the university for cheating. These results occurred irrespective of whether the stimulus person was a high achiever or an average achiever and the negative correlations were statistically significant in each case.

This second study that involved a transgression (cheating), maps more easily into the structural model of deservingness model that was presented in the previous chapter than does the first study. Cheating is a negative action that, in the scenario, led to a negative outcome (a penalty). Hence, in terms of the model, the outcome tended to be seen as deserved by observers or judges, but more so when the high achiever transgressed.

Subjects were generally more punitive toward the high achiever or tall poppy in this study and they reported feeling more pleased about the tall poppy's penalty. Why might this be so? Perhaps participants changed their perceptions of the high achiever and became suspicious of his or her past success, believing that the person's previous high performance at examinations might also have been the result of cheating. The benefits and privileges of high achievement might then be seen to be undeserved and considerations of justice and equity would require that the high achiever "pay the piper" and be punished more than the average achiever who cheated. Although both would deserve some sanction or punishment for cheating, the high achiever who had benefitted from his or her high status may be seen to deserve the stiffer penalty.

I have also argued (Feather, 1994a, p. 29) that high status may confer on a person extra responsibility to set a good example to others, although some idiosyncrasies may be allowed, depending on the extent of the deviation from social norms (Hollander, 1958, 1964). The high achiever who transgresses would therefore violate normative expectations about what is believed to be appropriate behavior from someone who occupies a high position, and would be judged to deserve a greater penalty when compared with the average achiever. This interpretation is consistent with the idea that perceived responsibility may also relate to the obligations that come with the role that a person occupies, an aspect of responsibility that I considered in Chapter 2.

Finally, a transgression such as cheating also provides an opportunity for observers to cut a high achiever down to size, bringing the tall poppy down so that he or she no longer represents high status and authority and is the subject of envy, but becomes more similar to others. This interpretation is similar to the way in which I interpreted the results of the first study, using a collectivist emphasis on equalitarian values. But, of course, other values would also be involved in judging a fall resulting from a misdemeanor when compared with a fall involving a decline in performance. In the former case, we are in the domain of moral transgressions; in the latter case in the achievement domain. Note also that participants in the second study reported feeling less pleased when the average achiever was punished, a finding that is consistent with the low ratings of pleasure that participants gave when the average achiever fell to near the bottom of the class. So in both studies there was evidence that the average achiever was treated more sympathetically when he or she suffered a fall.

RESPONSIBILITY AND DESERVINGNESS IN SUCCESS AND FAILURE SITUATIONS

I have described these two early studies in some detail because they introduced the deservingness variable, investigated the effects of status, and involved two quite different domains, achievement and morality, where the fall was either a decline in performance or a consequence of a moral transgression, namely, cheating. I will return to studies concerned with transgressions in the next chapter.

These two studies were followed by a number of other studies that were set within the context of achievement. Most of this research has been reviewed elsewhere (Feather, 1994a, 1996e). In the remainder of this chapter I will describe a selection of these studies that have particular relevance to the analysis of deservingness I have presented.

One investigation involved a complex mixture of variables and it extended the previous research by including a success condition as well as a failure condition, given the fact that the deservingness model applies to positive outcomes (such as success) as well as to negative outcomes (such as failure). The investigation included both types of outcome and it also added some new variables (e.g., envy, helping behavior) in order to test additional hypotheses. Full details of the investigation are provided elsewhere (Feather, 1992a). Here I present only a selection of those results that are relevant to the analysis of the deservingness model described in the previous chapter.

The study involved 689 male and female students who were sampled from high schools in metropolitan Adelaide, South Australia. They were presented with a scenario that described a student (gender unspecified) who was either a high achiever or an average achiever at school. Depending on experimental condition, they were either given no information about the stimulus person (no information condition), or they were told that the stimulus person was a student who "does not have a lot of natural ability but who puts in a lot of effort and studies very hard" (high effort/average ability stimulus person condition), or they were told that the stimulus person was "a real brain with loads of natural ability but does not put in a lot of effort and doesn't study very hard" (low effort/high ability stimulus person condition).

The scenario then went on to describe the stimulus person's performance in the final important matriculation examination at high school. The scenario described one of two possible outcomes. This outcome variation meant that the overall investigation could be divided into two parts. In Study 1 participants were given a scenario in which the high or average achiever continued to maintain his or her performance on the final examination. In Study 2 the stimulus person obtained a low mark on the final examination.

Study 1: A Success Outcome

Study 1 involved 169 participants. The scenario informed them that the stimulus person maintained the high or average performance level in the important matriculation examination at the end of Year 12 in high school. The high achiever went on "to get a top overall matriculation score (well above 400) in the final matriculation exams at the end of Year 12, about what was expected." The average achiever was described as going on "to get an average overall matriculation score in the final matriculation exams at the end of Year 12, about what was expected." So there was no change in performance in Study 1. The performance outcome in this study was basically a positive outcome.

These participants then used 7-point scales to rate the stimulus person on items that asked how pleased they privately felt that the stimulus person obtained the final score, whether the stimulus person deserved that final score, how responsible the stimulus person was for obtaining the final score, how much envy they privately felt toward the stimulus person because of the final score that was obtained, how much they thought the stimulus person should be praised for the final score that was obtained, and how pleased they thought the stimulus person would feel about the final score that was obtained. The main results for this part of the study are presented in Table 5.3.

Consistent with the analysis that I have presented, ratings of the stimulus person's responsibility for the outcome were significantly higher when his or her past performance could be attributed mainly to high effort (a controllable cause) when compared with the condition where the stimulus person's past performance could be mainly attributed to high ability (an uncontrollable cause). The two studies that I have already described, as well as the research that I reviewed previ-

**Table 5.3. Means of Dependent Variable and _F_ Values
for Main Effects from Univariate ANOVASs (Success Outcome)**

| Variable | Information about stimulus person | | | | |
	No information	High effort/ average ability	Low effort/ high ability	df	F for information
Responsible	5.75$_a$	6.04$_a$	4.69$_b$	2,163	13.01***
Deserve	5.80$_a$	5.96$_a$	5.02$_b$	2,163	6.47**
Pleased	4.94$_a$	5.05$_a$	4.06$_b$	2,162	8.72***
Envy	3.65	3.43	3.44	2,163	0.27
Praise	4.80$_a$	4.96$_a$	3.72$_b$	2,162	10.89***
Stimulus person's pleasure	5.43	5.32	4.89	2,163	1.94

| Variable | Achievement status | | | |
	Average achiever	High achiever	df	F for status
Responsible	5.29	5.61	1,163	2.40
Deserve	5.35	5.76	1,163	3.42
Pleased	4.20	5.07	1,162	16.04***
Envy	2.63	4.28	1,163	36.04***
Praise	3.84	5.03	1,162	24.25***
Stimulus person's pleasure	4.55	5.78	1,163	22.57***

Note: $N = 169$; minor variations in Ns occurred across variables due to missing cases. Means in each row not sharing a common subscript differ significantly, $p < .05$ (Tukey).
*$p < .05$ **$p < .01$ ***$p < .001$
Source: Feather (1992a). Reprinted by permission of the British Psychological Society.

ously (e.g., Weiner, 1995), showed that an important determinant of perceived responsibility is the degree to which the cause of a person's outcome is seen to be under his or her control.

The results in Table 5.3 also show that the mean ratings of deservingness, positive affect, and praise were significantly higher in the high effort/average ability condition than in the low effort/high ability condition. Again these results are consistent with the analysis that I have presented. These higher ratings occurred for a stimulus person who was perceived to be more responsible for the positive outcome and where the positive outcome could be assumed to follow positively valued high effort, given the stimulus person's record of high effort in the past. This combination of variables would lead to higher ratings of deservingness and higher ratings of positive affect. In the low effort/high ability condition, where the corresponding ratings were lower, the stimulus person was seen to be less responsible for the outcome, and the positive outcome could be assumed to follow negatively valued low effort, given the stimulus person's record of low effort in the past. This combination of variables would lead to lower ratings of deservingness and lower ratings of positive affect.

Other results from Study 1 showed that the high achiever was envied more than the average achiever, and the student participants also reported more pleasure and praise for the high achiever.

Study 2: A Failure Outcome

In Study 2 I presented the remaining 520 participants with a scenario where the stimulus person failed at the final matriculation examination at the end of Year 12 in high school, "with a low overall mark on the matriculation exams at the end of Year 12, a lot worse than was ever expected." I also varied information about the cause of the low performance in Study 2 by randomly presenting participants with one out of three variations of the scenario. In the first variation participants received no further information about the possible causes of the fall in performance; in the second variation they were told that the stimulus person became ill, contracting "a serious illness (an influenza virus) just before the exams"; in the third variation the scenario indicated that the stimulus person "slackened off in the second half of Year 12 and didn't put in the extra effort required." Note that the latter two variations were aimed at manipulating degree of controllability in order to affect judgments of responsibility, sickness being outside of the stimulus person's control, lack of effort being within the stimulus person's control. In addition, the third variation of the causal basis for the low performance presented participants with a cause that referred to a negatively valued action (lack of effort).

After they read the scenario participants rated the stimulus person on items concerning responsibility and deservingness for the outcome. In addition, they rated how sorry they privately felt for the stimulus person because of the low score, how unhappy they privately felt that the stimulus person obtained the low score, how pleased they thought the stimulus person would feel about the low score, and whether they would be in favor of letting the stimulus person "resit" a second examination with the opportunity of improving his or her score. So these variables overlapped with those used in the first part of the study, but they also took account of the negative outcome, a fall in performance, in regard to the types of affect that might be reported.

The main results are reported in Table 5.4. The strongest results occurred in regard to the effects of information about the stimulus person and information about the causes of the stimulus person's low performance. Consistent with the results for Study 1, the results in the top part of Table 5.4 show that the ratings of the stimulus person's

Table 5.4. Means of Dependent Variables and F Values for Main Effects from Univariate ANOVAs (Failure Outcome)

Variable	Information about stimulus person			df	F for information
	No information	High effort/ average ability	Low effort/ high ability		
Responsible	4.74_a	4.30_b	4.99_a	2,502	7.57***
Deserve	3.76_a	3.40_b	4.51_c	2,501	19.84***
Unhappy	3.76_a	3.87_a	3.06_b	2,501	10.18***
Sorry	4.28_a	4.47_a	3.59_b	2,502	12.63***
Stimulus person's pleasure	2.04	2.04	2.13	2,498	0.41
Redeem grade	5.61	5.86	5.54	2,501	1.72

	Achievement status		df	F for status
	Average achiever	High achiever		
Responsible	4.86	4.51	1,502	2.63
Deserve	4.15	3.65	1,501	7.56**
Unhappy	3.52	3.60	1,501	0.08
Sorry	3.82	4.39	1,502	10.40***
Stimulus person's pleasure	2.06	2.09	1,498	0.27
Redeem grade	5.60	5.73	1,501	0.50

Variable	Failure situation			df	F for situation
	No information	Sickness	Reduced effort		
Responsible	5.40_a	3.30_b	5.37_a	2,502	78.75***
Deserve	4.13_a	2.58_b	5.00_c	2,501	85.06***
Unhappy	3.33_a	3.85_b	3.51_a	2,501	3.96*
Sorry	4.04_a	4.99_b	3.27_c	2,502	39.11***
Stimulus person's pleasure	2.38_a	1.65_b	2.20_a	2,498	14.34***
Redeem grade	5.47_a	6.09_b	5.44_a	2,501	7.67***

Note: $N = 520$; minor variations in Ns occurred across variables due to missing cases. Means in each row not sharing a common subscript differ significantly, $p < .05$ (Tukey).
*$p < .05$ **$p < .01$ ***$p < .001$
Source: Feather (1992a). Reprinted by permission of the British Psychological Society.

responsibility for the low performance and deservingness for the low mark were related to information about levels of past effort and ability. But in this case the stimulus person whose past performance could be attributed to high effort was judged to be less responsible and less deserving of the low mark when compared with the stimulus person whose past performance could be attributed to low effort. Information about the stimulus person's past effort and ability apparently provided cues for judgments about his or her present responsibility for the low mark. Thus, the lower responsibility that was attributed to the high effort/average ability stimulus person was probably based on some appeal to uncontrollable factors (e.g., a difficult examination) as a cause of the stimulus person's failure.

In contrast, the low effort/high ability stimulus person could more easily be judged to be responsible for the low mark, given the information that this stimulus person was not usually hard-working. The higher deservingness ratings for this stimulus person would reflect this judgment of greater responsibility. The higher deservingness ratings may also reflect an inference that, for this stimulus person, low effort in the past (a negatively valued action) may have carried over to the present situation, influencing the failure (a negatively valued outcome).

Participants who responded to scenarios that involved the high effort/average ability person may also have inferred that his or her high effort in the past (a positively valued action) carried over to the present but then was followed by failure (a negatively valued action). According to the deservingness model, such an outcome would be seen to be less deserved for this type of stimulus person. Note also that participants also reported feeling significantly more unhappy and more sorry for the high effort/average ability stimulus person who received the low mark when compared with the low effort/high ability stimulus person.

More direct evidence that relates to the deservingness model comes from the comparison across the three conditions that varied information about the actual causes of the stimulus person's present failure. The results at the bottom of Table 5.4 show that the stimulus person was seen as less responsible for the low mark, less deserving of the low mark, and less pleased about the low mark when the cause could be attributed to sickness than when the cause could be attributed to reduced effort or when no information about cause was provided. Participants' own reported affective reactions and willingness to help the stimulus person mirrored these judgments. They reported feeling more unhappy about the stimulus person's failure, more sorry for the stimulus person, and more willing to let the stimulus person redeem his or her grade when the low grade could be attributed to sickness (an uncontrollable cause), than to reduced effort (a controllable cause), or to other unspecified factors (the no information condition).

Note that once again the results were consistent with the deservingness model. The low mark (assumed to be a negatively valued outcome) was judged to be more deserved when it followed reduced effort (also assumed to be negatively valued), and participants were less sympathetic and less willing to help the stimulus person in this condition. But, when uncontrollable sickness was the cause of the stimulus person's failure, participants judged the stimulus person as less responsible for the low mark, and they showed more sympathy and willingness to let the stimulus person resit the examination so as to attempt to redeem the low mark.

Correlations Involving Perceived Responsibility and Deservingness

Other detailed results from Study 1 and Study 2 are presented in the original report (Feather, 1992a). One final set of results will be reported here because it provides evidence about relations between deservingness, perceived responsibility, and the other dependent variables. Table 5.5 presents the correlations between these variables for each study, after collapsing across experimental conditions. Also reported in Table 5.5 are the partial correlations between deservingness and the other variables after controlling for the effects of perceived responsibility. The correlations in Table 5.5 are consistent with my analysis of deservingness. Ratings of responsibility and deservingness were positively correlated in both studies as would be expected when conditions were combined.

Also, when the outcome was success (Study 1), the correlations between reported positive affect and perceived responsibility and deservingness were positive, as would be expected, and they decreased in size when the responsibility variable was partialed out.

When the outcome was failure (Study 2), most of the correlations between the ratings of affect and perceived responsibility and deservingness were negative, as would be expected. And, again, these correlations decreased in size when the responsibility variable was partialed out.

In general, the correlations between deservingness and the other variables in each study were higher than the correlations between perceived responsibility and each of the respective variables. This difference suggests that deservingness was a stronger predictor of participants' reactions than was perceived responsibility. We will discover

Table 5.5.   Zero-Order and Partial Correlations (Controlling for Responsibility) between Deservingness and Other Variables

| | Success outcome | | |
| | Zero-order correlations | | Partial correlations |
Variable	Responsible	Deserve	Deserve
Responsible	—	.52***	—
Deserve	.52***	—	—
Pleased	.32***	.46***	.36***
Envy	.06	.17*	.16*
Praise	.36***	.38***	.23**
Stimulus person's pleasure	.29***	.38***	.28***

| | Failure outcome | | |
| | Zero-order correlations | | Partial correlations |
Variable	Responsible	Deserve	Deserve
Responsible	—	.42***	—
Deserve	.42***	—	—
Unhappy	−.08	−.20***	−.19***
Sorry	−.27***	−.40***	−.33***
Redeem grade	−.14**	−.16***	−.11*
Stimulus person's pleasure	.04	.17***	.17***

Note: Ns ranged from 168 to 169 in the success condition and from 516 to 520 in the failure condition. Tests of significance are two-tailed.
*p < .05   **p < .01   *p < .001
Source: Feather (1992a). Reprinted by permission of the British Psychological Society.

similar evidence that is consistent with this conclusion in some of the subsequent studies that will be reviewed in this chapter and the next.

Summary of Studies

I have presented the results of Study 1 and Study 2 in this investigation in some detail because they provided strong evidence that was generally consistent with the analysis of deservingness that I have presented. Clearly, judgments of deservingness were related to perceived responsibility. They were also related to the relation between a positively or negatively evaluated action (high or low effort) and a positively or negatively evaluated outcome (success or failure), as would be predicted from the deservingness model. Additionally, a stimulus person's perceived responsibility for an outcome depended upon whether or not the cause of the outcome was controllable or uncontrollable. Finally, both reported affect about the outcome and willingness to help the failed stimulus person were related to perceived responsibility and deservingness in the directions that one would expect.

Thus, as was the case in the two early studies of tall poppies that were described in the previous section, there were dependable relations between deservingness and causal ascriptions and between deservingness and reported affect.

STUDIES OF PUBLIC FIGURES

It could be argued that, by using hypothetical scenarios in the studies that have so far been described, I mapped into knowledge and linguistic structures that reflected normative sorts of rules that people fall back on when they are asked to respond to situations when information is relatively minimal. It may be the case that the psychological processes and responses that occur would be different in real-life contexts where the stimulus context is richer. The use of hypothetical scenarios would also move participants toward a "colder" cognitive style of analysis and may have the effect of reducing the impact of emotional states that would be aroused in actual situations where there is a high degree of personal involvement.

In defense of the scenario methodology, it can be said that the use of this type of procedure does enable one to manipulate and control the variables of interest, whereas, in real-life situations, such control is usually difficult to arrange or does not occur at all. Also, the scenarios that were used in the studies that I described in the previous sections were devised to be meaningful to the student participants who responded to them, focusing as they did on examination performance either at high school or at university. They were realistic scenarios, although necessarily stripped down in the information they presented.

In order to achieve greater realism I also conducted studies of high profile figures as part of the program of research concerning high achievers or tall poppies. These were people who were well known to the Australian public, constantly in the media, and the subjects of widespread attention. In this section I will describe two studies of public figures that I have conducted that provided results that are relevant to my analysis of deservingness.

A Study of Politicians, Entertainers, and Sporting Leaders

The first study involved leaders from the fields of politics, entertainment, and sport. Full details are provided elsewhere (Feather, Volkmer, & McKee, 1991). The participants were 377 students who were enrolled in introductory psychology courses at Flinders University. They completed a questionnaire that presented three well-known high achievers or tall poppies who came from one of three domains: politics, entertainment, or sport. The three tall poppies in each field were as follows: *Politics*, Robert Hawke (prime minister of Australia and leader of the Labor Party), Janine Haines (leader of the Democrat Party), and Andrew Peacock (leader of the Opposition and leader of the Liberal Party); *Entertainment*, Paul Hogan (leading actor), Kylie Minogue (leading actress and entertainer), and John Farnham (leading entertainer); *Sports*, Pat Cash (leading tennis player), Allan Border (leading cricketer), and Lisa-Curry Kenny (leading swimmer). Some of these high achievers might not be well known outside of Australia, but they were certainly leading figures in their field within Australia at the time of the study (1990) and highly visible to the public.

There were three versions of the questionnaire, each version containing one of the three sets of leaders. Participants answered a series of questions about each of the three tall poppies in the questionnaire they received. These questions concerned causal attributions, deservingness, positive affect, personality characteristics, and their feelings about a hypothetical fall of each leader. Participants also completed a measure of tall poppy attitudes (the Tall Poppy Scale) designed to assess their general attitudes toward tall poppies (whether they favored rewarding tall poppies or favored their fall), and a modified version of the Rosenberg Self-Esteem Scale (Rosenberg, 1965), which was used to obtain a measure of global self-esteem.

The causal attribution items involved 7-point scales and participants rated to what extent they thought the tall poppy's present high position was due to ability or talent, hard work or effort, outside or external assistance (e.g., publicity through the mass media, help from others), or opportunity or luck. Two deservingness items asked participants whether the tall poppy deserved to be in his or her high position and whether the tall poppy deserved to hold on to his or her present high position in the future. Three items asked similar questions about positive affect. Participants rated how pleased they were that the tall poppy held his or her present high position, how pleased they would feel if the tall poppy or leader were to rise even further, and how pleased they would feel if the tall poppy were to fall from his or her present high position. Again participants made these ratings by using 7-point scales.

Items concerning the personality characteristics of each leader involved semantic differential, bipolar adjective scales. Two composite measures were derived from factor analysis. These composite measures were used to assess the degree to which a tall poppy was self-centered and arrogant and the degree to which the tall poppy was a good mixer with high integrity.

The items concerned with a tall poppy's hypothetical fall asked participants to imagine that for some reason the tall poppy lost his or her high position. Participants then provided ratings about how they would feel about this fall if the tall poppy was responsible for it and then how they would feel if the tall poppy was not responsible for the fall. Using factor analysis, I derived three affect scales that related to the hypothetical fall. These respective scales reflected how sorry, pleased, and disturbed participants felt about the fall.

Table 5.6 presents the means for these variables across the three different fields, politics, entertainment, and sport, after combining data by averaging for the three tall poppies within each field. These results show that the high-achieving sports leaders were favored the most. Participants judged their success to be more attributable to ability and effort and less to external assistance when compared with the high profile politicians and entertainers. Good luck attributions were intermediate for the sports leaders. The sports leaders were also judged to be more deserving of their high achievement, to be less self-centered and arrogant, and to be higher on the good mixer/integrity variable when compared with the tall poppies in the other two fields. The affect reported by participants also tended to mirror these differences. For example, they reported feeling more pleased about the high achievement of the sports leaders, more pleased about a hypothetical rise in their achievement, and less pleased about a hypothetical fall. All of these differences were statistically significant.

These differences are relative to the particular public figures who were included in each field. However, they do provide a pattern of evidence that shows that judgments of deservingness were higher for tall poppies (the sporting leaders) whose achievement could also be attributed to their own skill and effort (implying that these tall poppies were seen as more responsible for their achievements), and higher for tall poppies who were viewed favorably in terms of their personality characteristics. The results also show that the kinds of affect that participants reported tended to be consistent with their deservingness ratings.

More detailed information about relations between variables is presented in Tables 5.7 and 5.8. These tables present the correlations for the total sample between the deservingness and affect variables, the causal attribution ratings, and the personality descriptions. These correlations

Table 5.6.   Mean Ratings on Variables for Tall Poppies
across Politics, Sport, and Entertainment

Variable	Midpoint of scale	Politics	Sport	Entertainment	Univariate F
Causal attributions					
Ability	4	4.71	5.73	4.58	45.12***
Effort	4	5.05	6.10	5.18	41.41***
Assistance	4	5.14	4.64	5.66	25.97***
Luck	4	4.00	4.44	5.29	48.24***
Deserve					
Present position	4	4.34	5.64	4.98	49.00***
Maintain position	4	4.08	5.11	4.60	28.70***
Pleased					
Present position	4	4.02	4.97	4.44	29.01***
Rise further	4	3.68	4.98	4.29	44.29***
Fall	4	3.80	3.21	3.65	13.38***
Personality					
Self-centered	36	35.28	30.01	31.37	24.33***
Good mixer	20	20.58	23.91	23.08	35.60***
Feeling about fall					
Responsible					
Sorry	6	3.30	3.63	3.52	0.57
Pleased	6	3.52	1.63	1.91	23.75***
Disturbed	8	3.10	2.24	1.26	11.34***
Not responsible					
Sorry	6	4.70	6.20	5.57	8.57***
Pleased	6	2.31	0.95	1.04	18.70***
Disturbed	8	4.51	4.30	2.87	7.42***

Note: Politics, $N = 124$; Sport, $N = 124$; Entertainment, $N = 129$. Minor variations in these Ns occurred due to missing cases.
*$p < .05$ **$p < .01$ ***$p < .001$

were based upon the average ratings for each variable across the three tall poppies each participant rated.

The results in Table 5.7 show that tall poppies who were judged to have achieved their success by ability and effort were also seen to deserve their success more. Participants also reported feeling more pleased about the present high achievement and the possibility of even greater success, and less pleased if a fall should occur, when the tall poppies' high achievement could be attributed more to ability and effort and when it was seen to be deserved. These relations were in the reverse direction when the achievement was attributed more to external assistance. The achievement was then judged to be less deserved and partici-

Table 5.7. Correlations between Deserve and Pleased Measures and Causal Attributions and Personality Characteristics

Variable	Deserve		Pleased		
	Present position	Maintain position	Present position	Rise further	Fall
Causal attributions					
Ability	0.61***	0.54***	0.49***	0.49***	−0.40***
Effort	0.64***	0.53***	0.52***	0.50***	−0.42***
Assistance	−0.21*'	−0.23***	−0.23***	−0.22***	0.30**
Luck	0.01	−0.03	−0.01	0.03	0.10
Deserve					
Present position	—	0.83***	0.69***	0.69***	−0.56***
Maintain position	0.83***	—	0.67***	0.70***	−0.61***
Personality					
Self-centered	−0.56***	−0.55***	−0.59***	−0.58***	0.53***
Good mixer	0.55***	0.51***	0.57***	0.56***	−0.50***

Note: Ns ranged from 345 to 367 due to some missing cases. Tests of significance are two-tailed.
*p < .05   **p <.01   ***p < .001
Source: Feather et al. (1991). Copyright 1991 by the Australian Psychological Society. Reproduced by permission.

pants reported feeling less pleased about present and even higher success and more pleased about a hypothetical fall.

The results in Table 5.7 also show that judgments of deservingness and ratings of positive affect were related to the personality characteristics of the tall poppies. The more participants perceived the tall poppies to be self-centered, the less the tall poppies were seen to deserve their success, the less the participants reported feeling pleased about the tall poppies' present high position and a hypothetical future rise, and the more participants reported feeling pleased about a hypothetical future fall.

These relations were in the reverse direction for tall poppies who scored higher on the good mixer variable. These tall poppies were seen to deserve their high position more and participants reported feeling more pleased about the success and less pleased about a hypothetical fall.

The results in Table 5.8 show that participants who reported feeling more sorry, less pleased, and more disturbed about the hypothetical fall of their tall poppies were in most cases also more likely to attribute the tall poppies' present high positions to ability and effort, less likely to attribute their high positions to external assistance, more likely to report that the tall poppies deserved their high positions and deserved to stay there, less likely to see the tall poppies as self-centered, and more likely to see them as good mixers.

Table 5.8. Correlations between Feelings About the Fall
and Causal Attributions and Personality Characteristics

| | Feelings about fall | | | | | |
| | Responsible condition | | | Not responsible condition | | |
Variable	Sorry	Pleased	Disturbed	Sorry	Pleased	Disturbed
Causal attributions						
Ability	0.21***	−0.29***	0.10	0.28***	−0.29***	0.15**
Effort	0.21***	−0.32***	0.07	0.29***	−0.29***	0.13*
Assistance	−0.15**	0.08	−0.20***	−0.14**	0.05	−0.14**
Luck	−0.07	−0.09	−0.16**	−0.03	−0.10	−0.11*
Deserve						
Present position	0.35***	−0.37***	0.12*	0.43***	−0.29***	0.15**
Maintain position	0.34***	−0.33***	0.16**	0.39***	−0.28***	0.14**
Personality						
Self-centered	−0.34***	0.31***	−0.14**	−0.43***	0.23***	−0.15**
Good mixer	0.38***	−0.33***	0.16**	0.49***	−0.30***	0.22***

Note: Ns ranged from 337 to 357 due to some missing cases. Tests of significance are two-tailed.
*$p < .05$ **$p < .01$ ***$p < .001$
Source: Feather et al. (1991). Copyright 1991 by the Australian Psychological Society. Reproduced by permission.

Finally, the manipulation of the tall poppies' responsibility for the hypothetical fall was associated with differences in reported affect, as one would expect (e.g., Weiner, 1995). Participants reported feeling more sorry, less pleased, and more disturbed about the fall of a tall poppy when the high achiever was described as not responsible for the fall than when he or she was described as responsible for it. Differences in the means for each of these measures of reported affect across the two responsibility conditions were highly significant ($p < .001$).

Thus, once again there was evidence to show that judgments of deservingness were related to the way participants attributed causality for the tall poppies' success and that participants' ratings of different types of affect were also associated in predictable ways to their deservingness judgments. There was also further evidence that affective judgments depended on the degree to which responsibility for a hypothetical fall could be assigned to a tall poppy. And there was evidence that both deservingness judgments and affective reports were related to how the tall poppies were viewed in relation to their personality characteristics.

The Rise and Fall of Political Leaders

The second study of public figures was conducted in 1992 and full details are provided elsewhere (Feather, 1993b). The study involved the top leaders of the two main political parties in Australia at the time. These leaders were Paul Keating (prime minister of Australia and leader of the Labor Party), John Hewson (leader of the Opposition and leader of the Liberal Party), and Bob Hawke (the ex-prime minister of Australia and ex-leader of the Labor Party). The Labor Party in Australia tends to be to the left of center in its ideology and policies; the Liberal Party tends to be more to the right of center.

Hawke had been displaced from office by Keating and had therefore suffered a dramatic fall. The study was conducted approximately three months after Hawke lost the prime ministership and was replaced by Keating. These events were still recent and topical.

There were 204 participants in this study. They were recruited from the general population of Adelaide, South Australia. These participants responded to a questionnaire that contained sets of items that concerned the three political leaders. These items were similar to those that have already been described in relation to the previous study of public figures. They included items concerned with causal attributions for Keating's and Hewson's present high position and for Hawke's fall, deservingness in relation to Keating's and Hewson's high achievement and Hawke's fall, personality characteristics in relation to each politician, and affective reactions to the high achievement of Keating and Hewson and to the actual fall of Hawke.

In addition, I included a single item measure of perceived responsibility. In the case of Keating and Hewson, participants were asked to suppose that, for some reason, each of these political leaders lost his present high position and then to rate how personally responsible they thought each leader would be for the fall. In the case of Hawke, the rating of personal responsibility applied to his actual fall.

As in the previous study, composite measures of personality characteristics and reported affect were obtained via factor analysis. These personality variables were very similar to those obtained previously and they were labeled "integrity" and "arrogance." The composite affect variables were identical to those obtained in the previous study and they reflected how sorry, pleased, and disturbed participants felt about the hypothetical fall of Keating and Hewson and the actual fall of Hawke. Participants also provided information about which political party they preferred or usually voted for.

The results of this study were generally consistent with those of the previous one. Here I focus only on a selection of results that are especially relevant to the deservingness variable and that followed hierarchical multiple regression analyses in which I controlled for the effects of voting preference (Liberal, Labor). In these analyses the effects of voting preference on the dependent variable were first determined by entering voting preference at the first step of the analysis. The remaining independent variables or predictors that were of interest in each analysis were entered at the second step of the analysis. This kind of analysis enables one to identify whether the variables entered at the second step significantly increased the variance accounted for in the dependent variable after controlling for political preference. The analysis also provides standardized beta coefficients for the set of independent variables that provide information about the relation between each predictor variable and the dependent variable, after controlling for the effects of other variables.

Table 5.9 presents the results of one of these analyses in which the dependent variables were the degree to which Hawke deserved his present position (the loss of his prime ministership) and deserved to maintain it and stay where he was, outside of politics. The independent variables or predictors that were included in the analysis were voting preference (entered at Block 1) and the personality variables (integrity, arrogance) and perceived responsibility for the fall (entered at Block 2).

The results in Table 5.9 show that the standardized beta coefficients were positive for perceived responsibility and negative for the integrity variable. Thus, the more Hawke was seen as responsible for his fall and as lacking in integrity, the more he was perceived to deserve his fall. Judgments of deservingness were therefore related to perceived responsibility and to personality characteristics in the directions that would be expected. These relations occurred after the effects of voting preference were controlled for at the first step of the analysis.

The results also show that the addition of the second block of variables significantly increased the variance accounted for in each dependent variable. The change in R^2 was statistically significant in each case.

Table 5.10 presents the results of a similar analysis in which reported positive affect or pleasure was the dependent variable. Again voting preference was entered as an independent or predictor variable at the first step of the analysis. Causal attributions, the two personality variables, and deservingness judgments were entered as independent variables or predictors at the second step of the analysis. Recall that the attribution variables and the deserve variable refer to the present position of each of the three tall poppies (high political office in the case of Keating and Hewson, loss of the prime ministership in the case of

Table 5.9. Standardized Betas and Multiple Correlations (Rs) for Deservingness as Dependent Variable and Voting Preference, Perceived Responsibility for Fall, and Personality Characterisitics as Independent Variables for Hawke

	Independent variables													
	Block 1			Block 2										
	Liberal vs. Labor voters			Integrity	Arrogance	Responsibility for fall						
Dependent variable	Beta	R	R^2	Beta	Beta	Beta	R	R^2	R^2 change	F change
Deserve position	.24**	.24	.06	−.25**	.12	.42***	.63	.40	.34	27.00***
Deserve to maintain	.13	.13	.02	−.15	.12	.25**	.40	.16	.15	8.23***

Note: Coding for voting preference was 1 = Labor, 2 = Liberal.
*p < .05   **p < .01   ***p < .001
Source: Feather (1993b). Copyright 1993 by the Australian Psychological Society. Reproduced by permission.

Table 5.10. Standardized Betas and Multiple Correlations (Rs) for Positive Affect as Dependent Variable and Voting Preference, Causal Attributions, Personality Characterisitics, and Deservingness as Independent Variables

Dependent variable	Block 1 Liberal vs. Labor voters			Block 2 (Independent variables)										
	Beta	R	R^2	Presence or lack of ability Beta	Presence or lack of effort Beta	Assistance or external forces Beta	Good or bad luck Beta	Integrity Beta	Arrogance Beta	Deserve Beta	R	R^2	R^2 change	F change
Pleased about position														
Keating	-.50***	.50	.25	.00	.05	.01	-.06	.21**	-.02	.53***	.83	.69	.44	27.15***
Hewson	.55***	.55	.30	-.05	.19*	-.03	-.01	.14	-.17*	.40***	.84	.71	.41	28.03***
Hawke	.21**	.21	.04	.05	.03	-.05	-.02	.02	.08	.66***	.74	.55	.51	22.21***
Rise further														
Keating	-.52***	.52	.27	-.08	.08	.04	.00	.12	-.08	.63***	.84	.70	.43	28.03***
Hewson	.65***	.65	.42	-.04	.14	-.02	-.07	.13	-.22***	.28***	.87	.75	.33	25.52***
Hawke	-.40***	.40	.16	-.07	-.08	-.03	.04	.07	-.18*	-.43***	.72	.51	.36	14.42***
Fall														
Keating	.53***	.53	.28	-.05	-.03	.06	.09	-.18*	.10	-.39***	.82	.68	.40	24.23***
Hewson	-.50***	.50	.25	-.01	-.18*	.04	.07	-.02	.37***	-.22**	.81	.65	.40	22.31***
Hawke	.38***	.38	.14	.00	.12	-.09	.00	-.22*	.07	.23*	.62	.38	.24	7.62***

Note: Coding for voting preference was 1 = Labor, 2 = Liberal.
$*p < .05$ $**p < .01$ $***p < .001$
Source: Feather (1993b). Copyright 1993 by the Australian Psychological Society. Reproduced by permission.

Hawke) and so they were phrased appropriately, depending on the present status of each leader (e.g., ability, effort, external assistance, and opportunity or luck for Keating and Hewson; lack of ability, lack of effort, external forces, and lack of opportunity or luck for Hawke).

The results in Table 5.10 show that, after controlling for voting preference and the other independent variables, the best predictor of reported pleasure was the degree to which a leader was seen to deserve his present position. All of the beta coefficients were statistically significant for the deservingness variable.

These coefficients were positive in regard to feeling pleased about Keating's and Hewson's present high political statuses, positive for feeling pleased about any further rise in status for each leader, but negative for feeling pleased about any hypothetical fall that either leader might experience. Thus, these results imply that participants reported feeling more pleased about a leader's success or any further success, and less pleased about a leader's fall, when they perceived that the leader was more deserving of the success.

When we consider judgments of deservingness for Hawke's present position (loss of high political office), again we find that the beta coefficients were positive in regard to feeling pleased about Hawke's fall and any further fall, but negative in regard to feeling pleased about any future rise in status that Hawke might experience. These results imply that participants reported feeling more pleased about Hawke's fall or any further fall, and less pleased should he rise again, when they perceived that Hawke was more deserving of his fall.

Again the addition of the second block of independent variables or predictors significantly increased the variance accounted for in the dependent variables. The change in R^2 was statistically significant in each case.

The results in Tables 5.9 and 5.10 also show that voting preference was a significant predictor for the dependent variables that were analyzed for the political leaders. For example, the standardized beta coefficients in Table 5.10 show that Liberal voters were less pleased about Keating's present high position, more pleased about Hewson's present high position, and more pleased about Hawke's fall when compared with Labor voters. These results are not surprising given the fact that Keating was the current prime minister and leader of the Labor Party, Hawke was the ex-prime minister and ex-leader of the Labor Party, and Hewson was the leader of the Opposition and leader of the Liberal Party at the time of the study. These kinds of differences also extended to most of the other variables that were measured in the study.

Table 5.11 presents an example of these differences between Liberal and Labor Party voters for Hawke, the fallen Labor leader. The results in Table 5.11 show that most of the differences in means were statistically

Table 5.11.   Means for Major Variables
for Hawke in Relation to Voting Preference

| Variable | Midpoint of scale | Voting preference | | t |
		Liberal	Labor	
Causal attributions				
Lack of ability	4	3.71	2.94	2.70**
Lack of effort	4	3.27	2.89	1.28
External forces	4	5.38	5.77	−1.40
Bad luck	4	2.77	3.06	−1.10
Deserve				
Present fallen position	4	4.64	3.58	3.22**
Maintain fallen position	4	4.65	4.17	1.51
Pleased				
Present fallen position	4	4.35	3.55	2.84**
Rise	4	2.44	3.90	−5.88***
Fall further	4	3.49	2.47	4.56***
Personality				
Integrity	24	25.31	30.61	−5.97***
Arrogance	20	24.01	19.14	5.53***
Actual fall				
Responsible	4	4.92	4.27	2.81**
Sorry	6	2.98	5.64	−5.41***
Pleased	6	4.71	2.52	3.91***
Disturbed	8	2.84	4.77	−2.67**

Note: Ns were 77 for Liberal voters and 64 for Labor voters. Tests of significance were two-tailed.
$*p < .05$ $**p < .01$ $***p < .001$
Source: Feather (1993b). Copyright 1993 by the Australian Psychological Society. Reproduced by permission.

significant and that they followed the direction of more Labor voter support for the ex-Labor leader. Labor voters judged lack of ability as a less important cause of Hawke's fall than Liberal voters. They also saw his fall as less deserved, reported less pleasure about his current fallen position, rated him higher on integrity and lower on arrogance, judged him less responsible for his fall, and reported feeling more sorry, less pleased, and more disturbed about his fall, when compared with Liberal voters.

Why focus on these results? They are relevant because a person's voting preference may be assumed to reflect underlying values and allegiance to the ingroup or favored political party as opposed to the outgroup or rejected political party. Hence, the relations between voting preference and such variables as deservingness and affective reactions to political success and failure may be interpreted in terms of the effects of the values that are associated with the ideology of each political party, and also in terms of ingroup versus outgroup loyalties that define the political identity a person expresses in the way he or she votes. I discussed the pervasive role of values in Chapter 3, especially in relation to their effects on how a person might evaluate the actions and outcomes of another. Ingroup/outgroup relations were discussed in Chapter 4 in the extended deservingness model, and they were represented in the model in terms of unit relations.

DESERVINGNESS, AFFECT, EMPLOYMENT, AND UNEMPLOYMENT

The studies that I have described so far in this chapter were primarily devised to investigate variables that I assumed would influence how people react to high achievers or tall poppies. These studies spanned both experimental and nonexperimental procedures in an attempt to move beyond the sometimes artificial experimental context to realistic situations involving actual tall poppies who either maintained their high positions or fell from the top of the ladder.

In the course of these studies it became apparent that there is an array of variables that affect how people react to tall poppies and that deservingness stands out as one of the important variables within this array. As I concluded in a review of these studies:

> One cannot generalize and say that people are negative toward all high achievers and like to see them fall. That would be the case for "bad" tall poppies who are seen not to deserve their high position but it is not likely to be the case for "good" tall poppies who are perceived to deserve their high status. Thus, an important variable that influences our attitudes toward specific tall poppies and how we react to their fall is the degree to which we construe their rise or fall as justly deserved. (Feather, 1996e, p. 240)

Furthermore, the influence of deservingness as a justice variable is not restricted to those who occupy positions of high status. This variable applies more generally to all sorts of status positions. For example, the average achiever who fails an examination due to lack of effort would be seen to deserve the failure more than an average achiever who failed because of sickness.

The tall poppy studies also provide information about variables that affect judgments of deservingness (e.g., causal attributions and perceived responsibility, the positive or negative actions taken by the other person, the personality characteristics of the other, ingroup/outgroup relations) and about the consequences of judgments of deservingness (e.g., reported affect, punitive or proactive behavior toward the other). So, a research program that developed from my curiosity about a commonly held Australian belief that Australians like to cut down tall poppies led me into a closer examination of what it means to deserve or not to deserve an outcome and to an analysis of the antecedents and consequences of judgments of deservingness.

The study to be described in this section was not part of the tall poppy research program. It was designed to relate to the extended deservingness structures that were presented in Chapter 4, specifically to the structures (Figure 4.4) where person (p) and other (o) are linked by positive or negative liking or sentiment relations.

The study also differed from the previous ones by investigating job-seeking behavior that led either to o's success or failure, after o had either exerted high or low effort to find a job. Again, the context was one of achievement or lack of achievement but, in this case, the outcome concerned employment or unemployment.

A further feature of the study was the attempt to discover whether the different variables in the deservingness model were equally important determinants of judgments of deservingness or undeservingness or whether some variables were more important than others. As I noted in the previous chapter, a basic assumption in the deservingness model is that perceived responsibility and the structure of the attitudinal relations in the person-action-outcome triad are key variables that affect deservingness judgments, especially when these attitudes are grounded in the stable and important values that person (p) holds. The results of the studies that I have described so far also showed that affective reactions are related to judgments of deservingness. People are more likely to report feeling pleased when they see another's outcome to be deserved, and to report negative feelings when the outcome is seen to be undeserved.

But would liking relations become more important determinants of reported affect when these are introduced into the extended model in Figure 4.4? I expected that relations between p and o would moderate judgments of deservingness and in consequence the reported affect associated with deserved or undeserved outcomes. For example, a liked o or an ingroup o would be seen to deserve a positive outcome more and a negative outcome less when compared with a disliked o or an outgroup *o*, and reported positive or negative affect associated with the positive or negative outcome would be consistent with these differences. I assumed that relations between *p* and *o* would be less important influences on deservingness judgments when compared with *o*'s perceived responsibility for an action and its outcome and *p*'s evaluation of *o*'s action and the outcome it produced. The *p/o* relations were thus assigned a moderating role, influencing reported affect mainly via their effects on deservingness.

This assumption, however, may not be valid. For example, perhaps liking relations between *p* and *o* have effects on reported affect that do not depend upon deservingness judgments. Person (*p*) might report feeling more pleased or less displeased about a liked *o*'s positive or negative outcome when compared with a disliked *o*'s corresponding outcome, irrespective of whether *o* was judged to deserve or not deserve the outcome. These affective reactions would still be consistent with Heider's (1958) balance principle, but they would depend on that part of the extended structure in Figure 4.4 that excluded *p*'s evaluation of *o*'s action.

Note that there is plenty of evidence to show that people who are seen to possess desirable traits are evaluated more positively and punished less for misbehavior than those who are perceived to be unattractive. Evidence from the studies from my research program that I have already reviewed is consistent with this conclusion. So are the results of many other studies (e.g., Berscheid & Walster, 1978; Darby & Schlenker, 1989; Kassin & Wrightsman, 1988; Kleinke, 1975; Stewart, 1980; Weiten, 1980). The present study, however, was specifically designed to test the effects of liking/disliking in relation to the extended deservingness model presented in Figure 4.4 and to provide evidence that would be relevant to the possibility that these relations may have effects on reported affect that are not mediated by judgments of deservingness.

Full details of the study are provided in Feather and Dawson (1998). The study involved 104 participants who were enrolled in undergraduate courses at Flinders University. Each participant completed a questionnaire that contained a hypothetical scenario in which either an unemployed male stimulus person (Brian) or an unemployed female stimulus person (Lisa) was described as seeking a job and either became employed or unemployed. We varied the degree of effort (high or low) that the stimulus person expended in seeking the job and the liking relations (like, dislike) that were described to exist between the participants and the stimulus person.

Figure 5.1 presents the eight structures that corresponded to the eight hypothetical scenarios that were employed. The four structures in

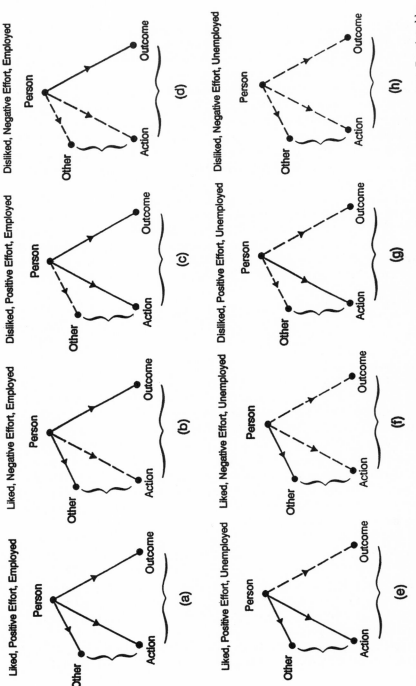

Figure 5.1. Balanced and unbalanced structures representing different experimental conditions. (*Source:* Feather & Dawson, 1998. Reprinted by permission of John Wiley & Sons, Ltd.)

the top half of Figure 5.1 correspond to the scenarios for which the outcome was employment (positively evaluated). The four structures in the bottom half of Figure 5.1 correspond to the scenarios for which the outcome was unemployment (negatively evaluated).

The following two examples show how the variables were manipulated in the scenarios. The first example presents the *liked, high effort* scenario with employed (positive) and unemployed (negative) outcomes. These scenarios correspond respectively to structures a and e in Figure 5.1.

> Lisa (Brian) is a relatively good friend of yours who you have known for about 5 years. You and Lisa (Brian) have a lot in common and you rarely have disagreements. Six months ago Lisa (Brian) completed a university degree with a major in Psychology. While Lisa (Brian) understands that jobs are difficult to find, she (he) wants to find work in psychology and she (he) has regularly visited the local CES (Commonwealth Employment Service) since finishing university. Lisa (Brian) has also applied for a number of jobs in psychology that have been advertised in the paper, and has attended a number of interviews. (*Employed outcome*: the last time you heard from Lisa (Brian) she (he) had found employment in the field of psychology and is now employed as a staff motivator and stress management advisor for a major business corporation.) (*Unemployed outcome*: although there are a number of other types of jobs available, Lisa (Brian) is still unemployed.)

The second example presents the *disliked, low effort* scenario with employed (positive) and unemployed (negative) outcomes. These scenarios correspond respectively to structures d and h in Figure 5.1.

> Lisa (Brian) is an acquaintance of yours who you have known for about 5 years but do not like. You and Lisa (Brian) have very little in common and you have had a number of disagreements. As a result of this, you rarely talk with Lisa (Brian), but you have heard about her (his) situation through a mutual friend. Six months ago Lisa (Brian) completed a university degree with a major in Psychology. While Lisa (Brian) understands that jobs are difficult to find, she (he) wants to find work in psychology but has visited the local CES (Commonwealth Employment Service) only once since finishing university. Lisa (Brian) only occasionally reads the employment section of the paper and is yet to apply for or attend any interviews for positions in psychology that have been advertised. (*Employed outcome*: the last time you spoke to your friend you heard that Lisa (Brian) had obtained employment in the field of psychology through a well-connected family member, and is now employed as a staff motivator and stress management advisor for a major business corporation.)

(*Unemployed outcome*: although there are a number of other types of jobs available, Lisa (Brian) is still unemployed.)

The eight scenarios were randomly distributed among participants, each participant responding to only one scenario. After reading the scenario participants responded to a number of items that concerned deservingness, perceived responsibility, affect, and the degree to which the stimulus person's actions were seen to be appropriate and positive behavior. We also included some additional items concerning affect (anger, sympathy) and welfare and family support in the unemployed condition of the study. Participants responded to these items by using rating scales that were numbered from 1 to 7, labeled at the extremes and at the middle (Feather & Dawson, 1998).

Table 5.12 presents the means for those variables that were common to both the employed and the unemployed conditions. These means show that when the outcome was employment, the liked stimulus person who displayed high effort attracted the most positive judgments. High ratings of responsibility, deservingness, positive and appropriate behavior, and pleasure about the stimulus person's success were reported in this condition as well as low ratings of resentment. This experimental condition corresponds to structure a in Figure 5.1. The experimental condition corresponding to structure d (disliked stimulus person, high effort, employed) also attracted positive judgments as far as responsibility, positive behavior, deservingness, and pleasure were con-

Table 5.12. Mean Scores for Variables Common to Both Employed and Unemployed Conditions

| | Employed condition | | | | Unemployed condition | | | |
| | Liked stimulus person | | Disliked stimulus person | | Liked stimulus person | | Disliked stimulus person | |
Variable	High effort	Low effort	High effort	Low effort	High effort	Low effort	High effort	Low effort
Responsibility	6.46	3.84	5.85	2.62	3.46	5.62	4.08	5.54
Positive behavior	6.62	3.08	6.15	2.31	5.92	2.23	5.08	2.46
Deservingness	6.54	4.54	5.54	3.85	2.31	5.23	2.85	5.08
Pleased	6.39	5.46	4.31	3.77	1.54	2.23	2.15	2.77
Resentful	1.46	2.31	3.23	2.85	1.46	2.92	2.15	2.62

Note: N = 13 for each of the eight experimental conditions.
Source: Feather & Dawson (1998). Reprinted by permission of John Wiley & Sons Ltd.

cerned. The corresponding means were much lower in the low effort condition.

When the outcome was unemployment, both the disliked stimulus person who displayed low effort and the liked stimulus person who displayed low effort attracted higher positive ratings for responsibility, deservingness, and pleasure about the stimulus person's failure, and lower ratings of positive and appropriate behavior when compared with the stimulus person who tried hard to get a job. Note, however, that judgments of pleasure were at the lower end of the scale. Participants did not report feeling happy about the stimulus person's failure to find employment. Clearly, therefore, information about effort was an important cue that influenced the judgments made by participants.

Statistical tests obtained from a multiple analysis of variance (MANOVA) showed that participants judged the stimulus person to deserve the outcome more, to see the stimulus person's behavior as more appropriate, and to report more pleasure about the stimulus person's outcome, when the outcome was employment rather than unemployment. Participants also judged the stimulus person as more responsible for the outcome, as displaying more positive and appropriate behavior, and they reported less resentment about the outcome when the stimulus person exerted high effort rather than low effort to find a job. They also judged the liked person as behaving more appropriately and positively than the disliked stimulus person, and they reported feeling more pleased and they reported less resentful about the liked stimulus person's outcome than about the disliked stimulus person's outcome. All of these differences (main effects from the analysis) were statistically significant. Details are provided in Feather and Dawson (1998).

A number of these main effects were qualified by statistically significant interaction effects. These interaction effects are reported in Tables 5.13 and 5.14. They relate specifically to the deservingness model and to the effects of liking/disliking. The results in Table 5.13 show that participants saw the stimulus person as more responsible for obtaining employment and more deserving of the employed outcome when it followed high effort rather than low effort. They also reported feeling more pleased about the stimulus person's successful employment in the high effort condition. These differences were reversed when the stimulus person failed to obtain employment. In the unemployed condition participants reported least pleasure when failure to get a job followed high effort rather than low effort, and they also judged the stimulus person as less responsible for the unemployed outcome and less deserving of this outcome when unemployment followed high effort rather than low effort.

Table 5.13.   Mean Scores for Univariate *F* Values for Effort by Outcome
Interactions

| Variable | Employed condition | | Unemployed condition | | *F* for interaction |
	High effort	Low effort	High effort	Low effort	
Responsibility	6.15a	3.23b	3.77c	5.58d	75.02***
Deservingness	6.04a	4.19b	2.58c	5.15d	55.22***
Pleased	5.35a	4.62b	1.85c	2.50d	8.14**

Note: Degrees of freedom were 1 and 96. Means sharing the same letter in each row did not differ
significantly from each other at $p < 0.05$ (Tukey test).
**$p < .01$ ***$p < .001$.
Source: Feather & Dawson (1998). Reprinted by permission of John Wiley & Sons Ltd.

Other results showed that participants reported more sympathy for
the stimulus person and less anger toward the stimulus person when
the unemployed outcome followed high effort rather than low effort.
They were also more supportive of financial assistance for the stimulus
person when the unemployment followed high effort rather than low
effort. All of these differences were statistically significant (Feather &
Dawson, 1998).

The differences in Table 5.13 are consistent with the deservingness
model and its related assumptions. We would expect that a person who
tried hard to find a job would be seen as more responsible for a successful outcome when compared with a person who exerted little effort.

Table 5.14.   Mean Scores for Univariate *F* Values
for Liking by Outcome Interactions

| Variable | Employed condition | | Unemployed condition | | *F* for interaction |
	Liked stimulus person	Disliked stimulus person	Liked stimulus person	Disliked stimulus person	
Responsibility	5.15a	4.23b	4.54b,c	4.81a,c	4.77*
Pleased	5.92a	4.04b	1.88c	2.46d	25.73***
Deservingness	5.54a	4.69b	3.77c	3.96c	3.04
Resentful	1.88a	3.04b	2.19a,c	2.38c	3.30

Note: Degrees of freedom were 1 and 96. Means sharing the same letter in each row did not
differ significantly from each other at $p < 0.05$ (Tukey test).
*$p < .05$ ***$p < .001$.
Source: Feather & Dawson (1998). Reprinted by permission of John Wiley & Sons Ltd.

Conversely, we would expect that a person who did not try hard would be seen as more responsible for failing to get a job when compared with a person who exerted a lot of effort. These differences in perceived responsibility were mirrored in the differences in judged deservingness, consistent with the assumption that perceived responsibility is a determinant of judgments of deservingness (Table 5.13).

In addition, however, the differences also relate to relations in the person-action-outcome triad. Positively valued actions (high effort) that led to a positively valued outcome (employment) were seen as more deserved and participants were less pleased about the outcome than was the case when negatively valued actions (low effort) led to a positively valued outcome (employment). The person-action-outcome triad is balanced in the former case and the result is consistent with the assumption that balance in the triad is associated with stronger judgments of deservingness. Also, negatively valued actions (low effort) that led to a negatively valued outcome (unemployment) were seen as more deserved, and participants reported less displeasure about the outcome, when compared with the situation where positively valued actions (high effort) led to a negatively valued outcome (unemployment). Again, the person-action-outcome triad is balanced in the former case and the result is consistent with the balance/deservingness assumption at the level of the triad.

The results in Table 5.14 show that participants reported feeling more pleased about a liked stimulus person's successful employment when compared with a disliked stimulus person's successful outcome. This difference was reversed when the stimulus person failed to find a job. Then participants reported feeling less pleased (or more displeasure) when the liked stimulus person remained unemployed than when the disliked stimulus person failed to obtain employment. These differences were statistically significant. Other differences in Table 5.14 were consistent with these results but not all of them were associated with statistically significant interaction effects.

Note that the results reported in Table 5.14 were independent of the amount of effort that the stimulus person exerted in looking for a job. Thus, the differences in Table 5.14 related more to relations within the person-other-action-outcome tetrad in Figure 5.1, excluding the person-action relation. A focus on this set of relations acknowledges that there were effects of liking/disliking on reported affect for the employed and unemployed outcome that did not depend on positively or negatively valued high or low effort as represented by the person-action evaluative relations. These tetrads were balanced for structures a and b, where all relations were positive, and also for structures g and h, where two relations were positive and two were negative. The tetrads were unbalanced for structures c, d, e, and f, where three relations were positive and one was negative. In balance theory terms the former structures (a, b, g, and h) are positive in sign and balanced; the latter structures (c, d, e, and f) are negative in sign and unbalanced. Reported feelings of pleasure about the employed or unemployed outcome were higher for the balanced tetrads.

Thus, the results of this study imply that liking/disliking relations between person (*p*) and other (*o*) may influence reported affect via deservingness as a mediator, and also independently of the person-action-outcome triad that I have assumed to be an important structural basis for judgments of deservingness and undeservingness. The latter form of influence may involve a more direct route to the affective system that is independent of intervening cognitive judgments, given the fact that liking/disliking and reported pleasure both clearly relate to the affective system.

A further important theoretical point that relates to the results I have reported involves an extension of the concept of perceived responsibility so that it applies not only to *o*'s action but also to *o*'s outcome. As presented in Chapter 4, the structural model of deservingness applies to situations where *o*'s action is followed by a positive or negative outcome, that is, the outcome depends or is contingent on the action. One can then assume that, in Heider's (1958) terms, other and action are linked by a positive unit relation and that action and outcome are also linked by a positive unit relation. The structures presented in Figures 4.3, 4.4, and 5.1 incorporate these positive unit relations.

However, there are many situations where a person's outcome may be attributed to causes other than that person's actions. The low effort/employed and high effort/unemployed conditions of the present study provide good examples. A person's success in finding a job despite low effort could be attributed to help from others, to an easy labor market, or to good luck; remaining unemployed despite a lot of effort directed toward finding a job could be attributed to a difficult labor market, to widespread intractable economic conditions, or to bad luck. In both the low effort/employed and high effort/unemployed conditions of the present study, the stimulus person was judged to be less responsible for the positive or negative outcome and also as less deserving of that outcome. We can assume that the outcome was not linked to *o*'s actions but to other causes.

This analysis leads to a distinction between a person's perceived responsibility for an action and his or her perceived responsibility for the outcome. A person may be seen as personally responsible both for an action and the outcome that follows from it. A person may also be seen as personally responsible for an action but not for the final outcome. What determines which of these two possibilities might occur? The important variable is whether the outcome is seen to be contingent on the action that the person takes or independent of the action that the person takes.

In *contingent* situations the perceived responsibility of o for the action would imply that o is also responsible for the outcome. In relation to the structures in Figures 4.3, 4.4, and 5.1, one can also assume that there would be a positive unit relation between other (o) and outcome. All relations in the other-action-outcome triad would then be balanced.

In *noncontingent* situations, however, the outcome could be attributed to other causes apart from o's action. In this case, the perceived responsibility of other (o) for an action would not necessarily imply that he or she was also responsible for the outcome. This independence between action and outcome could be represented by a null relation between action and outcome. There would be no other-action-outcome triad that could be described as balanced because action and outcome would not be linked by a positive unit relation.

In relation to the present study as shown in Figure 5.1, the high effort/employed conditions (structures a and c) and the low effort/ unemployed conditions (structures f and h) may be taken to imply contingent situations where o's outcome was contingent on o's action and where o would tend to be responsible for the outcome. These were the situations where ratings of deservingness and responsibility were highest.

In contrast, the low effort/employed conditions (structures b and d) and the high effort/unemployed conditions (structures e and g) may be taken to imply noncontingent situations where o's outcome was largely independent of o's action but could be attributed to other causes. These were the situations where ratings of deservingness and responsibility were lowest.

Similar distinctions to the one that I have made between perceived responsibility for an action and perceived responsibility for an outcome have been made in the literature (e.g., Brickman, Rabinowitz, Karuza, Coates, Cohn & Kidder, 1982; Karasawa, 1991; Weiner, 1995) in relation to onset and offset controllability. However, I have tied the distinction into the structural model of deservingness.

My distinction between contingent and noncontingent situations also has parallels in the literature. For example, it is consistent with Seligman's (1975) discussion of controllability and learned helplessness (see also Skinner, 1996) but again the distinction is used in the present context to clarify the structural model. As Feather and Dawson (1998) note:

> These two distinctions enable further elaboration of the structural model of deservingness ... so as to take account of unit relations between other (o) and outcome that may be coordinated to o's perceived responsibility for the outcome, and positive or null unit relations between action and outcome that may be coordinated to contingent and noncontingent relations respectively between o's behaviour and the outcome that occurs. (p. 19)

CONCLUDING COMMENTS

The research that I reviewed in this chapter involved a progression from the tall poppy studies in which, at least initially, deservingness was not given special emphasis, to more sophisticated studies where deservingness came to center stage in relation to the structural model.

These studies identified a number of variables that affected a person's judgments about the degree to which success or failure was deserved or undeserved. Here I briefly list these variables with selected examples from the results that I have presented.

1. Judgments of deservingness were related to causal attributions for the successful or unsuccessful outcome and to a person's perceived responsibility for the outcome. For example, whether or not a tall poppy deserved success was related to causal attributions to effort and ability; whether or not a political leader deserved to fall was related to perceived responsibility for the fall.

2. Judgments of deservingness were related to balanced as opposed to unbalanced relations within the person-action-outcome triad. For example, an unemployed person who engaged in positively valued behavior by trying hard to find a job was judged to deserve success more than one who engaged in negatively valued behavior by not exerting much effort; similarly, a student who did not study hard for a final examination was judged to deserve a low grade more than a student who did put in the necessary study.

3. Judgments of deservingness were related to like/dislike relations and to ingroup/outgroup relations that concerned person (p) and other (o). For example, a liked unemployed person was judged to deserve a positive outcome (finding a job) more when compared with a disliked stimulus person; political leaders belonging to the same party as the participants or judges were seen to deserve

their success more than political leaders belonging to the opposing party.

4. Judgments of deservingness were related to the perceived personality characteristics of o. Political leaders who were judged to be arrogant were seen to deserve their success less than political leaders who were seen not to be arrogant; political leaders with integrity were seen as more deserving of success than political leaders lacking in integrity.

The effects of all of these variables can be understood in terms of the structural model as described in the previous chapter.

Results from the studies also demonstrated links between deservingness and p's reported affect about o's outcome and between deservingness and p's willingness to provide assistance to o (e.g., to allow an unsuccessful student to resit an examination). The results also showed that deservingness ratings were better predictors of reported affect than were judgments of o's responsibility for an outcome, implying that judgments of deservingness, though linked to perceived responsibility, also bring in the effects of other variables, notably p's values and their influence on the way o's actions and outcomes are construed in evaluative terms. In addition, the results indicated that reported affect was also influenced directly by like/dislike relations between p and o.

These results were obtained from studies that focused on the context of achievement where outcomes could denote success or failure. They add to the literature that concerns reactions to success and failure and do so in relation to the deservingness variable. Note, however, that the focus has been on reactions to another's success or failure rather than on reactions to one's own success or failure. The latter question remains to be investigated in relation to the deservingness model.

It is also the case that the set of linkages that connect deservingness to antecedents, such as the general values that people hold, and to consequences such as affective reactions and behavior, needs to be specified in more detail for achievement situations so that the overall social-cognitive process can be clearly identified. I will return to this question in the final chapter.

Note that the studies that I described have focused on situations where outcomes are contingent on the actions that are taken. Noncontingent outcomes remain to be investigated in relation to the model. Do we say, for example, that a person deserved a huge win in a lottery when the outcome depended on chance? Positive affective reactions would surely accompany the win, but it would be stretching the language to say that the win was deserved. The person who won may see self or be seen by others as somehow in control of the win, having bought a lottery ticket, but that form of control is basically illusory when applied to the outcome (Langer, 1975, 1983).

It is clear, however, that deservingness is an important variable in the context of achievement or lack of it. We employ justice concepts when reacting to the success and failure of others and also in relation to our own positive or negative achievement outcomes. Our judgments about deservingness depend not only on the degree of responsibility that is assigned to other or to self. Our values are also involved in the way we evaluate the actions that are taken and the successful or unsuccessful outcomes that follow them. The structure of these evaluations of actions and outcomes, as well as our judgments of responsibility, are basic variables in the way deservingness is assessed. These assessments are in turn moderated by how much we like or dislike the other (o) who is being judged, and whether we perceive o as one of our own kind or belonging to an outgroup. Finally, the total set of variables has a structure, tending toward harmony and balance.

In the next chapter I will consider how deservingness can be incorporated into the analysis of retributive justice, dealing specifically with how people react to others who have committed an offense and, as a consequence, have suffered a penalty.

CHAPTER 6

A Social-Cognitive Process Model of Retributive Justice

This chapter extends the analysis of deservingness to the area of retributive justice. Research on justice has focused primarily on the fairness of procedures (procedural justice) and on the fairness of the way in which resources are distributed (distributive justice). For example, when new procedures are developed for promoting people within an organization, are these procedures fair? Are all candidates treated fairly? When rewards have to be distributed among individuals or group members, is the distribution a fair one in relation to principles of equity, equality, or need? To what extent does the nature of the distribution depend on the goals of the allocator (e.g., to improve performance, to increase group harmony, to relieve suffering, etc.)? There is now a relatively large literature on these topics that has recently been reviewed by Tyler and his colleagues (Tyler et al., 1997; Tyler & Smith, 1998). In contrast, the literature on retributive justice is more limited in quantity and is rather scattered according to whether the interest is in legal, psychological, or philosophical issues.

However, it can be argued that retribution, involving different forms of punishment reactions for crimes and other violations of social norms, is a basic part of social life. Indeed, Hogan and Emler (1981) proposed that, when compared with distributive justice, "the process of retribution is older, more primitive, more universal, and socially more significant. The two concepts are related in that they both rest on the norm of reciprocity, but distributive justice is a thin, unstable, and narrowly restricted derivative of retributive justice" (p. 131). Hogan and Emler came to that view on the basis of a number of considerations, namely, that rewards for good behavior are not always forthcoming (virtue is its own reward), whereas punishments for rule violations and bad behavior occur more reliably; that complex, institutionalized mechanisms have been developed for dealing with violations of social prohibitions but not for inequities in the way rewards are distributed; that questions of resource allocation are unlikely to arise when there is an abundance of resources; that communities usually punish those who violate social norms but they do not ordinarily compensate victims; and that people are aware of the social and personal costs that are involved if they behave in a deviant way, and these are assumed to be effective means of social control. Hogan and Emler argue that social control appears to depend more on punitive sanctions than on rewards for good behavior. They view retribution as a social concept that is a cultural universal, though it may take different forms as societies become more complex, formal, and bureaucratized. Retribution is also an important part of everyday life, as people respond to insults, taunts, and humiliations in their informal dealings with others (e.g., Goffman, 1971).

Issues concerned with retributive justice have also been discussed by Miller and Vidmar (1981) and more recently by Tyler et al. (1997). A consideration of retributive justice raises questions about responsibility, blame, social norms and values, and deservingness. As I indicated in the early chapters of this book, these questions have been debated in the philosophical, legal, and social psychological literatures concerned with the violation of social norms and with offenses against the legal order.

Miller and Vidmar (1981) propose that the motivation to punish others for rule violations can be related to concerns about behavior control and retribution. Behavior control relates to the present and to the future, and its basic concern is "with the elimination of some unjust behavior, either ongoing behavior or anticipated future behavior. It is fear of continued acts of injustice that motivates this type of punishment" (p. 146). Retribution is directed toward eliminating a sense of injustice that relates to some action that has already been performed. Hence, its orientation is more toward the past and with redressing wrongs that have been committed. Both kinds of motivation are assumed to be involved in most forms of punishment.

Miller and Vidmar (1981) define punishment as "a negative sanction intentionally applied to someone who is perceived to have violated a law, a rule, a norm, or an expectation" (p. 146). They acknowledge that punishment may serve other social and psychological functions in addition to those concerned with justice considerations, and that it can be applied not only to a single offender but also to a larger social group when "the purpose of the punishing act is general social deterrence, increased in-group cohesion, or the reactor's need for enhanced status or for social consensus regarding the correctness of the rule" (p. 148).

Miller and Vidmar's discussion of the psychology of punishment reactions draws on their distinction between behavior control concerns and retribution concerns. It considers each of these concerns in relation to the general motivations that are involved and also in relation to such variables as the nature of the rule that is violated and the offense, the characteristics of the rule violator, the relationship between the violator and the reactor, and individual differences among those who are reacting to the rule violation and the offender. In my analysis most of the variables that Miller and Vidmar mention can be incorporated into the deservingness model, assuming that a rule violation involves a negatively valued action that leads to a negatively valued outcome (a penalty or punishment).

The recent discussion of retributive justice by Tyler et al. (1997) also considers the nature of retribution, its underlying motivation, and its functions in society. These authors refer to both instrumental concerns at the personal level (e.g., punishing offenders may help prevent oneself from becoming a victim of crime) and more general relational concerns (e.g., protecting the group and maintaining social bonds). They also draw attention to the nature of the rule-breaking offense in relation to who is the victim (Is the victim an individual or a group?), what is lost (material resources or symbolic and status resources?), and the implications of these distinctions for the types of rules that can be broken and the ways in which retribution may occur following rule violation. Tyler et al. also consider criteria that may be used to evaluate justice or injustice when an offense has been committed, focusing on moral judgments of responsibility and blameworthiness and theoretical statements that refer to these variables, especially Heider's levels of responsibility (Heider, 1958), Shaver's (1985) conceptual model of blame attribution, and the model presented by Shultz, Schleifer, and Altman (1981) involving perceived responsibility as a mediator of how severely a rule-violator should be punished.

These different discussions are all relevant to the model that I will present in the next section. They consider the motivations for retributive justice and the variables that affect the way people react to violations of both formal and informal rules and social norms.

MODELING REACTIONS TO PENALTIES FOR OFFENSES

The model that I describe in this section was developed to account for how people react to penalties that are imposed when a person commits an offense (Feather, 1996c, 1998b). The model is presented in

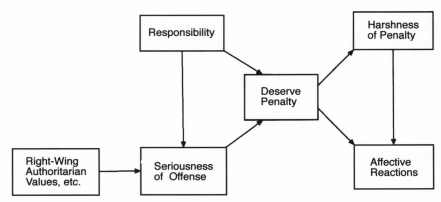

Figure 6.1. Social-cognitive process model for reactions to penalties. (*Source*: Feather [1996c]. Copyright © 1996 by the American Psychological Association. Reproduced with permission.)

Figure 6.1. It is a social-cognitive process model that assumes a structure of associations between variables and that also assumes some sequential ordering in the way in which events flow. Thus, individual differences in needs and values and the offender's perceived responsibility for the offense are both assumed to affect the degree to which the offense is perceived as serious; the offender's perceived responsibility for the offense and its perceived seriousness are both assumed to affect the degree to which the penalty is seen to be deserved; judgments of deservingness are assumed to affect reported affective reactions relating to the penalty and the offender and also to affect the degree to which the penalty is evaluated in terms of its harshness or leniency; and reported affective reactions are also assumed to be related to the perceived harshness/leniency of the penalty.

The variables that are contained in Figure 6.1 have been discussed in detail in previous chapters. Here I briefly review their status.

Perceived Responsibility

In Chapter 2 I noted that the concept of perceived responsibility has been extensively discussed in the legal, philosophical, and psychological literatures. I drew attention to the importance of personal causation and intentionality as important sources of evidence that permit a judgment of responsibility and also to role requirements and obligations that likewise affect the degree to which a person is seen to be responsible for an action or an outcome. I also referred to discussions of responsibility that distinguished different levels of responsibility (e.g., Hamilton & Sanders, 1992; Schlenker et al., 1994) and that linked judgments of responsibility to personal causation and to attributional processes (e.g., Shaver, 1985; Weiner, 1995). I also noted that perceived responsibility can be conceptualized as involving a relation of ownership and that, in Heider's (1958) terms, it can be represented by a positive unit relation, a form of representation that I used in previous models concerned with communication effects and causal attribution (Feather, 1964, 1967b, 1971a) and in the deservingness model that I presented in Chapter 4.

Figure 6.1 includes a link between perceived responsibility and the perceived seriousness of an offense. There is evidence to show that in situations where success or failure can be attributed to personal causation (e.g., effort), success is seen as more attractive (or positively valent) and failure is seen as more aversive (or negatively valent) when compared with situations where there is less emphasis on the self and personal causation (e.g., Feather, 1959a, 1959b, 1967c). A lot of the early research was framed within the context of a theory of achievement motivation that used concepts of motive, expectancy, and incentive value (Atkinson & Feather, 1966; Feather,1982b). In this context I assumed that the positive valence (or attractiveness) of success and the negative valence (or aversiveness) of failure would both be positively related to internal control of responsibility for an outcome, with success being perceived as more attractive and failure as more aversive the more a person is seen as responsible for the action and its outcome (Feather, 1982a, pp. 78–80).

We can extend this idea to judgments of the seriousness of an offense. An offense is a negative event, an event that is aversive (or negatively valent). An offense that can be attributed to accidental causes or to other mitigating circumstances is typically viewed as less serious and attracts less punishment and retaliation than the same offense committed with intention and after due deliberation (e.g., Crick & Dodge, 1994; Ferguson & Rule, 1983; Holtzworth-Munroe, 1992; Weiner, 1995, 1996). Murder is seen as a more serious crime than manslaughter. Thus, a person's perceived responsibility for an offense affects the degree to which an offense is seen to be serious. The greater the person's responsibility the more serious the offense is perceived to be.

Seriousness of an Offense

The negative valence or aversiveness of an offense can be related to a number of variables, one of which (perceived responsibility) I have already discussed. Some offenses are by their very nature more horrific than others (e.g., a cold-blooded murder versus a shoplifting offense). Empirical studies show that there is considerable agreement on how people rate the seriousness of various offenses depending on their nature (von Hirsch, 1986, pp. 78–79; von Hirsch & Jareborg, 1991). Criminal codes take account of the gravity of an offense when assessing penalties for guilt. Robinson and Darley (1995, pp. 157–160) propose that grading an offense for its seriousness depends on the seriousness of the harm caused by the offense, the offender's culpability level or blameworthiness, and on "the actual presence of the harm or evil of the offense and the strength of the person's causal connection with it" (p. 159). The negative quality of the offense, therefore, also influences its perceived seriousness, consistent with Lewin's (1936) assumption that one variable that determines positive or negative valence is the qualitative nature of the region (e.g., a wide, fast-flowing river has higher negative valence than a narrow, placid stream for a person who wants to cross it).

An offense may also acquire negative valence and be perceived as serious because it is a violation of social norms and upsets the social order, posing a threat both to individuals and to the wider community. The offense may also be seen to be linked with further negative consequences for those who are affected by it, leading to a set of future events that involve costs to the individual or the group. This latter possibility is consistent with the instrumentality theory of valence (e.g., Mitchell, 1982; Vroom, 1964). Recall also the more extensive discussion of valences that I presented in Chapter 3, where I referred to other theoretical contributions to the analysis of the determinants of valences (e.g., Brendl & Higgins, 1996; Maio & Olson, in press a, in press b).

More relevant, however, to the model presented in Figure 6.1 are influences on valences that involve a person's needs and values. As I proposed in Chapter 3, one can assume that a person's needs and values function to induce valences on objects and events (Feather, 1990a, 1992b, 1995b). They affect the way a person construes or defines a situation in terms of which objects, activities, or potential outcomes are seen as attractive and which are seen as aversive. In the case of an offense, a person's needs and values that are activated in a situation would affect how serious an offense is seen to be. People who place a high value on security, for example, may judge a burglary or break-in offense that results in theft and property damage to be more serious when compared with those for whom security as a value is less important. People who respect conformity may see violations of the law as more serious when compared with those who place a lesser value on conformity.

Some of these values (e.g., conformity, tradition, security) may cluster together in regard to particular types of personality (e.g., right-wing authoritarians). Hence, I have also included right-wing authoritarianism along with values in the link to perceived seriousness of an offense that is presented in Figure 6.1. I will return to a discussion of authoritarianism later in this chapter.

Deserving the Penalty

Figure 6.1 shows that judgments of the degree to which a perpetrator deserves the penalty that is imposed for the offense are linked to judgments of the perpetrator's responsibility for the offense and also to the perceived seriousness of the offense. These variables are part of the deservingness model presented in previous chapters. In the context of rule violations and offenses against the law, we have a situation where a negatively valued action (the offense) is followed by a negatively valued sanction or punishment (the penalty). In this case the person-action-outcome triad in the deservingness model is balanced. The triad is made up of two negative relations that represent negative evaluations of both the offense and the penalty (an outcome that would generally be seen to be aversive), and a unit relation that represents the fact that the penalty follows or is contingent on the offense.

Figure 6.2 presents the four structures that correspond to this type of situation, including relations between person (p) and other (o). As previously, a positive unit relation is represented by a solid bracket and a negative unit relation by a dashed bracket. A positive sentiment or attitudinal relation is represented by a solid line and a negative attitudinal or sentiment relation by a dashed line. Note that only structures b and d in Figure 6.2 are completely balanced. They represent situations where an outgroup member commits an offense and is punished (structure b) and where a disliked other commits an offense and is punished (structure d). We would expect that the penalty would be seen to be deserved for all of the situations represented by the structures in Figure 6.2, but that judgments of deservingness would be weaker when o is a member of p's ingroup (structure a) and when o is liked by p (structure c), than for situations that correspond to the two completely balanced structures in Figure 6.2 (viz., structures b and d). Judgments of deservingness would be higher the more the offense is seen to be serious and the more the offender is seen to be responsible for the offense.

Note that the latter prediction imports new variables, namely, degree of responsibility and degree of seriousness. I indicated in Chapter 4 that the deservingness model does not presently include strength of

INGROUP OTHER

OUTGROUP OTHER

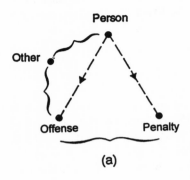

(a)

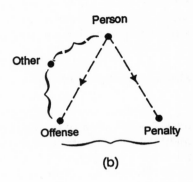

(b)

LIKED OTHER

DISLIKED OTHER

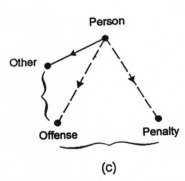

(c)

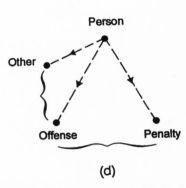

(d)

Figure 6.2. Four structures for situations where a negative action (an offense) is followed by a negative outcome (a penalty).

relations as a variable. It only includes relations that are positive or negative in sign. Here I assume that, in the context of negative actions that lead to negative outcomes, judgments of deservingness will be positively related to how serious the offense is seen to be and also to an offender's degree of responsibility for the offense. These differences in degree imply a form of representation in the structural model that takes account of the strength of relations, with an increase in perceived seriousness represented by an increase in the strength of the sentiment relation that links person to offense (Figure 6.2), and an increase in perceived responsibility by an increase in the strength of the perceived responsibility relation that links other to offense (Figure 6.2). Both increases would be associated with stronger judgments that the offender deserved the penalty.

The model deals only with cases where a person commits an offense and where a penalty is imposed. It would also be possible to formulate predictions that concern cases where a perpetrator commits an offense and is not detected. In these cases the perpetrator escapes punishment and may even derive benefit from the offense.

Note that the social-cognitive process model that I presented in Figure 6.1 is to some extent simplified and incomplete because I have not included relations between person (p) who is judging the offense and other (o) who has committed the offense (i.e., like/dislike relations between p and o, and ingroup/outgroup relations between p and o). These relations are included in Figure 6.2.

Thus, the analysis of deservingness presented in Chapter 4, which assumes a system of relations that tends toward harmony or balance, is also a central aspect of the model presented in Figure 6.1. In this model, judgments of deservingness may also relate to whether the person being judged is liked or disliked by the person making the judgment, or is seen to have a strong or a weak moral character, or is seen in some associative relation with the person (e.g., belonging to the same group) or as a member of an outgroup. These variables would be expected to moderate judgments of deservingness. For example, in the present context, a friend, or a person who is seen to have high moral integrity, or a member of a person's ingroup who has committed an offense and been found guilty, may be perceived to deserve a penalty less than a person who is disliked, or who is seen as not to be trusted, or who belongs to some outgroup.

Reactions to the Penalty and to the Offender

The right-hand side of Figure 6.1 contains variables concerned with how an observer or judge reacts affectively to the penalty and to the offender and how an observer or judge perceives the penalty that is imposed on the offender in terms of its harshness or leniency.

Evidence has already been presented in the previous chapter to show that deservingness is an important variable that influences how people feel about another's success or failure. For example, in the studies that were described, participants reported feeling more pleased about a politician's fall from a high position when the fall was seen to be deserved than when it was seen to be undeserved. They also expressed less sympathy for a student who failed an examination when the failure was judged to be deserved rather than undeserved, and they reported more pleasure when a student was judged to deserve success than when the success was seen to be less deserved. The evidence from these studies consistently demonstrated a link between judgments of deservingness and reported affect. This link is included in Figure 6.1. More specifically, it is hypothesized that the more a penalty is seen to be deserved, the more positive affect will be reported about the penalty that is imposed and the less sympathy will be reported for the offender.

Judgments of deservingness would also be expected to affect how a person responds to an imposed penalty in terms of its harshness or leniency. One might expect that strong judgments that a penalty is deserved will tend to be associated with judgments that the penalty is not too harsh. Justice would be seen to be done when harsher penalties are imposed on perpetrators of offenses whose deservingness is beyond doubt.

The social-cognitive process model in Figure 6.1 also includes a link between the perceived harshness-leniency of the penalty and reported affective reactions. More specifically, it is hypothesized that people will tend to report less positive affect about the penalty and more sympathy for the offender the more the penalty is seen to be too harsh rather than about right or too lenient. We can assume that people develop internalized standards about the appropriate levels of punishment for an offense that relate to their understanding of the law, the circumstances that surround the offense, and their own personality characteristics (Robinson & Darley, 1995). So, how they respond to a penalty would also reflect in part their beliefs about whether the penalty is an appropriate one.

By way of summary, the social-cognitive process model presented in Figure 6.1 was designed to capture a sequence of events that is assumed to occur when a person processes complex information about an offender and his or her crime or misdemeanor. When an offense has been committed, a person is assumed to form some judgment about its seriousness (negative valence) that depends in part on the person's own value system and on the offender's perceived responsibility for the offense. These two variables (seriousness and responsibility), along with relations involving person (p) and other (o) that are not represented in Figure 6.1, are assumed in turn to influence judgments about the degree to which the offender deserves the penalty, in accordance with the structural model of deservingness presented in Chapter 4. Deservingness is then assumed to be a central variable that affects judgments about harshness or leniency of the penalty, positive affect about the penalty, and sympathy for the offender. Affective reactions are also assumed to depend on how harsh or lenient the penalty is assumed to be.

It should be evident that this model incorporates a mixture of variables that spans both cognitive judgments and affective reactions. The model also takes account of individual differences in value priorities, interpersonal relations, and social identity, via their respective effects on component relations within the structural model of deservingness. It is therefore an integrative model that brings together cognitive, affective, and social psychological variables within the domain of retributive justice.

In the next sections I turn to studies that were designed to test aspects of this social-cognitive process model.

RESEARCH STUDIES

Because the two studies to be described in this chapter include a measure of right-wing authoritarianism, I turn first to a brief discussion of why this variable was included and how it is relevant to the social-cognitive process model.

Right-Wing Authoritarianism

The classic study of authoritarianism was reported nearly 50 years ago in *The Authoritarian Personality* (Adorno, Frenkel-Brunswik, Levinson, & Sanford, 1950). The approach taken in this comprehensive study used ideas from personality theory that were derived from psychodynamic or psychoanalytic theory and that emphasized childhood experience where there was harsh parental discipline, adherence to social codes, defenses against anxiety, and displacement of aggression.

In a later discussion of this approach Sanford (1973) referred to three major aspects of authoritarianism, namely, conventionalism, authoritarian submission, and authoritarian aggression. Conventionalism was conceived in psychodynamic terms as "a need to adhere strictly to conventional middle-class values, a disposition to feel anxious at the sight of or the thought of any violation of these values" (Sanford, 1973, p. 144). Authoritarian submission was conceived of "not as a balanced, realistic respect for valid authority but as an exaggerated, emotional need to submit" (Sanford, 1973, p. 144). Authoritarian aggression was assumed to involve displacement of hostility onto outgroups and was assumed to be especially manifested in ethnocentrism and prejudice.

The research program conducted by Adorno et al. (1950) used a variety of procedures that included questionnaires, projective tests, and in-depth interviews. The best-known instrument was the Fascism (F) Scale, which was designed to measure authoritarianism.

This seminal study of authoritarianism led to a spate of investigations and discussions that are too numerous to summarize here. The research has been reviewed and updated by a number of authors (e.g., Altemeyer, 1981, 1988, 1996; Brown, 1965; Christie, 1991, 1993; Eckhardt, 1991; Kirscht & Dillehay, 1967; Sanford, 1973; Stone, Lederer, & Christie, 1993).

In recent years there has been renewed interest in authoritarianism, stimulated in part by the publication of the results of Altemeyer's (1981, 1988, 1996) research program. Altemeyer (1981) also conceived of right-wing authoritarianism as a syndrome or pattern of personality traits that involved authoritarian submission, authoritarian aggression, and conventionalism. He defined authoritarian submission as "a high degree of submission to the authorities who are perceived to be established and legitimate in the society in which one lives" (p. 2), authoritarian aggression as "a general aggressiveness, directed against various persons, that is perceived to be sanctioned by established authorities" (p. 2), and conventionalism as "a high degree of adherence to the social conventions that are perceived to be endorsed by society and its established authorities" (p. 2). Thus, the right-wing authoritarian was viewed as more likely to submit to legitimate authority, more likely to display anger and to be punitive when norms or rules were violated, and more likely to follow conventional values when compared with the low authoritarian.

Altemeyer related authoritarianism to social learning rather than to personality dynamics based on psychoanalytic theory. Note that Adorno et al. (1950) included other features in their description of the authoritarian personality. For example, the high authoritarian was described as more likely to be intolerant of ambiguity when compared with the low authoritarian, wanting a more black-and-white view of the world. So Altemeyer's focus on the three traits of submission, aggression, and conventionality is a more restricted view of what authoritarianism involves when compared with the earlier Adorno et al. analysis.

An important contribution made by Altemeyer was his development of the Right-Wing Authoritarianism Scale (RWA Scale). The RWA Scale has good psychometric properties and Christie (1991) described it as currently the best measure of personal authoritarianism available. The items in the RWA Scale were written to reflect the pattern of the three personality traits that were conceived by Altemeyer to define right-wing authoritarianism. These items have undergone frequent revision in order to reflect changes in social attitudes and also in an effort to improve their test characteristics.

I used the RWA Scale in two of the studies that I will subsequently describe (see also Feather, 1993a). Whether one adopts a psychodynamic or a social learning approach, it is reasonable to assume that authoritarianism will be linked to the values that people hold. People who are authoritarian in outlook might be expected to place relatively high importance on values concerned with conformity, tradition, and security. They might also be expected to de-emphasize other values that connote a more liberal, open-minded, and hedonistic view of the world when compared with people who are low on authoritarianism.

There is already evidence to support this assumption from studies that have used the Rokeach (1973) Value Survey and the more extensive Schwartz (1992) Value Survey (e.g., Feather, 1971a, 1979, 1984; Rim, 1970; Rohan & Zanna, 1996). For example, I found that people who scored higher on a measure of conservatism (Wilson & Patterson, 1968) assigned more importance to values from the Rokeach Value Survey that were concerned with conformity and obedience to authority, and less importance to hedonistic, universalistic, self-directed and open-minded types of values (Feather, 1979, 1984). Conservatism is a variable that overlaps with right-wing authoritarianism in its features, though Altemeyer (1988) and Eckhardt (1991) draw some distinctions between the two variables.

Recently, Rohan and Zanna (1996) conducted a study of value transmission in families in which they administered both the Schwartz Value Survey (Schwartz, 1992) and Altemeyer's measure of right-wing authoritarianism (Altemeyer & Hunsberger, 1992) to male college students and their parents. They found that high authoritarians when compared with low authoritarians were significantly more likely to emphasize values concerned with *conformity, tradition, security, power*, and *benevolence* and significantly less likely to endorse values belonging to the *self-direction, stimulation*, and *universalism* value types. They also found that, consistent with Schwartz's (1992) assumption about the circular structure of value types (see Chapter 3), the correlations of the value types with right-wing authoritarianism tended to decrease monotonically as one moved round the circular structure of value types in both directions from the value with the highest correlation with authoritarianism (namely, *conformity*).

As I noted above, Altemeyer's conceptual analysis of authoritarianism emphasized conformity to legitimate authority and conventionalism as key aspects of the syndrome. The more psychodynamic interpretations of authoritarianism have also referred to the role of threat and the perception of a dangerous world as variables that are related to the formation of authoritarian beliefs and attitudes (e.g., Doty, Peterson, & Winter, 1991; Peterson, Doty, & Winter, 1993). Hence, there are also grounds for expecting right-wing authoritarians to be more security-conscious.

How does this value analysis of right-wing authoritarianism relate to the model presented in Figure 6.1? We can assume that a crime or offense would involve the violation of legitimate authority in the form of the rule of law. This violation may also be perceived to present a threat to personal security and the social order. It follows, on the basis of a motivational analysis that, when activated, values that relate to authoritarianism, either positively or negatively, will influence the way the offense is judged in terms of its seriousness. These values will influence the degree to which the offense is seen to have negative valence. Thus, high authoritarians, who may be assumed to place high importance on values concerned with conformity, tradition, and security, will be more likely than low authoritarians to view as serious offenses those that violate legitimate social norms sanctioned by authority. They would perceive these offenses to be more aversive and serious when compared with low authoritarians because of the way high authoritarian's values are structured. Depending on context, the high authoritarians may also take a different view of the offense because they place less emphasis on self-direction, stimulation, and universalism values when compared with low authoritarians.

Authoritarianism may also have other effects in addition to those that relate to the effects of activated values on the perceived seriousness of the offense. The tendency for authoritarians to be more punitive in their reactions has been documented in a number of studies (e.g., Altemeyer, 1981, 1988, 1996; Carroll et al., 1987; Peterson et al., 1993; Skitka & Tetlock, 1993). Thus, we would expect that authoritarians may not only be more likely to perceive crimes and misdemeanors as more serious when legitimate rules and laws are violated, they may also be more punitive toward offenders who have transgressed the law in the penalties that they believe to be appropriate.

The extensive review of research on authoritarianism by Christie (1993) also confirmed the positive correlation between authoritarianism and punishment across a number of studies and also indicated that the correlation may be moderated by such variables as the severity or seriousness of the crime, the status of the offender, and whether there were mitigating circumstances (e.g., Zwillenberg, 1983). Christie (1993) concludes that "authoritarians are not only more punitive in assigning sentences to target persons who are 'guilty' of committing crimes varying from trivial to extremely serious but are consistent in doing so across the range of severity of crimes" (p. 115). Christie also concludes that low authoritarians "give harsher penalties to high than low status individuals whereas high authoritarians show the opposite pattern especially strongly when the criminal is a low-status person committing a high-severity crime when there are mitigating circumstances" (p. 115). Moreover, "high scorers give relatively harsher sentences the more severe the crime as compared with low scorers" (p. 116).

I will return to the question of the status of the offender and how it moderates the effects of right-wing authoritarianism in a later section.

The Effects of Context

The context in which the offense occurs and the nature of the offense itself may also activate values in addition to those that relate to conformity, tradition, and security. For example, the offense may be set within the context of a sociopolitical protest where the offender is protesting against some event, such as nuclear testing or logging in a native forest, that violates universalistic values that are of concern to the welfare of society as a whole. Or the offense may be one against laws that restrict personal freedom and the right to express views that challenge a political party that controls a nation. People would differ in the values that are activated within these contexts and, accordingly, their judgments of the seriousness of the offense would differ. Thus, a person with strong universalistic values may see the offense committed by a "green" protester who is trying to protect native forests as less serious than a person whose universalistic values are weaker. A person who is strong on both self-direction and universalistic values may see an offense against a restrictive political regime as less serious than a person who puts less emphasis on freedom of thought and action and on the welfare of society.

Thus, the different contexts of an offense may elicit different values and patterns of values that affect the way an offense is perceived in terms of its seriousness.

Reactions to Offenses Committed by a Public Citizen

In this section I will describe two studies in which participants were presented with hypothetical scenarios, in each of which a member of the public was found guilty of violating a law and was assigned a penalty by the courts. The offenses were selected so as to vary in their severity (domestic violence, plagiarism, shoplifting, resisting a police order). Both studies included Altemeyer's measure of right-wing authoritarianism as a variable. The second study also included the Schwartz Value Survey (Schwartz, 1992). The studies were designed to test the pattern of linkages proposed in the social-cognitive process model presented in Figure 6.1.

Study 1. The first study involved 220 participants from the general population of metropolitan Adelaide, South Australia. Full details about the study and the procedures that were used are provided in Feather (1996c). Participants completed a questionnaire that contained three scenarios (domestic violence, plagiarism, shoplifting), each of which varied depending on whether the offender was a man or a woman and whether there were circumstances that might mitigate personal responsibility for the offense.

The domestic violence scenario described either a young married man (John) or a young married woman (Joan) who had been subject to verbal abuse from his wife (or her husband) over a number of years and who, under stress (or after some deliberation), threw a kitchen knife at his (or her) spouse, inflicting a serious wound. The offender was jailed for two years for the offense.

The plagiarism scenario described either a male student (Jim) or a female student (Anne) who got behind in writing an essay for a university course topic because of sickness (or because of lack of planning). Jim (or Anne) borrowed a friend's notes and plagiarized them by including identical material in his (her) essay. The plagiarism was detected and the student was awarded no mark for the essay.

The shoplifting scenario described either a male teenager (Mike) or a female teenager (Claire) who was pressured by friends to take expensive clothing from a supermarket without paying (or who stole the goods intentionally). The teenager was caught and fined $100 for shoplifting.

After reading each scenario participants used 7-point scales to rate the extent to which they believed the stimulus person was responsible for the offense and the extent to which they believed the stimulus person deserved the penalty. They also used 7-point scales to rate how much they disapproved of the offense and how serious they judged the offense to be. The latter two ratings were combined for each participant so as to provide a composite measure of the seriousness of the offense. Participants also checked whether they believed the penalty was either too lenient or soft (scored 1), about right (2), or too harsh or extreme (3).

In order to measure affective reactions, participants rated how they felt about the fact that the stimulus person received the penalty for the offense. They used 7-point scales to rate how angry, satisfied, disappointed, and pleased they felt about the penalty. A composite measure of positive affect about the penalty was derived via factor analyses (see Feather, 1996c for details).

Participants also answered two items that were more directed toward how they felt about the stimulus person rather than about the penalty that he or she received. They used 7-point scales to rate how sympathetic and concerned they felt for the stimulus person. These two ratings were combined for each participant to provide a measure of sympathy for the offender.

In addition, participants completed the 1982, 30-item version of the Right-Wing Authoritarianism Scale (Altemeyer, 1988, pp. 22–23).

The main interest here is in the relations between these variables. Table 6.1 presents their intercorrelations. The correlations were between composite scores that were obtained for each participant by computing the means for each variable for each participant across the three offenses. The statistically significant correlations in Table 6.1 show that the more responsible a stimulus person was seen to be for an offense, the more likely participants were to judge the offense as serious, the more the penalty was seen to be deserved, the less harsh the penalty was seen to be, the more positive affect about the penalty was reported by participants, and the less likely participants were to report sympathy for the offender.

Table 6.1. Intercorrelations between Variables Using Composite Scores

Variable	1	2	3	4	5	6	7
1. Right-wing authoritarianism	—	.05	.43***	.23***	−.27***	.21**	−.07
2. Responsibility for offense		—	.27***	.66***	−.44***	.46***	−.33***
3. Seriousness of offense			—	.45***	−.33***	.30***	−.13*
4. Deserve penalty				—	−.61***	.61***	−.44***
5. Harshness of penalty					—	−.49***	.51***
6. Positive affect about penalty						—	−.50***
7. Sympathy for offender							—

Note: N = 220, except for minor missing cases.
*p < .05, two-tailed   **p < .01, two-tailed   ***p < .001, two-tailed
Source: Feather (1996c). Copyright © 1996 by the American Psychological Association. Reprinted with permission.

The same pattern of statistically significant results was obtained for the seriousness variable. The more serious the offense was perceived to be, the more the offender was seen to deserve the penalty, the more likely participants were to judge the offense as too lenient or not harsh enough, the more participants reported positive affect about the penalty, and the less they reported sympathy for the offender.

Table 6.1 also shows that there was a statistically positive correlation between the degree to which the penalty was seen to be deserved and reported positive affect about the penalty. Thus, higher ratings of deservingness were associated with higher ratings of positive affect. There were also statistically significant negative correlations between deservingness and both the perceived harshness of the penalty and sympathy for the offender. Thus, the more a penalty was seen to be deserved, the more likely participants were to judge the penalty as too lenient or not harsh enough, and the less sympathy they reported for the offender.

There was also a statistically significant negative correlation between the perceived harshness of a penalty and reported positive affect about the penalty, and a statistically significant positive correlation between perceived harshness and sympathy for the offender. Thus, participants who judged the penalty to be too harsh tended to report less positive affect about the penalty and more sympathy for the offender. As would be expected, positive affect about the penalty and sympathy for the offender were negatively correlated.

How did right-wing authoritarianism relate to the judgments that participants made? Table 6.1 shows that there was a statistically significant positive correlation between authoritarianism and the perceived seriousness of an offense and a significant negative correlation between authoritarianism and the perceived harshness of the penalty. Thus, high authoritarians were more likely to view an offense as serious when compared with low authoritarians, and they also tended to perceive the penalty as too lenient or not harsh enough.

The degree to which the stimulus person was seen to deserve the penalty and the extent to which participants reported positive affect about the penalty were both positively and significantly related to right-wing authoritarianism. The correlation between authoritarianism and sympathy for the offender was nonsignificant.

The correlations reported in Table 6.1 are consistent with the set of relations proposed in the social-cognitive process model that was presented in Figure 6.1. The predicted associations between the various components of the model were obtained (namely, authoritarianism with perceived seriousness, responsibility with perceived seriousness, responsibility and perceived seriousness with deservingness, deservingness with reported affect, deservingness with perceived harshness, and perceived harshness with reported affect).

In order to obtain information about possible mediating variables and the structure of causal paths or relations that might underlie the pattern of correlations, I also conducted a path analysis of the correlations in Table 6.1. These analyses used hierarchical multiple regression analysis with listwise deletion of missing cases to generate the path coefficients. The path coefficients were obtained by regressing each variable on those variables that directly impinged on it in the path diagram presented in Figure 6.3. The analysis controlled for gender and age of participant, stimulus person gender, and mitigation at each step of the analysis. The path coefficients (standardized betas) that were obtained from this analysis are presented in Figure 6.3.

The statistically significant path coefficients in Figure 6.3 show that both perceived responsibility and authoritarianism predicted in the positive direction to the perceived seriousness of the offense, a result that is consistent with the social-cognitive process model. None of the other paths involving right-wing authoritarianism as a predictor were

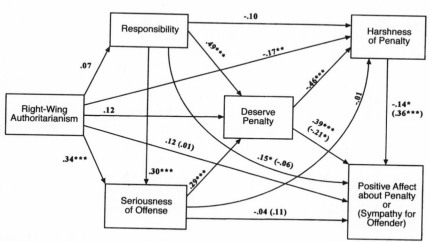

Figure 6.3. Path diagram linking variables for the composite of the three scenarios. Path coefficients for paths leading to reported sympathy are in parentheses. Statistically significant path coefficients (standardized betas) are indicated as follows: $*p < .05$, $**p < .01$, $***p < .001$. (*Source*: Feather [1996c]. Copyright © 1996 by the American Psychological Association. Reprinted with permission.)

statistically significant, except for the negative path linking authoritarianism to the perceived harshness of the penalty.

Also as assumed in the social-cognitive process model, both perceived responsibility and the perceived seriousness of the offense predicted in the positive direction to the degree to which the penalty was seen to be deserved. Both path coefficients were statistically significant. There was also a statistically significant positive path linking perceived responsibility to positive affect about the penalty.

The degree to which the offender was seen to deserve the penalty predicted in the negative direction to the degree to which the penalty was seen to be too harsh. As also assumed in the social-cognitive process model, deservingness predicted negatively to sympathy for the offender and positively to positive affect about the penalty. The respective path coefficients were statistically significant.

Finally, Figure 6.3 shows that the degree to which the penalty for an offense was judged to be too harsh predicted in the negative direction to positive affect about the penalty and in the positive direction to sympathy for the offender. These path coefficients were also statistically significant.

Taken together these results provide strong support for the pattern of linkages that I assumed would occur. The results of the path analysis are particularly compelling because the analysis controlled for the effects of other variables at each step of the analysis. It is clear that, in the context of the offenses that were investigated, right-wing authoritarianism mainly exerted its effects by means of the degree to which an offense was seen to be serious. Judgments of seriousness were also influenced by the offender's perceived responsibility for the offense. Both perceived seriousness and perceived responsibility affected the degree to which the penalty for the offense was seen to be deserved. Deservingness played a key role by affecting how participants reacted both to the penalty and to the offender. Reported affected reactions were also associated with judgments about the harshness of the penalty.

Study 2. The second study was basically a replication of the study I have just described except that it included the Schwartz Value Survey (Schwartz, 1992) in addition to the RWA Scale. It was therefore possible to check on the assumption that right-wing authoritarianism is associated with a set of values in which conformity, security, and tradition are emphasized and other values of a more liberal, open-minded, and hedonistic nature are downgraded. It was also possible to test the basic assumption that differences between high and low authoritarians in the way they judge the seriousness of an offense are related to their different value priorities.

The second study also involved a new scenario, one that was designed to target universalism values (Schwartz, 1992) and to elicit a wide range of reactions because of its controversial nature. This new scenario described a stimulus person (Jim) who was a member of a "green" group that promoted environmental conservation and protection. Jim joined with others in a protest demonstration against forestry employees who were cutting down trees for woodchipping in an old, established native forest. The forestry employers called in the police to stop the protest. Jim was one of the group who was arrested for refusing to obey a police order to stop obstructing the forestry workers as they cut down the trees. Jim was fined $200.

There were 181 participants in this study. They were again sampled from the general population of Adelaide, South Australia. After reading the scenario, they completed the measures of responsibility, deservingness, seriousness of the offense, harshness of penalty, positive affect about the penalty, and sympathy for the offender that have already been described in relation to Study 1.

Participants also completed the Schwartz Value Survey (Schwartz, 1992). Following Schwartz, the values were combined into ten different value types, namely, power, achievement, hedonism, stimulation, self-direction, universalism, benevolence, tradition, conformity, and security (see Feather, 1996c, for details). These value types have been described in Chapter 3 (see Table 3.2). Each participant's mean importance rating was obtained for each of these value types. Participants also completed the 1990, 30-item version of the RWA Scale (Altemeyer & Hunsberger, 1992). I do not present here all of the results of this study (see Feather, 1996c, for details) but only those findings that convey information about values. Table 6.2 presents mean scores and standard deviations for the ten value types as well as their correlations with right-wing authoritarianism.

Similar to the findings reported by Rohan and Zanna (1996), Table 6.2 shows that there were statistically significant positive correlations between authoritarianism and the rated importance for self of tradition, conformity, and security values, and statistically negative correlations between authoritarianism and scores for the hedonism, stimulation, self-direction, and universalism value types.

Table 6.3 presents the correlations between right-wing authoritarianism, the importance ratings for each of the value types, and the other variables that were included in the study. Here we can note the relatively

Table 6.2.   Means, Standard Deviations, and
Correlations between Value Types and Right-Wing
Authoritarianism, with Mean Value Held Constant

Value type	M	SD	Correlation with authoritarianism
Power	2.11	1.23	.02
Achievement	4.32	1.04	−.05
Hedonism	4.42	1.49	−.37***
Stimulation	3.65	1.46	−.36***
Self-direction	4.74	0.93	−.48***
Universalism	4.67	0.98	−.43***
Benevolence	5.00	0.88	.14
Tradition	2.75	1.27	.53***
Conformity	4.11	1.14	.57***
Security	4.25	1.07	.39***

Note: *N*s for the means varied between 177 and 181 because of missing cases. *N* = 159 for the partial correlations.
***$p < .001$, two-tailed
Source: Feather (1996c). Copyright © 1996 by the American Psychological Association. Reprinted with permission.

strong positive correlation between right-wing authoritarianism and the judged seriousness of the offense committed by the "green" protester; the positive correlations between importance scores for the tradition, conformity, and security value types and the judged seriousness of the offense; and the negative correlations between importance scores for the stimulation, self-direction, and universalism value types and the judged seriousness of the offense. All of these correlations were statistically significant and, together with the correlations reported in Table 6.2, they are consistent with the assumption that right-wing authoritarianism involves a particular syndrome of values and that these values together influence how an offense is judged in terms of its seriousness.

I again investigated relations between the variables by using path analysis. In the analysis I included scores on the universalism value type because I assumed that the woodchipping scenario used in the study would directly implicate these values that concern the welfare of society. Figure 6.4 presents the results of the path analysis.

For the most part the results in Figure 6.4 replicate those that have been presented in Figure 6.3 as far as the pattern of relations predicted by the social-cognitive process model is concerned. The new information in Figure 6.4 relates to paths that involve the universalism value type. Figure 6.4 shows that there were statistically significant negative paths linking scores on the universalism value type, to the perceived responsi-

Table 6.3. Correlations between Right-Wing Authoritarianism, Value Types, and Responses to Woodchipping Scenario, with Mean Value Held Constant

Variable	Responses to woodchipping scenario					
	Responsibility for offense	Seriousness of offense	Deserve penalty	Harshness of penalty	Positive affect	Sympathy for offender
Authoritarianism	.20*	.44***	.17*	−.23**	.34***	−.18*
Value types						
Power	.04	.06	.19*	−.17*	.13	−.17*
Achievement	.16*	.10	.23**	−.14	.21**	−.32***
Hedonism	−.04	−.14	.12	−.04	.04	−.12
Stimulation	.08	−.20**	.17*	−.04	.07	−.13
Self-direction	−.11	−.27***	−.13	.12	−.16*	.08
Universalism	−.26***	−.33***	−.40***	.32***	−.53***	.46***
Benevolence	.07	.10	−.06	.05	.04	.07
Tradition	.22**	.26***	.13	−.10	.23**	−.18*
Conformity	.11	.35***	.12	−.12	.24***	−.09
Security	−.07	.26***	.03	−.22**	.12	.00

Note: $N = 169$ for correlations involving authoritarianism. $N = 170$ for partial correlations.
$*p < .05$, two-tailed $**p < .01$, two-tailed $***p < .001$, two-tailed
Source: Feather (1996c). Copyright © 1996 by the American Psychological Association. Reprinted with permission.

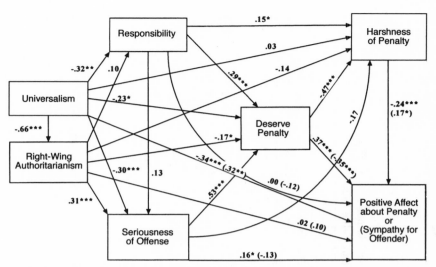

Figure 6.4. Path diagram linking variables for woodchipping scenario. Path coefficients for paths leading to reported sympathy are in parentheses. Statistically significant path coefficients (standardized betas) are indicated as follows: *p < .05, **p < .01, ***p < .001. (*Source*: Feather [1996c]. Copyright © 1996 by the American Psychological Association. Reprinted with permission.)

bility for the offense, to the perceived seriousness of the offense, and to the reported positive affect about the penalty. Universalism values predicted in the positive direction to reported sympathy for the offender.

The fact that the paths between universalism and perceived seriousness and between authoritarianism and perceived seriousness differ in their sign (negative and positive paths, respectively) implies that participants may have been involved in some degree of value conflict, with universalistic values confronting authoritarian values relating to conformity, tradition, and security or, in more specific terms, a concern for the environment conflicting with a concern for law and order.

Finally, the fact that universalistic values also had direct effects on reported affective reactions both to the penalty and to the offender suggests that in some contexts values, once activated, may have a direct role in generating positive or negative affect that is additional to their indirect effects on reported affect via perceived seriousness. There was no evidence that authoritarianism had direct effects on the affective measures for any of the scenarios.

Reactions to Offenses Committed by the Police

The offenses that were the subject of the two studies that I have just described were committed by a member of the public. How might right-wing authoritarians react to an offense that was committed by a person in authority, such as a police officer? There are well-publicized cases where the police have overstepped the bounds of duty and crossed into forbidden territory (e.g., the police harassment of Rodney King in Los Angeles).

There is not an extensive literature concerning the interactive effects of the status characteristics of offenders or rule violators and the personality characteristics of those who judge the offenders. The literature on crimes of obedience and vicarious responsibility where, for example, the perpetrator of an offense such as a war crime may justify the action in terms of following orders from a superior officer or conforming to notional expectations about what is expected (e.g., Kelman & Hamilton, 1989; Miller, Collins, & Brief, 1995), shows that these forms of justification are more likely to occur when the authority structure is well defined and where there is a strict set of role prescriptions that command obedience and conformity.

But how might right-wing authoritarianism interact with status to affect a person's judgments? Earlier in this chapter I noted that Christie (1993) concluded that low authoritarians tend to be more punitive toward high-status individuals than toward low-status individuals, whereas high authoritarians tend to show the reverse pattern, being especially punitive toward a low-status person who commits a serious crime when there are mitigating circumstances. Miller and Vidmar (1981) came to a similar conclusion after reviewing studies that mainly involved the California F Scale (Adorno et al., 1950). They reported evidence that suggested that low authoritarians and people with more liberal beliefs may sometimes want to exact more retribution when compared with high authoritarians, and those with more conservative social beliefs, especially in cases where the crime is especially serious and where the violator is a high-status person from whom one would expect a higher standard of conduct.

Altemeyer (1981, 1988) also reported findings from his research program that relate to the question of the interactive effects of right-wing authoritarianism and status characteristics. In one study he found that high scorers on the RWA Scale were more accepting of illegal acts when they were committed by government officials. Examples of these offenses were illegal wiretaps, illegal letter openings, illegal searches without warrants, and blocking peaceful protests that challenged government policies (Altemeyer, 1981, p. 229). Altemeyer also reported a study in which high authoritarians were less punitive toward Richard Nixon for his part in the Watergate cover-up. They also took longer to suspect and become convinced of Nixon's wrongdoing. Altemeyer (1981, p. 235) also reported findings from a study that showed that high authoritarians were less punitive toward a police chief who attacked a child molester when compared with low authoritarians, and they were much less punitive to the police chief than they were then the perpetrator of the attack was another prisoner. Findings for another case showed that high authoritarians tended to assign lighter sentences to an American air force officer who led unauthorized bombing raids against Vietnamese villages and was subsequently convicted of murder. All of these results are consistent with Altemeyer's (1981, 1988, 1996) discussion of right-wing authoritarianism as involving a strong respect for legitimate authority as well as an inclination to favor discipline and punishment and conformity to conventional values.

Note that these studies were concerned with the severity of the punishment rather than with the perceived seriousness of the offense. The former variable concerns the amount of retribution to be exacted; the latter variable is concerned with the negative valence or perceived aversiveness of the offense. It is the latter variable that is a component of the social-cognitive process model (Figure 6.1).

The study to be described investigated how right-wing authoritarianism and value priorities may moderate the perceived seriousness of an offense depending on the status characteristics of the perpetrator. I expected that right-wing authoritarians would view an offense more leniently when the offense was committed by a legitimate authority such as a police officer, whereas low authoritarians would judge the offense to be more serious. Authoritarians would be more likely to defer to the police because of their status. The police are seen as enforcers of the law with a legitimate right to discipline the public. This deference to authority would be consistent with the value priorities held by high authoritarians. The way they evaluated the seriousness of an offense would be influenced by their endorsement of conformity, tradition, and security values within their own value systems and by their de-emphasis of other values concerned with openness to change and with more universal, prosocial issues.

Low authoritarians, on the other hand, would be expected to be less likely to take account of the authoritative status of the perpetrator. One would expect them to be more sensitive to the nature of the offense and to the need to defend humane, liberal, and universalism values. Thus, a police offense that involved excessive violence against a group who was defending values concerned with the welfare of all would tend to be perceived as more serious by low authoritarians than by high authoritarians. Low authoritarians would be less influenced by the status of the police and more influenced by the fact that the police were violating deeply held values that were to the greater good of society as a whole. As indicated previously, the results of Study 2 that were presented in the previous section showed that low authoritarians tended to assign higher importance to universalism values concerned with human welfare (Table 6.3).

A citizen who breaks the law, however, would not be protected by the shield of legitimate authority that is afforded to the police by virtue of their role as enforcers of the law. An offense committed by a member of the public would be seen as violating social norms that are sanctioned by the legal system. Under these conditions one would expect that high authoritarians would be more disposed to uphold the law and to judge the offense as more serious when compared with low authoritarians, given the fact that, as we have seen, they assign more importance to conformity, tradition, and security values. In contrast, low authoritarians may be more protective toward the citizen who commits an offense, especially if the situation is one in which the offender is defending universalism values. The results of the two studies that were reported in the previous section, where the perpetrators of the offenses were members of the public, supported this analysis.

In summary, I expected that relations between right-wing authoritarianism and the perceived seriousness of the offense would be moderated by the degree to which the offender is seen to have legitimate authority. In the study to be described I predicted that (a) the perceived seriousness of an offense committed by the police will be *negatively* related to right-wing authoritarianism; and that (b) the perceived seriousness of an offense committed by a member of the public of unspecified status will be positively related to right-wing authoritarianism.

The study also allowed a further test of the social-cognitive process model. In addition, it enabled a comparison between the predictive power of this model with Weiner's (1995, 1996) analysis of social motivation. Recall that, in his analysis, judgments of responsibility have prime status as a determinant of reported anger, sympathy, and help-giving relating to a person who experiences a negative outcome. The social-cognitive process model incorporates perceived responsibility as an important variable, but it places it further back in the chain of events and assumes that judged deservingness is a more proximal influence on an observer's reactions to an offense.

Details of the procedures used in the study can be found in the published report (Feather, 1998b). There were 326 participants who were sampled from the general population of Adelaide, South Australia. They completed a questionnaire that contained either a scenario that described police action against a member of a "green" group protesting against destruction of trees in an old, established native forest (the *green protest scenario*) or a scenario in which detectives chased a car driven by juveniles (the *car chase scenario*).

In each case the police committed an offense. In the green protest scenario, Jim (a protester) was knocked to the ground by a police officer and had to be taken to the hospital for treatment of his injuries. Subsequently the case was heard in court and the police officer was required to pay $500 to Jim in damages. In the car chase scenario the detectives drove their car fast under unsafe conditions in pursuit of the juveniles. They lost control of their car, crashed into the juveniles' car, and injured them. The juveniles were taken to the hospital and were subsequently discharged. The detectives were charged with dangerous driving that caused injury to other persons. The case was heard by a tribunal and the detectives were reprimanded and demoted, losing salary and status in the organization.

In a subsequent development in the green protest scenario, Jim (the protester) was charged with refusing to obey a police order to stop obstructing the forestry workers as they cut down the trees in the old, established native forest. The charge was heard in court and Jim was fined $200. The subsequent development in the car chase scenario was that the juveniles were arrested for refusing to obey a police order. The charge was heard in court and the juveniles were put on probation and required to do 100 hours of community service.

The scenarios also varied mitigating circumstances for the authority figures (police officers, detectives). The mitigation versions of the scenarios indicated that the authorities were under orders from their superiors to stop the green protesters (in the green protest scenario) or ordered to apprehend the juveniles (in the car chase scenario). In the low mitigation scenarios no information about orders from superiors was provided.

After reading the first part of the scenario that related to the offense committed by either the police officer or the detectives, participants used 7-point rating scales to rate the high status offender on the dependent variables that have been described in the previous section (deservingness, responsibility, harshness, positive affect, sympathy). They then read the subsequent part of the scenario that described the offense committed by either the green protester or the juveniles and they used the same 7-point rating scales to rate the member of the public on the same set of dependent variables. Participants also completed the Schwartz Value Survey (Schwartz, 1992) and the Right-Wing Authoritarianism Scale (Altemeyer & Hunsberger, 1992).

The detailed results of this study are presented elsewhere (Feather, 1998b). Here I present a sample of the main findings. The analysis of the responsibility ratings for the police officer (green protest scenario) and for the detectives (car chase scenario) showed that the detectives involved in the car chase were judged to be less responsible for their offense when compared with the police officer who used too much force to stop the green protester. Participants may have viewed the actions of the detectives in driving at high speed in an attempt to catch the juveniles as more justified and perhaps even to be supported given the circumstances. In addition, the results showed that the police and the detectives were judged to be less responsible for their offense when they were described as following orders than when the scenario provided no information about orders from higher authorities.

The results also supported the different predicted relations between right-wing authoritarianism and the perceived seriousness of the offense, depending on the status of the offender. Table 6.4 presents the relevant correlations for the different experimental conditions. The correlations between right-wing authoritarianism and the perceived seriousness of the offense were positive and statistically significant for both the green protester and the juveniles, consistent with the results that were found in the two studies described in the previous section (Feather, 1996b). In contrast, the correlations between right-wing authoritarianism and perceived seriousness were negative for both the police officer and the detectives but statistically significant only in the case of the police officer. Further tests showed that the differences between the respective positive and negative correlations in each condition (green protest, car chase) were statistically significant (Steiger, 1980). Thus, there was strong evidence to support the prediction that relations between right-wing authoritarianism and the perceived seriousness of the offense would be moderated by the status of the offender. Status associated with the legitimate authority of the police officers and the detectives conferred on these authority figures a degree of protection when the judges were high in authoritarianism. They judged the offense to be less serious when compared with the judgments made by the low authoritarians. No such protection was afforded to the green protester and the juveniles who were members of the public. Their offense was judged to be more serious by high authoritarians when compared with low authoritarians.

Note also that the statistically significant correlations in Table 6.4

Table 6.4. Means, SD, and Correlations between Value Types, Right-Wing Authoritarianism, and Perceived Seriousness of Offense, with Mean Value Held Constant for Correlations Involving Value Types

Variable	M	SD	Right-wing authoritarianism	Seriousness of offense			
				Green protest scenario		Car chase scenario	
				Police officer	Green protester	Detectives	Juveniles
Value type							
Power	2.14	1.35	.16**	-.09	-.02	-.25**	.06
Achievement	4.32	1.15	-.02	-.08	.07	.04	.08
Hedonism	4.55	1.36	-.30***	-.04	-.13	-.11	-.14
Stimulation	3.79	1.39	-.33***	-.04	-.17*	-.06	-.22*
Self-direction	4.66	0.94	-.55***	.16*	-.17*	-.08	-.06
Universalism	4.51	1.05	-.41***	.30***	-.27***	.21*	-.15
Benevolence	4.85	0.99	.03	-.10	.14	.25**	-.01
Tradition	2.71	1.23	.46***	.05	.09	-.07	-.04
Conformity	4.08	1.32	.56***	-.29***	.40***	.08	.38***
Security	4.11	1.12	.44***	-.23**	.40***	-.05	.15
Right-wing authoritarianism	123.30	40.67	—	-.37***	.51***	-.11	.41***

Note: Ns for the partial correlations involving value types with seriousness were 165, 162, 135, and 137 for the police officer, green protester, detectives, and juveniles, respectively, and 280 for value types with right-wing authoritarianism; Ns for the correlations involving authoritarianism with seriousness of offense were 160, 160, 133, and 134 for the police officer, green protester, detectives, and juveniles, respectively.
*p < .05, two-tailed   **p < .01, two-tailed   ***p < .001, two-tailed
Source: Feather (1998b). Copyright © 1998 by the American Psychological Association. Reprinted with permission.

again show that high authoritarians when compared with low authoritarians assigned higher importance to tradition, conformity, and security values and lower importance to hedonism, stimulation, self-direction, and universalism values. These values in turn were related to perceived seriousness, although statistically significant correlations between value types and perceived seriousness were more in evidence for the police officer and the green protester.

The pattern of correlations between the dependent variables for each scenario was similar to that obtained in the previous studies. Here I only present the results of path analyses for the green protest scenario based on the intercorrelations between right-wing authoritarianism and the cognitive-affective judgments. Figures 6.5 and 6.6 present the results of these path analyses that again used hierarchical multiple regression analysis with listwise deletion of missing cases to generate the path coefficients. Each path analysis controlled for the gender and age of each participant at each step. In addition, the path analyses for the police authorities controlled for the orders/no orders experimental manipulation at each step by coding this variable as a dummy variable. In Figures 6.5 and 6.6 the standardized beta coefficients that relate to sympathy for the offender are given in parentheses.

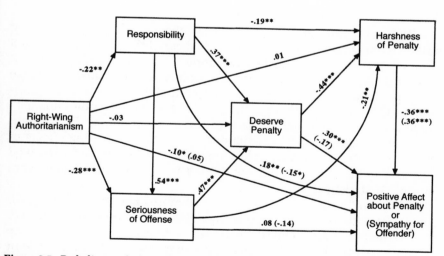

Figure 6.5. Path diagram linking variables for green protest scenario for police officer. Path coefficients for paths leading to reported sympathy are in parentheses. Statistically significant path coefficients (standardized betas) are indicated as follows: *$p < .05$, **$p < .01$, ***$p < .001$. (*Source*: Feather [1998b]. Copyright © 1998 by the American Psychological Association. Reprinted with permission.)

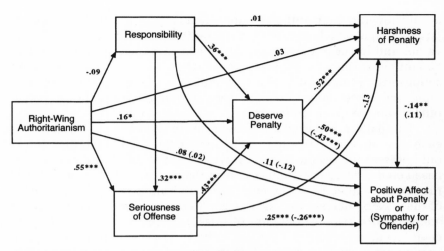

Figure 6.6. Path diagram linking variables for green protest scenario for green protester. Path coefficients for paths leading to reported sympathy are in parentheses. Statistically significant path coefficients (standardized betas) are indicated as follows: *$p < .05$, **$p < .01$, ***$p < .001$. (*Source*: Feather [1998b]. Copyright © 1998 by the American Psychological Association. Reprinted with permission.)

The main findings to note concern the path linking right-wing authoritarianism to the perceived seriousness of the offense. Figure 6.5 shows that there was a statistically significant negative path coefficient linking right-wing authoritarianism to perceived seriousness in the case of the police officer. Figure 6.6 shows a contrasting statistically significant positive path coefficient linking right-wing authoritarianism to perceived seriousness in the case of the green protester. These path coefficients again support predictions about the moderating effects of status on relations between right-wing authoritarianism and perceived seriousness but do so under conditions where other variables were controlled statistically.

The remaining path coefficients in Figures 6.5 and 6.6 are again consistent with the pattern of relations assumed in the social-cognitive process model as specified in Figure 6.1 and described in detail at the beginning of this chapter. As was the case in the two studies described in the preceding section, deservingness again occupied a central position, influencing both reported affect and the perceived harshness of the penalty.

Finally, I also conducted multiple regression analyses in order to determine whether deservingness mediated the effects of perceived responsibility on perceived harshness, reported positive affect, and reported sympathy. These analyses compared the present model with Weiner's (1995, 1996) model and they followed the guidelines proposed by Baron and Kenny (1986) in their discussion of tests of mediation. I do not report the results of these analyses here (see Feather, 1998b). It is sufficient to say that the results were consistent with the assumption that deservingness functions as a mediator between perceived responsibility and the dependent or outcome variables, although the mediation was not always complete. However, the results supported the view that models that include both perceived responsibility and deservingness as variables do provide a more complete analysis of reactions to offenses when compared with models that exclusively rely on perceived responsibility (e.g., Weiner, 1995).

CONCLUDING COMMENTS

The studies that I described in this chapter provided results that were generally consistent with the social-cognitive process model that I presented in Figure 6.1. This model explicitly allows for both person and situation variables in the analysis of reactions to the perpetrators of offenses by incorporating authoritarianism and values into the structure of relations between variables and by also considering the status of the offender as well as other aspects of the context of the offense that may have effects on components of the model (e.g., mitigating circumstances that may influence judgments of responsibility; severity of the penalty or sentence that may affect perceived harshness).

The focus on the effects of authoritarianism and values on perceived seriousness extends the analysis of the effects of values on valences that was presented in Chapter 3 to the specific case where observers judge the perceived aversiveness (or negative valence) of an offense. As indicated previously, differences in authoritarianism have usually been related to differences in the severity of punishment that judges or observers impose on the perpetrator of the offense (e.g., Altemeyer, 1981, 1988, 1996; Christie, 1993; Miller & Vidmar, 1981). Much less attention has been given in the literature to the perceived seriousness of the offense. This variable is an important component of the social-cognitive process model. Its inclusion enables representation of the effects of needs and values in regard to how they affect the perceived aversiveness of an offender's actions. These effects are assumed to depend on how strong the needs and values are for the person and on whether the situation is such as to engage them (Feather, Chapter 4, 1990a).

The results also showed that the degree to which an offender is judged to deserve the penalty that is imposed for an offense is an important mediating variable that is related to both perceived responsibility and to the perceived seriousness of the offense and that in turn affects the cognitive and affective reactions of a judge or observer. Deservingness is a justice-related variable that is often overlooked in social psychological research but one that is of central importance. A detailed hierarchical multiple regression analysis reported in Feather (1998b) showed that its inclusion in the regression equation significantly added to the variance accounted for in the outcome variables.

How might research on the social-cognitive process model be extended? First, we need to apply the model to a wide range of different offenses that vary in their nature, their severity, and in the circumstances under which they were committed (e.g., Robinson & Darley, 1995). The studies that I described in the present chapter sampled different offenses but it is possible to go further. Such an extension may have important theoretical consequences. For example, it may show that there are limits to the high authoritarians' protection of authority figures. High authoritarians may move away from protecting a high-status offender when the offense is especially serious and cannot be justified in terms of fluid role expectations. We require research that investigates the reactions of high and low authoritarians to offenses that exceed the normal expectations associated with the authority figure's role (e.g., an unprovoked killing of an offender; a cold-blooded attack by police on rule-violators) and that also extends the inquiry to severe offenses that are unrelated to the authority figure's role (e.g., a rape committed by a high-status politician). Some offenses that involve a profound disrespect for the law and that also reflect an unbridled pursuit of pleasure and a threat to security and personal safety may be especially condemned by high authoritarians, irrespective of the authority status of the perpetrator. These future investigations may be informed by research that has studied the conditions under which high status acts as a liability or as a shield (e.g., Hollander, 1958, 1964; Rosoff, 1989; Skolnick & Shaw, 1994, 1997; Wiggins, Dill, & Schwartz, 1965). A further issue is whether the effects of authoritarianism can be accounted for mainly in terms of authoritarian values or whether we also need to consider psychodynamic concepts (e.g., ego-defenses) in order to give a fuller account of the dynamics of authoritarianism (e.g., Adorno et al., 1950).

We also need further research that varies other characteristics of the offender in addition to his or her status as a legitimate authority and research that takes account of relations between the judge or observer and the offender. For example, in the study of offenses committed by the police officer and the detectives, it may be assumed that the high authoritarians held values that they would see as congruent with those held by these authority figures (e.g., conformity to the law, security), and that the value fit would not have been as close for the low authoritarians. The results showed that the high authoritarians tended to protect the legitimate authorities under these conditions when they judged the seriousness of their offense. But would they do the same for high-status violators who were perceived to have values that were different or less congruent with their own values? For example, would high authoritarians be more likely than low authoritarians to defer to a prominent politician (e.g., a senator) who resisted the police and enlisted support from the public to stop logging in a native forest? Research by Mitchell and Byrne (1973) showed that the perceived similarity between an offender and a person reacting to an offense affected the assignment of guilt and the recommended punishment. When attitudes were similar, authoritarians were less certain of a defendant's guilt than egalitarians. When attitudes were dissimilar, authoritarians recommended more severe punishment for the defendant than egalitarians.

I take up some of these issues in the next chapter where the focus is on the social identity of the offender (ingroup versus outgroup) in relation to the judge or observer and on the perceived moral character of the offender.

CHAPTER 7

Social Identity, Moral Character, and Retributive Justice

The structural model of deservingness presented in Chapter 4 included relations between person (p) and other (o) as variables that were assumed to moderate p's judgments of deservingness. These relations could be unit relations that represented ingroup or outgroup membership involving p and o or sentiment or attitudinal relations that represented like/dislike relations between p and o.

In this chapter I describe studies from my research program that investigated variables that relate to these person-to-other relations and that were targeted to their effects on how people react to perpetrators of offenses who are found guilty and punished. Would observers or judges be more lenient toward offenders who are perceived as ingroup members and similar to themselves when compared with outgroup offenders who are perceived as dissimilar? Would they also be more lenient toward offenders who are seen to possess high moral character when compared with offenders who are given a low rating as far as their moral character is concerned?

The conceptual analysis incorporates the social identity of the offender and the perceived moral character of the offender into the social-cognitive process model via their moderating effects on deservingness. (Both of these types of variables were discussed in detail in Chapter 4.) Here I will present in summary form evidence of their effects in the particular context of retributive justice.

INGROUP/OUTGROUP EFFECTS
ON REACTIONS TO OFFENSES

The two studies described in this section used hypothetical scenarios. One study concerned a dispute involving domestic violence; the other involved a drug-smuggling offense. Because these studies used scales that were identical to those that were described in the previous chapter, I will not present a detailed description of procedures in each case but will focus instead on the scenarios that were presented to participants and on those results that are relevant to the effects of social identity.

Reactions to a Domestic Dispute

The scenario involving the domestic dispute was presented as one of the three different scenarios used in the first study, which was described in the previous chapter (p. 184). The situation presented in the scenario was one in which either a husband or a wife threw a kitchen knife at his or her spouse following years of verbal abuse, inflicting serious injury. The incident occurred either following stress or after deliberation and thought. The perpetrator of the offense was found guilty and was subsequently sent to jail for two years.

The 220 participants in the study provided their reactions to this situation of domestic violence by rating the perpetrator's responsibility for the offense; the degree to which he or she deserved the penalty; the seriousness of the offense; whether the penalty was too lenient, too harsh, or about right; any positive affect about the penalty; and their sympathy for the offender. The detailed scenarios that were used have been presented in a previously published report (Feather, 1996a).

I expected that participants' reactions to this offense would be more negative when the perpetrator was the husband rather than the wife. The evidence shows that men are physically more violent and aggressive than women (Eagly & Steffen, 1986; Geen, 1998) and that women are more likely to use indirect forms of verbal aggression (Lagerspetz, Bjorkqvist, & Peltonen, 1988). Most domestic violence cases in the courts involve abusive husbands rather than wives, although the woman is often blamed for inciting the abuse or for not leaving the husband (Claes & Rosenthal, 1990; Frieze, 1979; Geen, 1998, pp. 339–341; Kristiansen & Giulietti, 1990; Pierce & Harris, 1993; Summers & Feldman, 1984; Walker, 1984). The results of a study by Pierce and Harris (1994) show that participants judged a husband more severely than a wife when either was the perpetrator of domestic violence. When the husband was the perpetrator, he was seen as more responsible for the offense, more deserving of conviction, more likely to have offended in the past, more likely to be reported to the police, more likely to be left by the victim for good, and less liked than when the wife was the perpetrator of the dispute.

These kinds of differences would reflect widely held social beliefs about the dynamics of domestic violence, beliefs that assign more blame to the male partner in serious domestic disputes that result in physical injury. These beliefs are probably shared by most men and women, and they may also be linked to other beliefs about differences in aggression and power that are associated with a person's gender.

Of more interest in the present study is the possibility that the gender of the judge or observer may moderate the general tendency to react more negatively to the husband who is the perpetrator of physical violence in a domestic situation when compared with the wife who commits the same offense. Would those who react to the offense be influenced by whether the perpetrator of the offense is of their same gender? Would men be relatively more sympathetic in various ways to the husband than women judges or observers and would women be relatively more sympathetic to the wife?

I chose a domestic violence situation because it is one that involves a serious and realistic conflict between two people who differ in gender. Conflict or competition between husband and wife would increase the salience of group membership, just as would also occur, for example, when different sporting teams compete in an important contest or groups or nations are in conflict (e.g., Feather, 1990b; Hogg & Abrams, 1988; Turner et al., 1987). The conflict that occurs in a domestic dispute would be expected to prime thoughts about social identity in the judge or observer, activating social categories that are defined by male or female gender. When gender becomes salient as a category, thoughts about one's own gender and gender role are likely to occur, and there may be some identification with the perpetrator who has the same gender as the judge. The perpetrator is then seen in terms of a social category that is part of the definition of one's social self, and the identification that occurs with the self-related categorization may be accompanied by a degree of in-group bias and outgroup denigration (e.g., Hogg & Abrams, 1988; Oakes, Haslam, & Turner, 1994; Tajfel & Turner, 1986; Turner et al., 1987). Thus, it was expected that, in the present context, there may be evidence of favorability toward a perpetrator of domestic violence when he or she was the same gender as the person who is judging the offense, as well as some evidence of denigration of the victim who was of opposite gender.

These hypotheses about gender biases in judgments drew upon ideas from social identity theory, but other theoretical interpretations are also possible. For example, Ho and Venus (1995) found that gender influenced respondents' judgments in a situation where a woman retaliated against a violent husband by killing him. Female participants in their study made less severe judgments about the woman's guilt and sentencing when compared with male participants. Ho and Venus interpreted these results in terms of a defensive attributional bias on the part of the female participants (e.g., Shaver, 1970, 1985). They assumed that the female participants may have perceived some similarity between themselves and the battered woman in terms of their shared gender and were therefore more defensive of the woman. Note also that the female participants may have had more knowledge and understanding of the battered woman's situation (Greene, Raitz, & Lindblad, 1989; Saunders, Lynch, Grayson, & Linz, 1987). They were thus making their judgments using different knowledge structures and different perspectives.

Differences in the way men and women react to a domestic dispute may also reflect their beliefs about power differences in society associated with gender as a status variable (e.g., Claes & Rosenthal, 1990; Dutton, 1992, 1995). Women may regard a wife's negative actions toward a husband as more justified because she is perceived to have less power in the domestic relationship. Men may construe the wife assailant as challenging social differentials in power that favor themselves and, because of this challenge, they may evaluate the wife less favorably. These interpretations assume that normative beliefs about the way power functions in society may then become contextualized in relation to a domestic dispute where there is partner abuse.

How did male and female participants react to the domestic violence scenario in the present study? The results from a multivariate analysis of variance (MANOVA) showed some clear differences in the way the husband was judged when compared with the wife. Participants perceived the husband to be more responsible for the offense than the wife, and they also perceived the penalty to be harsher for the wife than for the husband. They also judged the husband to deserve the penalty more than the wife and the offense to be more serious when it was committed by the husband. They reported more positive affect about the penalty that was imposed when the offense was committed by the husband, and more sympathy for the wife. Thus, for all of the variables, there was a strong evidence that the participants were more favorable toward the wife who committed the identical offense than toward the husband. The results for the wife are consistent with findings from a study by Hillier and Foddy (1993) that showed that a wife who was the victim of an assault was blamed less by female participants than by male participants. The results are also consistent with findings by Pierce and Harris (1994) and may be seen to reflect generally held beliefs about male aggression, male power, and male responsibility in domestic disputes (e.g., Dutton, 1995; Gerber, 1991).

Was there any evidence of bias in the judgments, depending on the gender of the participant? Table 7.1 presents the results from the MANOVA for those variables for which there was a statistically signifi-cant interaction effect involving the gender of the participant and the stimulus person in the scenario (husband, wife). These significant inter-action effects occurred for the perceived seriousness of the offense, for judgments that the perpetrator deserved the penalty, and for reported positive affect about the penalty. The female participants perceived the offense as more serious than male participants when it was committed by the husband, but the corresponding difference in means was not statistically significant for the wife. The female participants also judged the wife to deserve the penalty less when compared with the male participants. They also reported less positive affect about the penalty when the wife was punished for the offense and more sympathy for the wife when compared with the male participants. The corresponding differences in means were not statistically significant for the husband.

These results are consistent with the implications of social identity theory (e.g., Hogg & Abrams, 1988; Oakes et al., 1994; Tajfel & Turner, 1986), but more so for the wife. They may be interpreted in terms of social identity theory as indicating some ingroup bias on the part of the female participants when they made judgments about the wife and some out-

Table 7.1. Means and F Values in Relation
to Stimulus Person and Gender of Participant

	Means				
	Husband		Wife		F for
Variable	Males	Females	Males	Females	interaction
Seriousness of offense	11.57a	12.32b	10.75c	10.19c	4.34*
Deserve penalty	4.92a	5.19a	3.87b	3.09c	5.18*
Positive affect about penalty	16.92a	17.81a	13.75b	10.66c	6.22*
Sympathy for offender	8.77a	8.54a	10.11b	11.40c	3.10

Note: Degrees of freedom for the F values were 1,208. Means sharing the same letter in each row did not differ significantly from each other at $p < .05$ (Tukey test).
*$p < .05$
Source: Feather (1996a). Reprinted by permission of Kluwer Academic/Plenum Publishers.

group bias directed against the husband. Thus, the female participants were more favorable toward an offender who had the same gender as themselves, and they showed some discrimination against the husband. The only evidence that the male participants favored their own gender was that they judged the husband's offense as less serious than did the female participants. It is probably more accurate, however, to focus on the differences rather than to use the language of bias and discrimination, given the fact that we have no objective information against which bias can be assessed.

An important feature of the present study is that the scenarios involved a conflict situation. I found evidence from a study of allocation behavior that showed that participants tended to favor a same-sex stimulus person in a situation where a male stimulus person competed with a female stimulus person and where rewards were distributed (Feather, 1990b). Again it can be assumed that social identity in terms of gender became salient because of conflict or competition (see also Hogg & Turner, 1987).

The differences that were obtained in these studies should be set within the context of the general beliefs that people may hold about gender similarities and differences. In the present study, for example, the female participants may have seen the wife as defending herself in a long-standing relationship where there was a history of conflict, a situation where the wife was more vulnerable and deserving of support. They may have perceived her action as justified given the circumstances. They may also have made their judgments on the basis that the wife should be supported more because of her relative lack of power in the relationship (e.g., Dutton, 1992, 1995). The female participants may also have engaged in a certain amount of defensive attribution (Shaver, 1970, 1985), identifying with the wife, feeling threatened by her negative outcome, and trying to excuse her actions in various ways. The male participants may have appealed to some other beliefs. They may have seen the wife as causing the dispute, instigating aggression as well as challenging male supremacy (e.g., Saunders, 1988). They were, therefore, less generous toward the wife when compared with the female participants. Note, however, that, as I reported previously, all participants viewed the husband more negatively than the wife, and they mainly took the side of the wife rather than the husband when making their judgments about the perpetrator and the offense.

Were there any effects that related to the experimental manipulation of stress versus deliberation in the scenarios? Briefly, the offense was perceived as more serious in the stress condition than in the deliberation condition when it was committed by the wife. Also, the wife was seen to deserve the penalty more in the stress condition than in the deliberation condition. In contrast, the husband was seen to deserve the penalty more in the deliberation condition than in the stress condition. These effects were statistically significant. Perhaps the wife was blamed more for not being in control in the stress condition, whereas, in the deliberation condition she may have been seen as planning a justified action to defend herself against her husband's continuing verbal harassment. The husband who committed the deliberate act of physical violence may have been seen as a cold-blooded attacker, using aggression and power for his own ends, whereas, he may have been partly excused in the stress condition for losing control (Feather, 1996a).

Finally, the correlations between deservingness and perceived responsibility and the other variables that were measured in the study are reported in Table 7.2. These correlations are consistent in their direction with those that I have reported in previous chapters (Table 5.5, p. 142; Table 6.1, p. 185) and they show that participants' reactions were more strongly related to deservingness than to perceived responsibility. They are again consistent with my argument that judgments of deservingness are farther along in the chain of events than judgments of responsibility, and that they depend not only on the way responsibility is assigned for an action and its outcome but on other variables as well, especially on how the action and the outcome are evaluated in positive or negative terms. In the previous chapter I reported evidence (p. 201) that supported the assumption that deservingness may have the role of a mediator between perceived responsibility and the way people react to outcomes (see Feather, 1998b, for details).

In summary, the results of this current study of reactions to a situation of domestic violence provided some support for a theoretical analysis based on social identity theory, but the results may also be inter-

Table 7.2. Correlations between Deserve Penalty and Other Variables for Domestic Violence Scenario

	Correlations				
Variable	Responsibility	Seriousness	Harshness of penalty	Positive affect	Sympathy
Responsibility for offense	—	.36***	−.50***	.61***	−.43***
Deserve penalty	.65***	.39***	−.67***	.75***	−.59***

Note: $N = 216$. Tests of significance are two-tailed.
***$p < .001$.

preted in terms of patterns of belief that relate to male and female gender. The two types of interpretation are not mutually exclusive. Social identity theory has to take account of the wider context of judgment and the structure of beliefs that relate to particular situations.

Reactions to a Drug-Smuggling Offense

The second study to be described in relation to person (p) and other (o) relations and the possible effects of social identity and self-categorization used scenarios that described a drug-smuggling offense that was committed by either a white, Anglo-Australian male or by an Asian male. Would the ethnic identity of the perpetrator affect the way people react to an offense? Would someone with Asian background be judged differently for the same offense by predominantly white Australians when compared with someone of Anglo-Saxon or Anglo-Celtic background? On the basis of social identity theory we might expect that the Australian judges would show some ingroup bias that would be reflected in a tendency for them to favor the perpetrator of the offense when he was described as an Australian with Anglo-Saxon background (i.e., as a member of the ingroup) when compared with a perpetrator who was described as an Asian who had previously immigrated to Australia (i.e., as a member of an outgroup).

The study to be described tested this prediction using a sample of 170 students who were enrolled in undergraduate courses at Flinders University (Feather & Oberdan, in press). These students completed a questionnaire that contained a scenario in which either an Anglo-Australian male or an Asian male was detected at Bangkok airport with a quantity of cocaine in his suitcase. He was arrested and imprisoned. Subsequently, following representations from the Australian government and negotiations through diplomatic channels, the final penalty that was imposed was ten years imprisonment.

We also varied mitigating circumstances in the scenarios. In one condition (high responsibility) the stimulus person in the scenario was described as a drug dealer who intended to sell the cocaine in Sydney. In another condition (low responsibility) the stimulus person was described as being approached by a man at his hotel who asked him to carry a suitcase for him into Australia that he claimed contained some extra bottles of Scotch whiskey. The man was described as offering the stimulus person $100 to carry the suitcase, which in fact contained the cocaine. The stimulus person was thus an unknowing pawn.

With these experimental manipulations there were four different versions of the scenario. Participants responded to the version they received by using 7-point scales to rate the degree to which the perpetrator deserved the penalty that was imposed, his responsibility for the offense, the perceived seriousness of the offense, the perceived harshness of the penalty, any positive affect about the penalty, and the degree of sympathy for the offender. The items used were identical to those already described for the previous studies except that, as was the case in the study of police and public offenders (Feather, 1998b), perceived harshness was rated on a 7-point scale rather than by using the three-category scale (too lenient, too harsh, about right).

Participants also used 7-point scales to rate the extent to which they thought the drug smuggler was justified in the actions he took, the extent to which they thought the drug smuggler could be excused because of the presence of mitigating circumstances, and the extent to which they thought the drug smuggler could be blamed for the offense. Finally, they completed the 1990, 30-item version of the Right-Wing Authoritarianism Scale (Altemeyer & Hunsberger, 1992).

We expected that information about mitigating circumstances would reduce the perpetrator's perceived responsibility for the offense. We also expected that social identity effects on judgments would be moderated by the degree to which our participants held high or low authoritarian values. As noted in the previous chapter, the evidence shows that high authoritarians tend to be more punitive in their reactions to offenders when compared with low authoritarians (e.g., Altemeyer, 1981, 1988; Christie, 1993). The study of police versus public citizen offenders described in Chapter 6 (p. 197) also showed that right-wing authoritarianism interacted with the status of the offender to affect the judgments made by participants in regard to the seriousness of the offense. By extension, we hypothesized that negative reactions by high authoritarians would be more extreme toward an outgroup offender who was perceived to have lower status when compared with a higher status, ingroup offender. In contrast, low authoritarians may either show an absence of discrimination, discounting or ignoring status differences, or they may display some positive bias toward an outgroup offender when compared with an ingroup offender.

This line of argument assumes that high authoritarians will tend to see outgroups as having lower status than themselves when the outgroup is dissimilar and the categorization is based on ethnicity, although these judgments would also be affected by objective information about an outgroup and its status in the wider community. Early research (Adorno et al., 1950) linked authoritarianism with ethnocentrism, with high authoritarians being more ethnocentric and dismissive of outgroups than low authoritarians. We expected, however, that the differences that might occur in our study in relation to right-wing authoritarianism might occur in subtle ways when the bias is negative, given social constraints against displaying prejudice or bias in a blatant manner (e.g., McConahay, Hardee, & Batts, 1981; Pettigrew & Meertens, 1995).

We also expected that authoritarianism might interact with the information provided to participants about mitigating circumstances. In the studies described in the previous chapter I assumed that the values held by high and low authoritarians would affect the perceived seriousness of the offense committed, but it is likely that high and low authoritarians may also differ in the way they process information. The early research in *The Authoritarian Personality* (Adorno et al., 1950) described authoritarians as less able to tolerate ambiguities (see also Feather, 1971b). Rokeach (1960) also described authoritarians as close-minded, having a black-and-white view of the world and being less able to tolerate intermediate shades of gray. By implication, it seemed possible that high authoritarians in the present study might be less willing to attend to or to accept information about a perpetrator's degree of responsibility in the drug-smuggling scenario. This information would change the nature of the offense, mitigating the crime for the perpetrator who was used as a pawn and who acted without full knowledge. Low authoritarians might be more willing to take this information into account. To test these ideas we investigated the possible interactive effects of responsibility information and authoritarianism in relation to the different dependent variables included in our study.

Here I present only a limited selection of the results of this study, focusing more on those findings that relate to interactive effects (see Feather & Oberdan, in press, for more details). The data were analyzed using a 2 × 2 × 2 multiple analysis of variance (MANOVA) involving ethnic identity and responsibility information as the first two factors in the analysis and right-wing authoritarianism (high or low) as the third variable. Participants were classified as high or low in authoritarianism in terms of whether they were above or below the median of the distribution of authoritarianism scores.

This analysis showed that it was the manipulation of responsibility information that had the major effect on participants' judgments. Participants who were told that the drug smuggler acted intentionally and with full knowledge of what he was doing judged him to be more responsible for the offense and to deserve the penalty more when compared with participants who were told that the stimulus person acted without the intention to smuggle drugs and without full knowledge of what he was doing. Participants who were given the high responsibility information also judged the offense to be more serious, were more likely to judge the penalty as not too harsh, reported more positive affect about the penalty and less sympathy for the perpetrator, perceived the perpetrator as less justified in the actions that he took, judged the perpetrator's offense as less excusable, and reported that they blamed the perpetrator more for the offense (see Feather & Oberdan, in press, for details).

There was no evidence that participants were more positive toward the Anglo-Australian offender when compared with the Asian offender. The results, however, showed that participants who were high in right-wing authoritarianism judged the offense to be more serious when compared with participants who were classified as low in right-wing authoritarianism, consistent with the results presented previously for public citizens who were without any special legitimate authority (Feather, 1996c, 1998b; Chapter 6, p. 186).

Table 7.3 presents results pertaining to the statistically significant interaction effects obtained from the analysis. These results show that right-wing authoritarianism interacted with responsibility information to affect participants' judgments about the perpetrators' deservingness. The high authoritarians showed less discrimination in their judgments of deservingness when compared with the low authoritarians. Consistent with our hypothesis, they were less sensitive to the responsibility information than were the low authoritarians, but this effect occurred only for the deservingness variable.

The results in Table 7.3 also show statistically significant interaction effects for positive affect and the justify variable that involved the interaction of right-wing authoritarianism and ethnic identity. High authoritarians reported more positive affect about the penalty and judged the offense as less justified when it was committed by an Asian offender than by an Anglo-Australian offender. In contrast, the low authoritarians showed the reverse pattern. They reported less positive affect and judged the offense as more justified when it was committed by an Asian offender than by an Anglo-Australian offender. Thus, as we predicted, discrimination on the basis of the perpetrator's ethnic identity was influenced by the level of right-wing authoritarianism, but again the effect was limited in scope, involving only two variables.

Table 7.4 presents the correlations between the dependent variables. These correlations show a similar pattern of relations to that described in Chapter 6 for responsibility, seriousness, deservingness, harshness, positive affect, and sympathy (see Table 6.1, p. 185). The new information contained in Table 7.4 relates to the justify, excuse, and blame variables. Perceived justification and excusability tended to be

Table 7.3. Mean Scores for Statistically Significant Interaction Effects and Univariate F Values from Analysis of Variance

Variable	Low authoritarianism Low responsibility	Low authoritarianism High responsibility	High authoritarianism Low responsibility	High authoritarianism High responsibility	F values for interaction effect
Deserve penalty	3.38_a	6.27_c	4.47_b	$5.95_{c,d}$	$9.60**$

Variable	Low authoritarianism Anglo-Australian	Low authoritarianism Asian	High authoritarianism Anglo-Australian	High authoritarianism Asian	F values for interaction effect
Positive affect about penalty	18.61_a	16.95_b	$17.46_{a,b}$	19.33_d	$4.03*$
Justify	1.70_a	2.20_b	2.49_b	$1.79_{a,d}$	$7.01*$

Note: Means in the same row that share a subscript do not differ significantly from each other at $p < .05$ (Tukey test).
$*p < .05$ $**p < .01$
Source: Feather & Oberdan (in press). Copyright by the Australian Psychological Society. Reproduced by permission.

Table 7.4. Correlations between Dependent Variables
after Partialing Out Effects of Responsibility Information and Ethnic Identity

	Seriousness of offense	Deserve penalty	Harshness of penalty	Positive affect about penalty	Sympathy for offender	Justify offense	Excuse offender	Blame offender
Responsibility for offense	.16*	.35***	-.06	.23**	-.20*	-.24**	-.41***	.51***
Seriousness of offense	—	.24**	-.28***	.23**	-.14	-.40***	-.16*	.05
Deserve penalty		—	-.42***	.62***	-.42***	-.17*	-.39***	.36***
Harshness of penalty			—	-.42***	.40***	.16*	.09	-.14
Positive affect about penalty				—	-.44***	-.25**	-.33***	.37***
Sympathy for offender					—	.10	.15	-.25***
Justify offense						—	.28***	-.15
Excuse offender							—	-.43***

Note: Degrees of freedom = 150 for partial correlations. Tests of significance are two-tailed.
*p < .05   **p < .01   ***p < .001.
Source: Feather & Oberdan (in press). Copyright by the Australian Psychological Society. Reproduced by permission.

lower the more the offender was seen to be responsible for the offense, the more serious the offense was seen to be, the more the offender was judged to deserve the penalty, the less the penalty was judged to be too harsh, and the less positive affect about the penalty was reported by participants. Justification for the offense and the degree to which the offense was judged to be excusable were positively correlated. All of these correlations were statistically significant.

The results in Table 7.4 also show that relations involving the blame variable followed the same pattern as those involving perceived responsibility and that these two variables were positively correlated. These results suggest that participants may have found it difficult to distinguish between responsibility and blame, although these two variables can be distinguished at the conceptual level. As noted previously, Shaver (1985) proposed that the assignment of blame for a negative outcome involves a complex process of social attribution. A person may be seen as responsible for a negative event but may not be blamed for it because the person can justify the action or excuse it in some way. Our results show that blame and responsibility were related in very similar ways to other variables, and they suggest that more detailed and subtle manipulations may be necessary to distinguish between them at the empirical level.

In relation to the present context of discussion, however, the main point about the results of the study is the absence of social identity effects. The manipulation of ethnic identity was not associated with direct effects on participants' judgments. There was no evidence that the predominantly white Australian participants favored the Anglo-Australian offender in various ways when compared with the Asian offender, a difference that would be consistent with social identity theory, which assumes that members of an ingroup will tend to view their group more positively than an outgroup, thereby reinforcing their social identity and maintaining or enhancing their self-esteem.

How do we account for the failure to find social identity effects? As noted previously (Chapter 4, p. 100), studies that have investigated positive distinctiveness have found a rather complex pattern of results (e.g., Brewer, 1993; Brewer & Brown, 1998; Hinkle & Brown, 1990), and social identity theory continues to be qualified in order to take account of this complexity. Consistent with the point that I made previously, the effects would be expected to occur when the social category (in this case ethnicity) was especially salient, as when an Australian is more aware of his national identity when he or she visits a foreign country, or on days that celebrate the nation and its achievements, or when there is conflict or competition between individuals or groups, as was the case in the domestic violence study or would occur in sporting competitions, in other contests, or, at the extreme, in wars between nations.

The effects would also be influenced by the norms and beliefs of those who make the judgments. In a student sample, for example, norms of fairness may be more evident than in a less selected sample, mitigating discrimination against an outgroup and reducing any bias that favored a perpetrator who could be classified as sharing the same social identity as the judge. Jetten, Spears, and Manstead (1996) found that committed group members considered ingroup bias to be inappropriate when such bias was inconsistent with group norms of fairness. Thus, social identity theory has to take account of considerations of justice.

Also relevant is a body of research concerned with whether jurors are more lenient toward defendants who are similar to themselves. Kerr, Hymes, Anderson, and Weathers (1995) call this the *similarity-leniency hypothesis* and they refer to texts on legal tactics that show that this hypothesis appears to be widely accepted by attorneys in the United States as a valid basis for selecting jurors. They also cite research that seems to support the similarity-leniency hypothesis when it applies to various dimensions of juror-defendant similarity, which include language, general social attitudes, ideology, lifestyle, gender, and race. One Australian study by Amato (1979), for example, found evidence supporting the hypothesis when the offense was a political burglary committed by either a radical left defendant or a radical right defendant and when participants were classified in terms of their political attitudes (from far left to far right). The hypothesis, however, was not supported in this study when the offense was a terrorist bombing committed by either a radical-right or radical-left defendant. This result suggests that support for the hypothesis might be less forthcoming for very serious offenses.

Kerr et al. (1995) caution against overgeneralization of the similarity-leniency hypothesis, and they present both theoretical reasons and evidence to suggest that there are limits to it. They acknowledge that the strength of the similarity-leniency relation may depend on the personality of the juror and also on the social identity and group membership of the defendant (Tajfel & Turner, 1986). There may, however, also be occasions when a similar defendant receives harsh treatment, especially when he or she poses a threat to the positive image of the ingroup. In such cases the defendant may be viewed as a "black sheep" (Marques, 1990; Marques & Paez, 1994; Marques & Yzerbyt, 1988) and derogated and excluded from the group. By implication, the black sheep research would suggest that a highly deviant ingroup member who violated group norms and committed a serious crime would be dealt with more harshly when judged by ingroup members who are strongly identified with the ingroup. Kerr et al. present some evidence that indicates that support for the similarity-leniency hypothesis seems to depend on whether the evidence is weak or strong and on whether the jurors making the judgment are majority or minority members of the jury.

We found some evidence for the similarity-leniency effect in the present study but only for the predominantly white Australians who were high authoritarians. As the results in Table 7.3 show, the high authoritarians reported less positive affect about the penalty and they judged the offense as more justified when it was committed by the Anglo-Australian offender than by the Asian offender. The low authoritarians showed the reverse pattern. They reported more positive affect and they judged the offense as less justified when it was committed by the Anglo-Australian offender than by the Asian offender. So the high authoritarians displayed a positive bias toward the Anglo-Australian and a negative bias toward the Asian offender. In contrast, the low authoritarians showed a pattern of reverse discrimination, displaying positive bias toward the Asian offender and negative bias toward the Anglo-Australian offender, but these effects were limited to two variables (see also O'Driscoll & Feather [1985] for further evidence of positive bias among participants low in ethnocentrism). The results of a study by Mitchell and Byrne (1973) also produced limited results. In a study of a stealing offense they found that, when certainty of guilt was the dependent variable, high authoritarians who shared similar attitudes with a defendant were less certain of the defendant's guilt than were low authoritarians (or egalitarians). The authoritarians in the dissimilar attitude condition recommended more severe punishment for the defendant than did the participants in the other three conditions of the study.

Rector and Bagby (1997) also presented evidence suggesting that the conditions under which one might find a similarity-leniency effect in juror decision making are likely to be complex. They found that black Canadian participants in a mock jury trial imposed a guilty verdict more frequently when the victim was a black ingroup member. However, their verdict decisions were not related to the race of the defendant, nor were there more subtle differences in their verdicts that related to the interaction between the race of the defendant and the race of the victim. The discriminatory bias that the black Canadians showed did not carry through to jurors' sentencing decisions. In contrast, in a previous similar study, Bagby, Parker, Rector, and Kalemba (1994) found that white jurors' prejudicial perceptions were based "more on the race of the defendant and negatively biased towards the White in-group defendant" (p. 80). Rector and Bagby point to the need for further studies of jury decision making that take account of minority issues and the ethnic composition of juries.

A recent collection of articles concerning the O. J. Simpson trial also points to the complex nature of the variables that influenced observers' judgments about the trial and the verdict. In a summation of the contributions made in these articles Fairchild and Cowan (1997) concluded that "The recurrent theme to emerge from our collection of studies is that race, or ethnicity, served merely as a proxy for other cultural or experiential variables that provided meaning to the group differences in trial perceptions or reactions to the verdict." Differences in the way whites and blacks reacted to the trial and the verdict would reflect "their attitudes toward the legal system ..., perceptions of institutional racism ..., the amount and quality of interracial attitudes and behaviors ..., or the salience of race or gender as an aspect of personality" (p. 585). Fairchild and Cowan, and other contributors to the set of articles, point to the effects of shared cognitions and affects and to the effects of intergroup processes that become engaged when there is social conflict that relates to inequality and social justice. Thus, "it is not definitive, in assessing attitudes toward Simpson's guilt or trial, whether someone is Black or White, Latino or Asian, male or female or feminist; what matters is how these social categories are reflected in different experiences and how those experiences are folded into the personalities of the individuals involved" (Fairchild & Cowan, 1997, pp. 587–588).

It is evident, therefore, that the effects of social identity and similarity among juror, defendant, and victim on reactions to an offense are by no means simple, and they may depend on the nature of the crime, the dimension of similarity along which comparisons are made, the norms and beliefs of those who make the judgments, the strength or weakness of the evidence, the personality of the defendant, the strength of identification with the ingroup, and other variables.

Finally, I note that again there was an association between right-wing authoritarianism and how serious the drug smuggling was judged to be by participants. The high authoritarians viewed the offense as more serious when compared with the low authoritarians for the stimulus persons in the scenarios who were not authority figures but members of the public. As before, we can assume that the values held by the high authoritarians in contrast to the low authoritarians influenced the judgments of seriousness that were made.

A further theoretical point that I made is that high authoritarians may have a more black-and-white view of the world than low authoritarians (Adorno et al., 1950), a cognitive difference that would also affect their judgments. Indeed the results showed that they took less account of the context of the offense, judging the penalty to be more deserved, even when there was evidence of mitigating circumstances in the sense that the stimulus person had been duped to carry the cocaine. The low authoritarians showed more discrimination in the low responsibility condition, judging the offender to be less deserving of the penalty (Table 7.3). This result suggests that we need to take account not only of value differences between high and low authoritarians but also of cognitive differences that relate to their belief structures when studying the effects of authoritarianism on how people react to offenses.

MORAL CHARACTER AND REACTIONS TO OFFENSES

In this final section I will describe two studies in which information designed to vary the perceived moral character of an offender was presented to participants and the effects of this variation were investigated in relation to how participants reacted to each offense. The first study presented information about two offenses, one that involved child abuse, the other an arson offense. The second study was concerned with a motor vehicle accident offense involving a driver who used excessive speed.

Both studies represent attempts to obtain some understanding of how the perceived moral character of an offender might affect variables included in the deservingness model and the social-cognitive process model. As mentioned previously, the study of moral character has been relatively neglected in both social psychology and personality research. I assume that judgments of moral character primarily develop from information and knowledge about a person's behavior that is either communicated directly by observation of that person's positively or negatively valued actions, or indirectly via reports of that person's reputation and character. In relation to the structural model of deservingness, the primary link is between the judge or person (p) and other (o). When o is perceived to have high moral character there would be a tendency for p to view o in a positive light; when o is perceived to have low moral character, he or she would be viewed more negatively.

Reactions to Child-Abuse and Arson Offenses

This study (Feather & Atchison, 1998) presented participants with two scenarios (child abuse, arson). The scenarios varied depending on whether the stimulus person had advantaged or disadvantaged status and in terms of whether the stimulus person achieved that status by his or her own controllable actions. By an advantaged status position we mean one that most people would positively value (e.g., having a good job, attending a high-quality school). By a disadvantaged status position we mean one that most people would negatively value (e.g., being unemployed, being a single parent).

We assumed that people often use the advantaged or disadvantaged status of another person as a basis for judging that person's moral character. Their judgments would depend on the degree to which they assigned positive or negative value to the actions that led to the status position and on the degree to which the person was seen to be responsible for those actions. Thus, a person whose advantaged or disadvantaged status was seen to follow positively valued, controllable actions that have occurred consistently over time and situations would be judged by observers to have high moral character. A person whose advantaged or disadvantaged status was seen to follow consistently occurring negatively valued, controllable actions would be judged to have low moral character. In the case of politicians, for example, observers might judge the politician as having high or low integrity or as displaying arrogance or humility, based in part on knowledge about the politician's usual behavior (see Chapter 5). A single event, such as a good deed or reprehensible conduct, may also provide information that is used to form a judgment of moral character in the absence of more complete information and, as stated previously, judgments of moral character may also be based on information that is received from others or via the mass media.

When a status-based judgment of moral character is made in relation to the perpetrator of an offense, it may moderate the judgments that an observer makes. Some evidence for this assumption is already available. In an early study of the decisions of simulated jurors, Landy and Aronson (1969) concluded that their results suggested that "both the character of the defendant and the character of the victim are important variables in the severity of the sentence imposed" (p. 151). Sociologists have also argued that status may acquire moral meaning, becoming linked to moral worth (e.g., Douglas, 1970). Similar early references to moral worth and status were also made by Steffensmeier and Terry (1973) and by White (1975), among others.

Other studies have drawn attention to the perceived characteristics of the offender and their effects on judgments. The results of these studies may be interpreted as reflecting the effects of perceived differences in moral character. For example, Weiten (1980) found that a defendant in a simulated court case was less likely to receive a severe penalty for a serious offense (driving recklessly and accidentally causing the death of a two-year-old child) when the person was described as a high school graduate who was warm, helpful, and cooperative and who also acted as a coach for little league baseball than when the defendant was described negatively as a cold, impolite, and self-centered high school dropout who gambled. Darby and Schlenker (1989) found that a child who was described as having a good rather than a bad reputation, or who expressed remorse rather than lack of remorse for damaging another child's bicycle, was judged to be more likable, as having better motives, as not intending to do the damage, as being less blameworthy, and as showing more sorrow for the damage. In a study by Baldwin and Kleinke (1994), perceptions of a drunk driver's character (being reckless versus being careful and disciplined) and judgments about how much the driver deserved to be punished added significant variance over the perceived severity of a car accident when predicting recommended fines and prison sentences.

In other research, Stewart (1980) found that the perceived attractiveness of the defendant was predictive of both minimum and maximum sentences in actual court cases; the more attractive the defendant, the less severe the imposed sentence. He also noted that the effects of offender attractiveness on sentencing might depend on the nature of the crime (see also Sigall & Ostrove, 1975). There is also a body of research that shows that people who possess desirable traits tend to be evaluated more positively and to be punished less than those who are perceived to be unattractive (e.g., Berscheid & Walster, 1978; Kassin & Wrightsman, 1988; Kleinke, 1975).

I have focused so far on conditions where status may be used as a cue for judging good or bad moral character and on the effects of perceived moral character on how people react to the perpetrator of an offense. However, there might be effects of status that may be interpreted in terms of processes that do not involve perceptions of moral character as a mediator. For example, Hollander (1958, 1964) argues that high status leaders may build up "idiosyncrasy credit" to allow them to deviate from group norms within limits without being sanctioned by their groups. Their high status would then act as a shield. Large deviations from group norms may, however, result in a leader being punished (see Levine, 1989; Ridgeway, 1978; Rosoff, 1989; Wiggins, Dill, & Schwartz, 1965), and that leader's high status would then act as a liability. I noted this concept of idiosyncrasy credit when discussing processes that might be involved in people's reaction to tall poppies or high achievers who suffer a fall from their high positions (Chapter 5, p. 134).

The results of a study of reactions to criminal offenses by Skolnick and Shaw (1994) show that whether status acted as a shield or a liability depended on whether the crime was related to the profession of the offender. A high status offender (a licensed psychotherapist) was judged more harshly than a low status offender (a graduate student taking courses in clinical psychology) when the major crime (the forcible rape of a client) was professionally related, but the low status offender was judged more harshly than the high status offender when the major crime (insurance fraud) was unrelated to the profession or role of the perpetrator. However, Skolnick and Shaw (1994) found no support for a prediction based on Hollander's (1958) idiosyncrasy credits model or the Wiggins et al. (1965) status liability model, namely, that status effects would be moderated by crime severity, with more serious crimes reflecting greater deviations from group norms and therefore having different effects depending on the status of the offender.

The study to be described (Feather & Atchison, 1998) relates to the distinction between status as a shield and status as a liability because we assumed that perceptions of high moral character attached to a status position would function to shield a person when he or she commits an offense or suffers a negative outcome, mitigating the negative reactions that might occur, whereas perceptions of low moral character attached to a status position would act as a liability, magnifying the negative reactions that might occur. Thus, the perception that an offender is basically a good person will help to shield or protect that offender from negative reactions when he or she commits an offense. The perception that an offender is basically a bad person will function as a liability, magnifying negative reactions when he or she commits an offense.

There were 79 participants in the study and they responded to two scenarios that were presented in counterbalanced order. One scenario (the mother scenario) described an offense involving child abuse. The other scenario (the student scenario) described an arson offense where a student set fire to a school. Each scenario was varied in four different ways, depending on whether the stimulus person in the scenario had advantaged or disadvantaged status and on whether the status was achieved by controllable actions or because of the actions of another person.

The mother scenario described the case of a young mother who abused her five-month-old daughter. The mother was described as either a 24-year-old single mother (disadvantaged status) or a 24-year-old married mother (advantaged status). The single mother status was further described as either resulting from the mother's deliberate decision to become pregnant and to raise the child on her own (controllable status), or from becoming pregnant and then being left by her partner before the child was born (uncontrollable status). In the case of the married mother, her status was described as resulting from either choosing to get married and wanting to start a family immediately (controllable status) or from being pressured by others to marry and have a child (uncontrollable status).

The student scenario described a young student in ninth grade who broke into and attempted to burn down the secondary school that he was attending. The student either attended a rough inner-city public high school (disadvantaged status) or a more prestigious private boys' college (advantaged status). The student either chose to go to the school that he attended (controllable status) or was sent to that school by his parents (uncontrollable status).

Each scenario also contained some information about mitigating circumstances. The defense argued by the young mother was that her child constantly cried and was difficult to handle and that she could not cope with the pressure. The defense argued by the student was that he tried to burn down the school in an effort to obtain attention to the fact that he had previously been harassed by a teacher and the harassment had been ignored by the school.

When we devised these scenarios we assumed that both the positively or negatively valued actions taken by each stimulus person and prevailing social norms would affect participants' perceptions of advantaged or disadvantaged status. Thus, it was assumed that the status of the married mother who chose to follow the socially acceptable path of marriage and parenthood would be viewed more positively than that of the single mother who departed from social norms and chose to be a single parent, and that the status of the student who chose to attend the prestigious private boys' college would be viewed more positively than the status of the student who chose to go to the rough inner-city high school. These assumptions are reasonable ones to make in the Australian context, though we would expect some differences between how people react, depending on their own beliefs, attitudes, and values.

The participants in the study used 7-point scales to rate the degree to which they thought the stimulus person in each scenario was decent, reliable, worthy, and respectable (see Feather & Atchison, 1998, for details). On the basis of the results of a factor analysis these ratings were combined for each participant so as to obtain a composite measure of moral character for the mother and for the student.

Participants also used 7-point scales to rate the degree to which the cause of the offense committed by the stimulus person was controllable and manageable, and the degree to which they thought the stimulus person was personally responsible for committing the offense (see

Feather & Atchison, 1998, for details). Again the results of a factor analysis supported combining these ratings into a composite measure of perceived responsibility for each participant.

We also obtained ratings on a 1 to 7 scale of how angry each participant felt that the stimulus person committed the offense, how serious they saw the offense to be, and the extent to which they thought the stimulus person deserved to be punished. Participants were also told that the mother was sentenced to one year in jail and that the student was sentenced to 30 hours of community service, and, in each case, they were asked to rate whether this penalty was too lenient, about right, or too harsh.

Full details of the results are presented in the published report (Feather & Atchison, 1998). Here I focus on a sample of the findings. The statistically significant status by controllability interaction effects are of particular interest. Table 7.5 presents the relevant means and F values for these interaction effects that were obtained from the analysis that was conducted.

The results in Table 7.5 show that offenders with advantaged status were perceived to have stronger moral character, to be less responsible for the offense, and to be less deserving of punishment when the advantaged status was an outcome of the offender's controllable actions than when the status was outside of the offender's control. All of these differences were statistically significant ($p < .05$) when the simple effects were tested.

In contrast, offenders with disadvantaged status were perceived to have weaker moral character, to be more responsible for the offense, and

Table 7.5.   Mean Scores and F Values
for Status by Controllability Interaction Effects

Variable	Disadvantaged status		Advantaged status	
	Uncontrollable	Controllable	Uncontrollable	Controllable
Perceived moral character	4.13_a	3.08_b	3.51_b	4.44_a
Responsibility for offense	5.93_a	6.25_a	5.93_a	5.21_b
Deservingness of punishment	5.26_a	5.83_a	5.63_a	4.64_c

Note: Means in a row that share the same letter do not differ significantly from each other at $p < .05$ (Tukey test).
Source: Feather & Atchison (1998). Copyright 1998 by the Australian Psychological Society. Reproduced by permission.

to be more deserving of punishment when the disadvantaged status was an outcome of the offender's controllable actions than when the status was outside the offender's control. However, only the difference that involved perceived moral character was statistically significant ($p < .05$) when the simple effects were tested.

These results support our predictions about perceived moral character. Offenders with advantaged status were judged to have higher moral character when their status could be attributed to positively valued actions for which they were perceived to be responsible when compared with offenders whose advantaged status was not attributable to their own controllable actions. Offenders with disadvantaged status were judged to have lower moral character when their status could be attributed to negatively valued actions for which they were perceived to be responsible when compared with offenders whose disadvantaged status was not attributable to their own controllable actions.

Note also that the results in Table 7.5 show that the largest difference between means was obtained for all three variables when the comparison was between controllable actions leading to disadvantaged status and controllable actions leading to advantaged status. Thus, the status effects were most pronounced when advantaged or disadvantaged status followed controllable actions.

How were judgments of moral character related to the other dependent variables in our study? Table 7.6 presents the correlations between these variables for the mother scenario and for the student scenario, combining the controllable and uncontrollable conditions. Of interest here are those correlations that involve perceived moral character. These correlations show that, when the stimulus person was perceived to have higher moral character, he or she was less likely to be seen as responsible for the offense and less likely to be seen as deserving of punishment. Participants also tended to report less anger about the offense and they were more likely to judge the penalty as harsh, when the stimulus person was judged to have higher moral character. Further analyses supported the assumption that perceived moral character mediated some of the effects of the experimental manipulations (see Feather & Atchison, 1998, for details). The correlations involving the remaining dependent variables in Table 7.6 show a similar pattern to that obtained in other studies (e.g., Table 6.1, p. 185; Table 7.4, p. 217).

Was there any evidence that status acted as a shield to protect the offender in various ways? The results show that status shield effects were present when information about both status and the conditions of its occurrence led to higher judgments of moral character. Thus, both advantaged status and the fact that the status was achieved by positive

Table 7.6. Correlations between Dependent Variables for Mother Scenario and Student Scenario

Variable	Perceived moral character	Responsibility for offense	Anger about offense	Seriousness of offense	Deservingness of punishment	Harshness of penalty
Perceived moral character	—	-.34**	-.40***	-.17	-.52***	.56***
Responsibility for offense	-.34**	—	.68***	.47***	.73***	-.46***
Anger about offense	-.30**	.30**	—	.47***	.75***	-.42***
Seriousness of offense	-.22	.43***	.48***	—	.41***	-.31**
Deservingness of punishment	-.38***	.54***	.36***	.51***	—	-.57***
Harshness of penalty	.36***	-.52***	-.25*	-.35**	-.33**	—

Note: Ns for the correlations varied between 73 and 77 because of missing cases. Correlations for the mother scenario are above the diagonal; correlations for the student scenario are below the diagonal. Tests of significance are two-tailed.
*$p < .05$ **$p < .01$ ***$p < .001$
Source: Feather & Atchison (1998). Copyright 1998 by the Australian Psychological Society. Reproduced by permission.

actions for which the person was responsible conferred some protection for the offender against more extreme negative judgments (Table 7.5). However, there may be limits to this finding. The shield or protection may operate only up to a point, depending on how serious the offense is seen to be, the nature of the social role that the violator occupies, and what the offense reveals about the values and character of the offender. More research is needed on the boundary conditions that concern status shield and status liability effects. After reviewing some of the literature concerning status differences and opinion deviance within groups, Levine (1989) concluded that "research designed to test Hollander's idiosyncrasy credit notion has yielded a rather confusing melange of results," and that studies of opinion deviance suggest that "high status deviates are severely punished for major interference with group goal attainment, only mildly punished for minor interference, and highly rewarded for facilitation of goal attainment" (p. 215). The results of the Feather and Atchison study imply that we also have to examine the beliefs that surround status, in particular whether a person achieved the status by positively or negatively valued means or whether it was imposed on the person by forces beyond his or her control.

Finally, it might be argued that the scenarios that we used in this study presented stories that would evoke other kinds of attributions in addition to attributions about moral character. These unmeasured attributions might have influenced participants' reactions to the offender and to his or her offense. For example, the unmarried mother who left her partner to bring up her child on her own may have been seen as impulsive and lacking in judgment; the married mother who was forced into marriage and into having a child may have been seen as passive and weak; the student who chose the rough inner-city school may have been seen as unwise and rebellious. Participants may have based their judgments on these inferred personality attributes rather than on perceived moral character. As noted previously, however, variables that concern personality and character are not easy to disentangle (Chapter 4) and personality attributes may carry moral overtones. Even the personality dimensions described as the "big five" (Costa & McCrae, 1992) could be construed in terms of characteristics that are more or less valued. Moreover, the variables that we used to measure moral character (decency, reliability, worthiness, and respectability) had face validity (though they might be improved and added to in future studies) and the experimental manipulations did produce the predicted differences in perceived moral character (Table 7.5).

The Feather and Atchison study is a step in the direction of redressing the neglect of moral character as a variable and the results show that it has a role, along with other variables, in the analysis of how people react to the perpetrators of offenses.

Reactions to a Motor Vehicle Accident

The second study that included moral character as a variable used a different type of scenario, one that involved a motor vehicle accident. The experimental manipulation of moral character was more direct than the more indirect manipulation that was used in the Feather and Atchison (1998) study.

Details of the study are provided in the report by Feather and Deverson (in press). There were 153 participants in the study who were sampled from undergraduate courses in psychology at Flinders University in Adelaide, South Australia. These participants responded to a scenario that could take one of eight different forms depending on whether the stimulus person in the scenario was male or female, whether or not there were mitigating circumstances, and whether the stimulus person was described as having high or low moral worth.

The scenarios described a male or female driver who was involved in a motor vehicle collision while returning home from a business meeting. The scenarios with a high level of mitigating circumstances described the presence of heavy rain and a slippery road; those with a low level of mitigating circumstances stated that there were witness accounts that the driver was traveling at high speed. The driver of high moral worth was described as a very dependable and trustworthy person; the driver of low moral worth was described as not very dependable and a bit untrustworthy. The outcome in each scenario was a 12-month suspension of the driver's license and payment of $500 for damages.

Participants used scales numbered from 1 to 7 to rate the stimulus person in regard to deservingness of the penalty, responsibility, seriousness of the offense, harshness of the penalty, positive affect about the penalty, and sympathy for the driver. The items used to measure each of these variables were identical to those already described for the previous studies except that, as in the Feather and Oberdan (in press) and Feather (1998b) studies, harshness was measured on a 7-point scale.

The measure of perceived moral character was the same as that used in the Feather and Atchison study and involved rating the stimulus person on a scale of 1 to 7 in relation to decency, reliability, worthiness, and respectability. In addition, participants used a 1 to 7 scale to rate how much they might like the stimulus person on further acquaintance and how much they might like to have him or her as a friend.

We also assessed stereotyped attitudes regarding male and female drivers by asking participants to estimate on a scale from 0 to 100 the proportion of women they considered to be safe drivers and the proportion of men they considered to be safe drivers. The measure of stereotyping was obtained by subtracting the male driver proportion from the female driver proportion. Positive scores indicated a bias in favor of female drivers; negative scores indicated a bias in favor of male drivers.

The results of a $2 \times 2 \times 2$ MANOVA are presented in Feather and Deverson (in press). These results showed that there were strong effects of mitigation. The driver who speeded (low mitigation) was judged to be more responsible for the accident and to deserve the penalty more when compared with the driver whose accident occurred under slippery road conditions (high mitigation). Participants in the low mitigation condition also rated the accident as more serious and the penalty as more toward the lenient side. Participants also reported more positive affect about the penalty and less sympathy for the driver when mitigation was low rather than high. All of these differences that emerged as main effects of mitigation from the analysis were statistically significant.

In addition, the results of the analysis showed that participants rated the female driver as having higher moral character than the male driver and they also reported liking the female driver more. As far as the effects of moral worth were concerned, participants reported higher ratings of moral character for the driver in the high moral worth condition when compared with the driver in the low moral worth condition. Participants also reported more sympathy and more liking for the driver in the high moral worth condition, and they also tended to judge the penalty as harsher in this condition. The differences that emerged either as main effects of the gender of the driver or as main effects of moral worth were statistically significant.

There were no statistically significant interaction effects that emerged from the MANOVA. However, a further analysis of the stereotyping variable showed that female participants rated female drivers as safer than male drivers, but the difference in ratings for male and female drivers was negligible for the male drivers. In terms of social identity theory, these results indicate ingroup bias as far as gender stereotyping was concerned but only for the female participants (see Feather & Deverson, in press, for details).

We also conducted multivariate analyses that were based on the intercorrelations between variables that are reported in Table 7.7. As was the case for the studies reported in Chapter 6, we used path analysis. Two path analyses were conducted, each using hierarchical multiple regression with listwise deletion of missing cases to generate the path

Table 7.7. Correlations between Dependent Variables

Variable	Responsibility for offense	Deserve penalty	Seriousness of offense	Harshness of penalty	Moral character	Positive affect about penalty	Sympathy for driver	Liking for driver
Responsibility for offense	—	.72***	.45***	-.42***	-.10	.62***	-.32***	-.01
Deserve penalty		—	.36***	-.55***	-.15	.67***	-.41***	-.12
Seriousness of offense			—	-.15	-.09	.43***	-.18*	-.03
Harshness of penalty				—	.23**	-.59***	.48***	.14
Moral character					—	-.27***	.32***	.58***
Positive affect about penalty						—	-.55***	-.27***
Sympathy for driver							—	.35***
Liking for driver								—

Note: Ns for correlations ranged from 147 to 153 due to missing cases. Tests of significance are two-tailed.

*p < .05   **p < .01   ***p < .001

Source: Feather & Deverson (in press). Reprinted by permission from the *Journal of Applied Social Psychology*, V. H. Winston & Sons, Inc., 360 South Ocean Boulevard, Palm Springs, FL 33480.

coefficients. The first path analysis was restricted to those variables that were affected by the experimental manipulation of mitigation, namely, responsibility, deservingness, seriousness, harshness of penalty, positive affect, and sympathy. The second path analysis included those variables that were affected by the experimental manipulation of moral worth, namely, harshness of penalty, moral character, liking, and sympathy. We also included positive affect about the penalty in this analysis. The results of these path analyses are presented in Figures 7.1 and 7.2.

The statistically significant path coefficients in Figure 7.1 show a pattern of path coefficients that is generally consistent with the structure found before for other types of offense (Feather, 1996c; Chapter 6, Figures 6.3 and 6.4), except that the paths linking seriousness of the offense to deservingness, and deservingness to sympathy, were not statistically significant. There were, however, positive paths between responsibility and seriousness, between responsibility and deservingness, between deservingness and positive affect about the penalty, between seriousness and positive affect, and between harshness of the penalty and sympathy for the driver. There were negative paths between mitigation and responsibility, between deservingness and harshness, and between harshness and positive affect.

These results show that mitigation had strong effects on the driver's perceived responsibility for the accident and that the effects of perceived

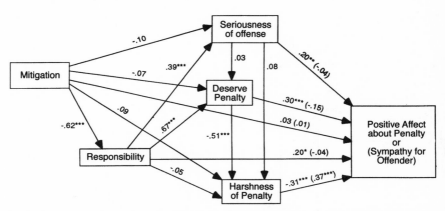

Figure 7.1. Path analysis involving mitigation and variables relating to social-cognitive process model. Path coefficients for reported sympathy are in parentheses. Statistically significant path coefficients (standardized betas) are indicated as follows: *$p < .05$, **$p <$ .01, ***$p < .001$. (*Source:* Feather & Deverson [in press]. Reprinted by permission from the *Journal of Applied Social Psychology*, V. H. Winston & Sons, Inc., 360 South Ocean Boulevard, Palm Springs, FL 33480. All rights reserved.)

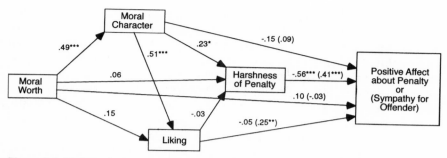

Figure 7.2. Path analysis involving moral worth, moral character, harshness of penalty, and liking and affective variables. Path coefficients for reported sympathy are in parentheses. Statistically significant path coefficients (standardized betas) are indicated as follows: $*p < .05$, $**p < .01$, $***p < .001$. (*Source*: Feather & Deverson [in press]. Reprinted by permission of from the *Journal of Applied Social Psychology*, V. H. Winston & Sons, Inc., 360 South Ocean Boulevard, Palm Springs, FL 33480. All rights reserved.)

responsibility on harshness of the penalty and reported positive affect about the penalty were mainly mediated by deservingness and by perceived seriousness, although, as in the Feather (1998b) study, full mediation in the sense discussed by Baron and Kenny (1986) was not always obtained.

The statistically significant path coefficients in Figure 7.2 show that there were positive paths between moral worth and moral character, between moral character and liking for the driver, between moral character and harshness of the penalty, between harshness and sympathy for the driver, and between liking and sympathy. There was a negative path between harshness and positive affect about the penalty.

These results show that, in the context of the present study, information about moral worth in the scenarios had strong effects on perceived moral character and that the direct and indirect effects of moral character were limited to judgments about the harshness of the penalty and to variables that were interpersonal in nature (liking, sympathy) and that involved the affective system (positive affect). These findings are similar to those obtained by Feather and Dawson (1998) in their study of how people react to another's success or failure to find employment (see Chapter 5, p. 164). They varied like/dislike relations in their scenarios and found that this manipulation affected how pleased participants were when the stimulus person either found a job or remained unemployed. In the present study perceived moral character had a direct effect on liking that then flowed through to affect sympathy for the driver.

Note, however, that, in contrast to the results of the Feather and

Atchison (1998) study described in the previous section, there was no evidence from the present study to show that judgments of responsibility and deservingness were related to the perceived moral character of the offender (Table 7.6). This difference may relate to the nature of the offense. The driving offense involved property damage and there was no serious injury to either driver. The offenses that were described in the Feather and Atchison study (child abuse, arson) clearly had harmful effects on other people. As noted in Chapter 4, most moral values are concerned with desirable ways of behaving toward other people (e.g., being honest, responsible, loving, and helpful) (Rokeach, 1973), and developmental theorists introduce an interpersonal emphasis in the higher stages of moral reasoning (e.g., Gilligan, 1982; Kohlberg, 1984; Turiel, 1983). We may have found similar effects to those found by Feather and Atchison if, in the scenarios that we used, the driver of the other car had been seriously injured. The moral character of the offending driver may then have become a more relevant variable in regard to how participants reacted in terms of responsibility and deservingness.

Finally, the relative absence of social identity effects in the present study (except for the stereotyping measure) may have been due to the fact that group membership involving gender categories was not especially salient. As noted previously, social identity effects involving ingroup favoritism and negative appraisals of the outgroup would be more likely to occur in situations where there is an obvious context for comparison and where social categories are activated, as when groups are in competition or conflict and when identification with the ingroup is strong.

CONCLUDING COMMENTS

The studies described in the present chapter extended the analysis or retributive justice to situations where the effects of the social identity of the offender and the moral character of the offender were under scrutiny. The results of these studies help to clarify the conditions under which social identity effects and moral character effects might be expected to occur. Clearly, there is scope for a lot of further research into both the conceptual status of these variables and their effects on how people react to the positive and negative outcomes of others.

CHAPTER 8

Final Reflections

I have presented a conceptual analysis of deservingness that includes variables from different areas of psychology, especially motivational psychology, social psychology, cognitive psychology, and the psychology of personality, and that also makes use of concepts from legal theory and the psychology of justice. I then showed how this deservingness model may be applied to the analysis of how people react to the positive or negative outcomes of others. This application first considered reactions to the success or failure of students in an examination setting, and it was then extended to the achievements or failures of tall poppies or people who occupy very high positions in their chosen pursuits. Subsequently, the model was integrated into a social-cognitive process model that was applied to the analysis of situations involving retributive justice, in which people react to situations where offenses are committed and where penalties are imposed. These theoretical accounts were tested in various ways in different experimental settings and by using multivariate procedures.

My aim in conducting this analysis was to bring the concept of deservingness to center stage and to show how we can use judgments of deservingness to further our understanding of how people react to positive and negative outcomes. The analysis has both theoretical and applied interest. Much of the research that was reported related to relatively underresearched topics, namely, the study of retribution and punishment and the study of achievers who occupy high status positions.

The approach that I adopted has a number of distinctive features. First, it acknowledges that how we react to the positive or negative outcomes of others depends not only on features of the immediate situation but also on aspects of our own selves, and especially on the needs and values that are activated within any particular context. The way we perceive and structure the immediate environment in terms of its meanings and possibilities depends not only on the situation itself but also on what we bring to it by way of our own needs, values, beliefs, and expectations. The research that I described provided firm evidence for the effects of variables that were manipulated in the scenarios presented to participants, and value variables that were personal in nature that related to those who judged the other's action and outcome. The interaction of these variables led to differences in the way our participants reacted to the situations presented to them. I have taken Lewin's (1951) prescription seriously that progress in psychological analysis depends on theoretical models that include both the person and the perceived environment, and that once we have developed these types of models we should go out and apply them.

Second, the models that I presented incorporated justice variables that have been extensively discussed by legal theorists and philosophers and that have also been considered by social psychologists concerned with issues of responsibility, deservingness, and entitlement. In the analysis of deservingness I presented a structural model that takes both values and perceived responsibility into account, and that also acknowledges the possible effects of relations between person (p) and other (o) in regard to shared or disparate social identities and like/dislike relations. Again the influence of Lewin (1951) is apparent in the assumption that a person's needs and values will affect the way he or she evaluates specific actions and outcomes. Added to that is the influence of Heider (1958) that is apparent in the assumption that relations within the deservingness model tend to be structured in the direction of achieving harmony or balance. The deservingness model also enables the representation of other legal concepts such as mitigation and justification in terms of their effects on perceived responsibility and on how an observer perceives the actions of the other. For example, information that the road was slippery might help to mitigate a driver's responsibility and subsequent blame for an accident; or a driver's act of speeding might be seen as justified in terms of an important goal like getting a sick person to a hospital quickly.

Third, the emphasis on deservingness goes beyond those analyses that assign prime status to judgments of responsibility (Weiner, 1995, 1996). In my analysis the judgment of whether another person deserves a particular outcome presupposes a judgment of responsibility. A null relation between other (o) and action disconnects o from the action and its outcome, and therefore implies that o has no perceived responsibility for the action that led to the outcome. Other (o) cannot then be said to deserve or not deserve the positive or negative outcome that followed the action. Where the situation is one that involves o's perceived responsibility, however, it is necessary to separate a judgment of responsibility from a judgment of deservingness. A judgment of deservingness would then depend not only on o's perceived responsibility but also crucially on how o's actions and outcomes are evaluated in regard to whether they are positively valent (or attractive) or negatively valent (or aversive). Recognition of this point means that there can be a disjunction between perceived responsibility and deservingness. For example, people can be held responsible for outcomes that they are perceived not to deserve. Research by Pepitone and L'Armand (1996) also incorporates variables that concern valence, but in their analysis the perception of justice and injustice in life events depends upon the relation between the valence of the person being observed (good or bad) and the valence (positive or negative) of the outcome experienced by that person. My analysis is more extensive and it gives a lot of weight to evaluative relations within the deservingness triad. Judgments of deservingness are farther along in the chain of events than judgments of responsibility, and they are assumed to be better predictors of how people react to positive and negative outcomes. The evidence that I reported supported this assumption.

Fourth, the structural model of deservingness may be applied to positive outcomes as well as to negative outcomes. The analysis is not restricted to outcomes that are harmful, having negative consequences for others or for self. A focus on negative outcomes has implications for the kinds of variables that can be examined and some of these variables are not appropriate in situations where the outcomes are positive. For example, concepts such as mitigating circumstances, justification, negligence, and blameworthiness that come from legal theory are relevant to the analysis of reactions to negative outcomes but not to positive outcomes that are associated with benefit to a person. These kinds of variables have been incorporated into theoretical analyses that have been concerned with the attribution of blame and with other reactions to outcomes that are associated with harm (e.g., Shaver, 1985; Shultz & Darley, 1991). The deservingness model that I presented has a much wider scope of application because it is also relevant to positive outcomes in a person's life.

It may be the case that there are some differences in the underlying processes that are involved in the way people react to harm versus benefit that are still to be determined. For example, Shultz and Schleifer (1983) discussed some possible asymmetries between harm and benefit in the judgments of ordinary observers, referring to proposals by D'Arcy (1963), Schleifer (1973), and Feinberg (1968). However, their own empirical research found a fairly close correspondence between the results they obtained for benefit and the results they obtained for harm (Shultz & Schleifer, 1983; Shultz, Schleifer, & Altman, 1981).

Fifth, my discussion of the deservingness model was based on the case where outcomes could be seen to be contingent on the other's actions. This contingency was represented by a positive unit relation between action and outcome in the diagrams that were presented (Figures 4.2, 4.3, and 4.4). I also noted, however, that there are cases where outcomes are independent of a person's actions and can be attributed to other causes, such as the effects of situational forces or chance events that are outside the person's control. A noncontingency between action and outcome can be represented by a null relation so that action and outcome are not linked at all.

Note, however, that positive unit relations between an action and an outcome may sometimes be induced so as to achieve a balanced deservingness triad. An induced positive unit relation would be more likely to occur when a positive action and a positive outcome occurred in close conjunction, or when a negative action and a negative outcome occurred in close conjunction. A person may then see the outcome or event as produced by the action, even though it can be attributed to other causes. Personal causality may then be assumed, involving an illusion of control (Langer, 1975, 1983).

Sixth, the deservingness model in its more complete and extended form (Figures 4.3, 4.4) incorporates person (p) and other (o) into the structures, thereby enabling the representation of relations between p and o and the responsibility relation between o and action. Thus, the model connects with social psychological analyses that have been concerned with interpersonal attitudes and relations and with social identity, as well as incorporating legal and attributional concepts that are involved in the concept of perceived responsibility.

FURTHER EXTENSIONS

There is room for further research on the models that I have presented. In this section I will briefly outline some possibilities.

Effects of Relations Between Person and Other

I assumed that relations between person (p) and other (o) would have moderating effects on judgments of deservingness, that is, how the person is seen in terms of liking, ingroup or outgroup membership, or moral character will affect the degree to which that person is seen to deserve or not to deserve an outcome. As noted previously, however, like/dislike relations may have their primary effect on affective responses to another's outcome rather than on more cognitive judgments about deservingness (Chapter 5). We need more research on that topic.

The concept of moral character was discussed mainly in relation to its likely basis in p's direct knowledge about o's positive or negative past actions (e.g., Has o acted with integrity or dishonesty?), and also in relation to other more indirect information reflecting public opinion that might be available to p about o's reputation (e.g., Does the mass media present o as a person who shows concern for others?). These perceptions of moral character were assumed to affect p's positive or negative evaluation of o, as reflected in like/dislike relations with consequent effects on affective reactions. Perceptions of moral character may also modify p's evaluation of o's current actions so that these actions are seen in a more positive or negative light. However, whether judgments of perceived responsibility and deservingness are also affected by information about moral character may depend on whether the situation is one that elicits moral values or is outside the moral realm.

Social identity effects on judgments may also depend on a range of variables, such as strength of identification with the group or social category, whether there is a salient basis for comparison between groups, the importance of the dimension along which comparison occurs, the normative structure that is part of a person's subjective knowledge, the status and homogeneity of the group, whether the group is formed in the laboratory or is a naturally occurring group, or other variables that have been discussed by social identity theorists. Clearly, there is need for more research on the effects of these different variables on judgments of deservingness and on other reactions to outcomes across a range of different situations.

The status of the other person who is being judged (e.g., whether it is legitimate status or otherwise; whether it is earned or achieved status or ascribed status on the basis of other criteria) also requires more investigation in regard to its effects on judgments of deservingness. The vertical dimension in society, involving status differences, has largely been ignored in social psychology.

Incorporating the Self into Deservingness Structures

The deservingness model includes other (o) as an element in the relational structure. I noted previously that it would be possible to replace other (o) by self in the diagrams presented in Figures 4.3 and 4.4. One could then represent relations between person (p) as observer or judge and self. For example, does person like or dislike self, or perceive self as good or bad?

POSITIVE SELF-EVALUATION

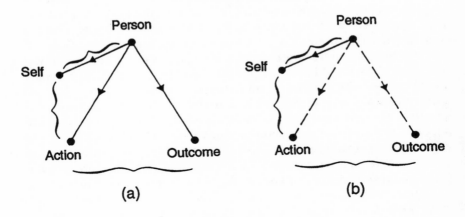

(a)   (b)

NEGATIVE SELF-EVALUATION

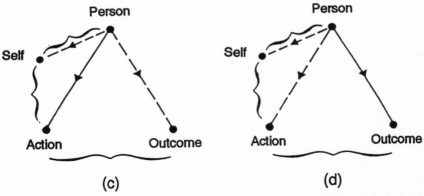

(c)   (d)

Figure 8.1. Balanced and unbalanced structures involving attitudinal (sentiment) and unit relation and including self as an element.

The signed digraphs in Figure 8.1 show how the incorporation of self into the structures can be accomplished. In these structures I assume that person "owns" self, and that this linkage or association can be represented by a positive unit relation. The other elements and relations within the four structures in Figure 8.1 have the same meaning as presented in Chapter 4. The four structures contain positive and negative sentiment or attitudinal relations between person and self that correspond to like or dislike, or to positive or negative evaluations of self. These relations may be coordinated to differences in self-esteem, where self-esteem is defined either in terms of global measures (e.g., Rosenberg, 1965) or in terms of more differentiated measures (e.g., Marsh, 1990; Marsh & Hattie, 1996).

Bringing self into the deservingness structures would have interesting implications concerning how a person reacts to his or her own positive or negative outcomes. When self is viewed positively, there may be a tendency for person (p) to assign more personal deservingness when positive outcomes occur, and less personal deservingness when negative outcomes occur than would be the case when self is viewed negatively. Affective reactions to the positive and negative outcomes would tend to follow these judgments of deservingness, consistent with previous discussion.

There may also be a tendency for person (p) to see a positively valued or liked self as more responsible for positive actions that lead to positive outcomes, and less responsible for negative actions that lead to negative outcomes, when compared with a negatively valued or disliked self. Thus, there may be a variety of different self-enhancement and self-deprecation reactions depending on the way person views self. These reactions would again be expected to follow the balance principle, reflecting balancing forces within the person-self-action triad in the direction of self-consistency.

This kind of analysis provides a new direction for research into self-related processes in that it includes both values and justice variables in the analysis. These variables are assumed to affect a person's judgments about self-related outcomes and the emotional reactions that follow these judgments. I would expect that affective reactions such as pride, shame, and guilt would depend on a person's positive or negative view of self, on the person's evaluation of the actions that led to a positive or negative outcome, and on the degree of perceived responsibility for the action and its contingent outcome. These kinds of emotions have been discussed by Weiner (1986, 1992, 1995) in relation to his attributional theory of motivation and emotion.

The model presented in Figure 8.1 provides another way of examining them. For example, feelings of pride would be expected to occur more predictably when p has positive rather than negative self-regard and when p sees self as responsible for a success outcome that follows a positively valued action (e.g., high effort), where the action's positive valence depends on underlying competence values (e.g., achievement values). I would expect that this combination of variables would also be associated with stronger judgments by p that he or she deserves the success than would occur if p's self-regard were negative.

Feelings of guilt would be expected to occur when p has negative rather than positive self-regard and when p sees self as responsible for a positive outcome that advantages self and that follows a negative action (e.g., dishonest behavior), where the action's negative valence depends on underlying moral values (e.g., prosocial or benevolence values). I would expect that this combination of variables would also be associated with stronger judgments by p that he or she does not deserve the positive outcome than would occur if p's self-regard were positive. Feelings of guilt may also occur when p's action has negative effects on another person, especially on one who is liked or is a member of p's group.

A Social-Cognitive Process Model for Positive Outcomes

The social-cognitive process model described in Chapter 6 concerns the analysis of how people react to offenses and to the penalties that are imposed on a guilty offender as a consequence. The same form of analysis can also be used in relation to positive outcomes where a person succeeds at a task or achieves some positive goal that is associated with a reward or some other positive consequence.

Figure 8.2 presents a social-cognitive process model for this type of situation where another's action or performance is followed by a positive outcome and an associated reward. This diagram can be read in much

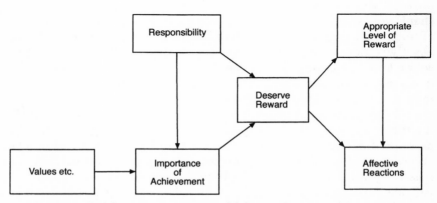

Figure 8.2. Social-cognitive process model for reactions to positive outcomes.

the same way as the parallel diagram concerned with reactions to offenses (Figure 6.1). I assume that the positive valence of an achievement, represented by its perceived importance in Figure 8.2, will depend both on the degree to which the person is seen to be responsible for the achievement and on the needs and values that the judge or observer holds. That is, a success or achievement will have higher positive valence when a person's perceived responsibility for the success is greater and when achievement needs and values are stronger. Theory and research in achievement motivation provide some evidence for these assumptions (Feather, 1967c, 1968, 1982a; Weiner, 1992, 1995).

Perceived responsibility for the achievement and the perceived importance of the achievement are then assumed to influence the degree to which the reward for the achievement is seen to be deserved. The degree to which a person is seen to deserve the achievement and its associated reward would be positively related to the degree of perceived responsibility when the action leading to the positive achievement is positively evaluated. Judgments of deservingness would also be higher for achievements that have higher positive valence and are viewed as more important.

Deservingness, in turn, would predict both the appropriate level of the reward and affective reactions to the positive outcome and to the reward. The more the person is seen to deserve the reward, the more appropriate a higher level of reward would be seen to be, and the more positive the affective reactions that are associated with the positive outcome would be.

Finally, higher levels of reward would be expected to be associated with more positive affective reactions under conditions where the reward is seen to be deserved. These affective reactions may involve feelings of pleasure about the reward and praise and support for the successful achiever.

The model presented in Figure 8.2 provides a basis for further research. Such research should also include investigation of those cases where a success or an achievement follows negatively valued actions and where it is seen to be undeserved. In these cases reward may be seen to be inappropriate and affective reactions to any such reward may be negative and accompanied by condemnation of the successful achiever.

The research on high achievers or tall poppies described in Chapter 5 provides evidence of positive or negative affective reactions to another's high achievement when the achievement is seen to be either deserved or undeserved. The achievement context, however, may also elicit other types of emotion such as envy and resentment, which require much more research in the future (Feather, 1994a, 1996e).

Application to Procedural and Distributive Justice

The research described in the latter part of this book concerned retributive justice, where some form of penalty or punishment is imposed for a negative event. Two other areas that have been more extensively investigated in justice research concern procedural justice, where the focus is on how people react to procedures that are seen to be fair or unfair, and distributive justice where the fairness or unfairness of distributions or allocations is the main focus of concern.

Theories and research relating to the two areas have been reviewed by Tyler et al. (1997) and Tyler and Smith (1998). Other recent contributions have proposed an integration of the two areas (e.g., Brockner & Wiesenfeld, 1996; Van den Bos, Lind, Vermunt, & Wilke, 1997; Van den Bos, Vermunt, & Wilke, 1997; Van den Bos, Lind, & Wilke, in press). For example, the proponents of fairness heuristic theory (Van den Bos, Lind et al., 1997; Van den Bos, Vermunt et al., 1997; Van den Bos et al., in press) propose that, when the context of judgment provides incomplete information or information that is difficult to interpret, people may process information heuristically. The limited context forces them to take cognitive shortcuts, precluding the more systematic and controlled processing suggested in some justice theories. For example, the evidence from some of the studies that relate to fairness heuristic theory indicates that, in the absence of information about the outcomes of others, people may use information about procedural fairness when judging whether outcomes are fair or unfair; or they may give more weight to either procedural or outcome information, depending on which type of information was available first. The evidence also shows, however, that the distinction between procedural justice and distributive justice is still an important one when people think about justice.

In the context of the deservingness model, procedural justice relates to how an observer or judge evaluates the specific actions taken by another person (Lind & Tyler, 1988; Thibaut & Walker, 1975; Tyler & Lind, 1992), that is, it relates to whether person (*p*) views the actions taken by other (*o*) as positive or negative. The variables discussed previously that affect the assignment of positive or negative valence to another's actions are therefore also relevant to the analysis of procedural justice. The perceived justice of procedures would be related to the observer's own needs and values and to the context in which the procedures occur, a context that includes the person who is enacting the procedures, the other person or group that is subject to them, whether people have "voice" or an opportunity to have their say, and sets of rules, norms, and legal prescriptions. For example, a person who sets a high value on honesty would be more likely to see somewhat dubious procedures that were used to elect a person to a position as more negative when compared with someone who values honesty less; high status members of a group would tend to perceive treatment by a high status, ingroup member as more positive when compared with treatment from a low status, outgroup member (cf. Heuer, Blumenthal, Douglas, & Weinblatt, in press). These differences would be qualified by the nature of the treatment itself and the degree to which it conforms to agreed-upon rules and legal prescriptions, and also by a person's own view of self (positive or negative) when the treatments apply to self. In the latter case, for example, a person with high self-esteem may see disrespectful treatment as more negative when compared with a person whose self-esteem is much lower (cf. Heuer et al., in press). Assuming that outcomes are specified and can be positively and negatively evaluated, these differences in the way a procedure is evaluated would flow through to effect deservingness judgments in a manner consistent with the implications of the extended deservingness model presented in Chapter 4.

The conceptual analysis of deservingness can also be applied to how people judge the fairness of distributions of rewards. For example, one might ask whether Person A deserves a higher reward than Person B when there is a set of rewards to be allocated (e.g., Adams, 1965). This judgment may depend upon the respective inputs of each person, upon the needs and values of the judge or observer, and upon contextual variables that relate to group, culture, and the aims or goals that the allocator is attempting to achieve via the allocation (e.g., enhanced performance, social harmony). For example, in a situation where the goal is to enhance the performance of the group, higher rewards may be seen to be more deserved when they are associated with higher performance for which a group member is seen to be responsible. The higher performance would have higher positive valence, consistent with the group goal and with achievement values. I would expect that judgments of higher deservingness would be stronger among judges or observers who hold stronger achievement values and when the situation makes these values salient.

In contrast, when the goal is to achieve harmony within the group, differences in performance among group members would become less important as a basis for allocation, and allocations would be more influenced by egalitarian values. The issue of deservingness may then become less important in this type of situation where a person's performance is less relevant and where more general goals of group harmony and cooperation are more salient.

Studies from my research program concerned with the allocation of rewards in both laboratory and realistic situations support the role that values play in the way allocations are made and in how people react to those allocations (Feather, 1990b; 1991; Feather & O'Driscoll, 1980).

The Role of Affect

My analysis has assumed that affective reactions to positive and negative outcomes follow cognitive judgments, especially judgments of deservingness or undeservingness. It could be argued, however, that the causal direction is from affect to cognition rather than from cognition to affect, that is, the outcome may lead to a rapidly occurring positive or negative feeling that then influences the cognitive judgments that are made. For example, feeling happy about an outcome may lead to the judgment that the outcome is deserved; feeling disappointed or sad about an outcome may lead to the judgment that the outcome is undeserved. Thus, an immediately occurring emotional state variable may have direct effects on cognitive judgments.

The anger or distress that people experience about a heinous offense may also lead them into a process of defensive attribution (e.g., Lerner & Miller, 1978; Shaver, 1970) in which they demand a scapegoat and bias their judgments of responsibility and deservingness accordingly.

The general question concerning the causal direction of the linkage between cognition and affect is a complex one that is not easy to resolve (e.g., Forgas, 1995; Parkinson, 1997; Parkinson & Manstead, 1992; Schwarz, 1990; Schwarz & Clore, 1996; Zajonc, 1980, 1998). It is like the question of which came first, the chicken or the egg. The effects of each variable are probably reciprocal with cognition influencing affect and affect influencing cognition. Both variables are intertwined and difficult to separate in empirical studies. Moreover, in the deservingness model the values held by people are assumed to be linked to the cognitive-affective system so that the judgments made in regard to the evaluation of actions and outcomes have some grounding in affect.

A recent study by J. Lerner, Goldberg, and Tetlock (1998) explored the joint impact of accountability, anger, and authoritarianism on attributions of responsibility and punitiveness toward defendants in a set of four vignettes that varied the conditions under which each defendant harmed another person in a work situation. They found that, when participants were not subsequently accountable to another person for their judgments, self-reported anger primed via a video clip they watched carried over to affect their judgments of punitiveness toward the defendant who committed the offense. When participants were told they would be accountable to another person for their judgments, self-reported anger did not influence punitiveness. Instead there was evidence that the degree to which the defendant was seen to act intentionally and with free will rather than being coerced predicted punitiveness. Lerner et al. (1998) proposed that this attenuation of the effects of anger in the accountable condition was probably the result of more nuanced, systematic cognitive processing, "a conscious monitoring of mental processing in which accountable participants ask themselves the question: What justification do I have for assigning blame and assigning punishment" (p. 571). In the not accountable condition this systematic cognitive processing would be less likely to occur because participants were not required to defend their judgments to another person. In this case the effects of anger followed a more simplified or heuristic route, less complicated by conscious, rational processes. This distinction between systematic processing and a simpler mode of reaction is consistent with M. Lerner's (1987) distinction between rational, controlled responses that take account of the normative framework and that are more likely to occur when there is less emotional involvement and more primitive, scripted responses that are based on early learning and that are more likely to occur under conditions of high emotional involvement. J. Lerner et al. also found that the anger-primed participants made more punitive judgments and that punitiveness was also higher for high authoritarians than for low authoritarians.

Further research could attempt to disentangle the effects of cognition and affect in the context of judgments of responsibility and deservingness, though that will be no easy task.

We also need more research that investigates the conditions under which judgments of deservingness are based on preconscious automatic cognitive processes as opposed to conscious and systematic cognitive processes. Does the former route to judgment occur more under conditions of high personal involvement as Lerner claims? Cognitive theorists and researchers in the areas of attitude theory and persuasion have argued that "mindless" behavior and the use of easy decision rules or heuristics may be more likely to occur when, for example, a person has low motivation to think about an issue, is limited in the capacity to think about an issue because of lack of knowledge, and is in a situation where there is insufficient information to enable the person to come to a considered judgment (e.g., Ajzen, 1996; Chaiken, 1987; Chaiken, Wood, & Eagly, 1996; Petty & Cacioppo, 1986). Recall also that heuristic fairness theory assumes that people may make snap judgments about fairness when there is incomplete information or when the information is difficult to process and interpret. Sometimes people use quick decision rules when the information is complex and there is pressure to respond quickly.

I would not want to discount the importance of automatic processes that occur outside of conscious awareness or heuristic processes that may underlie some judgments of deservingness. The automaticity may also relate, however, to the degree to which the underlying cognitive structures involve balanced or harmonious sets of relations. Earlier in Chapter 4, I suggested that judgments of deservingness may be relatively quick or automatic when relations in the corresponding deservingness structures are balanced. Under such conditions a person might not think much about the reasons for his or her judgment. The decision is an easy one for the person to make. Thinking would be more likely to occur, however, when there are unbalanced relations in the corresponding deservingness structures. The imbalance or lack of harmony has to be resolved in some way and systematic processing of information would then become more evident.

Balance Assumptions

I assumed that relations within the structures contained in the deservingness model tend toward a state of harmony or balance (Heider, 1958). I also noted that these structures do not presently allow for the representation of the strength of relations but only for their sign (positive or negative). I drew attention to recent developments in cognitive theory (e.g., Read & Miller, 1994) that take account of knowledge structures and that set the balance principle within the context of cognitive models, enabling a treatment of strength of relations and modes of resolution of imbalance.

Recently, Eagly and Chaikin (1998) provided a discussion of classical balance theory and a summary of more recent developments in which the principle of balance is considered in relation to more complex cognitive theories. Eagly and Chaikin refer in particular to cognitive principles inherent in the associative network analysis of memory and in connectionist models involving local constraint-satisfaction networks that use the language of nodes, linkages, and spread of activation (e.g., Anderson, 1983; Judd & Krosnick, 1989; McClelland & Rumelhart, 1981; Read & Miller, 1994; Shultz & Lepper, 1996; Smith, 1998; Spellman, Ullman, & Holyoake, 1993; Thagard, 1989). Eagly and Chaikin argue that restating balance theory in terms of these kinds of models brings in propositions that are not part of balance theory but supplement it, thereby permitting new approaches to some of the old problems of balance theory, such as how to conceptualize strength of relations and different ways of resolving imbalance. Consideration of these new developments is beyond the scope of the present book but it should be possible to relate them to the deservingness model and use them to extend the analysis.

My discussion of the structural model of deservingness has focused on possible changes in relations within each structure when the structure is unbalanced. However, people confronted by inconsistency may also attempt to resolve the imbalance by seeking out new information that might help to eliminate or reduce the imbalance (e.g., Eagly & Chaikin, 1998; Feather, 1967a, 1969c; Festinger, 1957, 1964; Frey, 1986). For example, a parent whose child received a low grade at school might look for mitigating circumstances that would soften a judgment that the child deserved the low grade, seeking out new information that would result in a higher degree of balance.

The search for new information, however, may not only be motivated by a need to achieve consistency in a person's cognitions. The search may also be determined by a need to find information that is useful in regard to achieving other specific goals (e.g., Feather, 1967a). In a court of law, for example, a defense lawyer arguing a case will be alert to any evidence that indicates that there were circumstances that would help to mitigate the alleged offense with which the defendant is charged. The lawyer in pursuit of a not-guilty verdict might also seek information that supports the good character of the defendant. This new evidence may have the effect of creating inconsistencies in the minds of the jurors, increasing the possibility that the offender will be found not guilty or charged with a lesser offense.

Further research using the deservingness model should investigate actual behaviors, such as information seeking, as well as cognitive restructuring that might follow states of imbalance.

Further Comment on Actions and Outcomes

The deservingness model discussed in this book has been applied to instrumental behavior sequences where outcomes follow actions. This contingency was represented by a positive unit relation between action and outcome. It was also noted that there are many cases where outcomes are seen as not contingent on a person's actions and where a null relation between action and outcome can be assumed.

It is important to note that the outcome that is referred to in the model is an outcome that applies to the actor and not to someone else.

For example, consider an offense where a person stabs another person and causes serious injury. The outcome considered in the deservingness model is not the injury to the other person but the consequence of the action in relation to the person who performed it. In this case, the outcome would be a penalty for the offense should the person be found guilty. Similarly, the outcome for an unemployed person who is seeking a job might be finding employment or not finding employment. The outcome is tied to the actor and to his or her performance. Feinberg (1970) made the same point when he wrote that "If a student deserves a high grade in a course, for example, his desert must be in virtue of some fact about *him*—his earlier performances, say, or his present abilities" (p. 59).

A further point concerns whether positive and negative outcomes attract consequences that are explicitly recognized in the form of rewards or punishments or benefits or costs that may also extend into the future. Most of the scenarios used in the research described in this book concerned this kind of situation where, for example, rewards (e.g., grades on an examination) or punishments (e.g., penalties for an offense) were specified. Sometimes, however, an outcome does not receive explicit recognition in this way but p might say that o deserves to be rewarded or deserves to be punished.

These kinds of situations, where there is an absence of more explicit and tangible recognition of positive and negative outcomes, are worth examining in the future. In these situations, the assumed punitiveness of right-wing authoritarians may become evident when there is a judgment that the perpetrator deserves to be punished and when the observers or judges are free to impose their own penalties (e.g., Altemeyer, 1981; Christie, 1991). Consistent with this research literature, we would expect high authoritarians to impose stiffer penalties when compared with low authoritarians. The studies of retributive justice described in previous chapters did not provide this freedom because the penalties were already determined in the scenarios that were used. The emphasis was on relations between assumed values (authoritarian or otherwise) and the perceived seriousness of the offense.

There is also need for more detailed analysis of relations between the perceived level of a reward or punishment that is a consequence of some positive or negative outcome and the degree to which the reward or punishment is seen to be deserved. Under what conditions will o be seen to receive too much reward or punishment or not enough reward or punishment? Answers to these questions will depend on information about the normative beliefs or expectations that people hold about what levels of rewards or punishments are appropriate (cf. Robinson & Darley, 1995; von Hirsch, 1986).

When o is judged to deserve more or less reward or punishment than he or she received, the discrepancy may itself be a condition for positive or negative affect (e.g., anger, sympathy) and for subsequent attempts to resolve the discrepancy. These attempts may take the form of providing o with more or less reward or punishment so as to bring the outcome into line with normative expectations. For example, parents who believe that their child deserved a higher examination grade than he or she received may recompense the child in other ways (e.g., by some special reward); employees in an organization who believe that a worker who violated union rules was not punished sufficiently may impose other penalties (e.g., a degree of social ostracism) to redress the discrepancy. Thus, as was the case with some other examples provided in the previous section, perceived inconsistencies within a structure may lead to behavioral attempts to resolve the inconsistencies as well as to cognitive restructuring.

We must also acknowledge that outcomes and their consequences are often tied to a person's status and role and occur in the absence of any action that the person takes. A child, for example, may receive an inheritance upon the death of a parent; a son might become king upon the death of a monarch. Do we say that the child deserves the inheritance or that the son deserves to be king? Probably not. These are examples of outcomes that seem to fall outside the deservingness model presented and they relate more to formal rules of entitlement where a person has legal rights.

A similar question relates to need. Do we say that a needy person deserves to be assisted? We may feel strongly that assistance should be provided on the basis of need, but we may not want to relate the "oughtness" of this assistance to deservingness. As Feinberg (1970) states:

> It is only in respect to compensation that need can be a desert basis. A man with a chronically sick wife or child deserves compensation since through no fault of his own he has a greater need than others.... But need is never a desert basis for any other form of treatment. In fact, in respect to most other modes of treatment, desert is *contrasted* with need. (p. 93)

For example, in a competition we give the prize to the person who deserves it by virtue of a winning performance rather than to the person who might need it the most. Consistent with this argument and in the interests of precision, I would prefer to restrict the use of the concept of deservingness to outcomes that can be clearly related to a person's actions and that are tied to the person rather than to someone else.

Psychology and the Law

Throughout this book I have attempted to draw attention to the way legal theorists have discussed some of the basic concepts (e.g., responsibility, desert) that are central to the models that I have presented. My discussion of the legal literature has necessarily been selective and it has avoided many of the subtle and intricate issues that legal theorists raise. I have been more concerned with establishing some core meanings of different concepts and with proposing a psychological rather than a legal analysis.

Many of the concepts and issues considered by legal theorists are relevant to psychological theories that focus on human agency, personal causation, the processing of information, attribution theory, the influence of social norms and values, social judgment, and other topics. There is a fertile area for collaboration between psychologists, sociologists, and legal theorists that is increasingly being acknowledged by the creation of cross-disciplinary journals (e.g., *Law and Human Behavior, Social Justice Research*) and by the publication of jointly authored monographs (e.g., Robinson & Darley, 1995).

By way of example, further research on the interface between psychology and the law might give more attention on the one side to the various ways in which alleged perpetrators try to avoid accountability for an offense (e.g., by denial, demurrers, justifications, excuses, etc.) and, on the other side, to the strategies that people use to assign credit to themselves for positive outcomes so that any consequent reward is seen to be deserved. We also need more research on the relations between perceived responsibility and the role and status of the person who is being judged, as well as further investigation of how individuals come to judge responsibility in relation to perceptions of cause (e.g., how they weight necessary versus sufficient cause, the directness or remoteness of the cause, and the contribution of the alleged perpetrator to the causal matrix) (Greene & Darley, 1998). Research by the author (Feather, 1985) has shown, for example, that causal attributions for unemployment were related to general conservatism as measured by the Wilson and Patterson Conservatism Scale (1968), to conservative voting preference, and to some of the terminal and instrumental values from the Rokeach Value Survey (Rokeach, 1973).

The attitudes that people hold toward particular laws and to the legal system are also worthy of further study. For example, people will probably see an offense as less serious when the offense violates a law that they perceive to be unjust than when the law is seen to be just and fair. For example, those who regard a strict law against abortion as unjust would view abortion as a less serious offense in certain circumstances when compared with those who believe that the law is just. Attitudes toward a law that relates to a specific offense would depend on a number of variables, among which would be the values that these attitudes express. As proposed in the social-cognitive process model (Chapter 6), values that are relevant to the offense that violates a law would influence the perceived seriousness of the offense, with consequent effects on judgments of deservingness and, via the mediation of deservingness, on other reactions that flow from these judgments. In general, as others have argued (e.g., Robinson & Darley, 1995, 1997), specific laws and legal codes that are in basic disagreement with community values are likely to inspire moral contempt and a consequent undermining of legal authority.

Methodological Issues

The studies from my research program that have been described in this book relied almost exclusively on procedures in which participants responded to hypothetical scenarios rather than to real-life events. I justified this procedure on the basis of the importance of maintaining experimental control over the variables that were of major interest. I attempted to devise realistic scenarios that would activate relevant values among participants. Results of the studies show that this research strategy was successful.

Clearly, however, it would be advantageous for both theoretical and empirical reasons to supplement the use of scenarios with studies that investigate reactions to real-life events where there may be strong beliefs and attitudes and high levels of feeling and emotion. My use of public figures in the studies of tall poppies drew from real life. Similarly, it should be possible to deal with actual court cases where high profile defendants are the focus of the media spotlight as has been done, for example, in the studies of reactions to the O. J. Simpson case referred to in the previous chapter. One could then apply the models described in this book by obtaining the public's views about responsibility, seriousness, and deservingness in regard to the alleged offense, the alleged perpetrator, and any penalty that might be imposed in the event of a guilty verdict. Such studies would lack the advantages of experimental control, but they would have high ecological validity.

CONCLUDING COMMENTS

An important assumption in the structural model of deservingness is that our perceptions of the actions and outcomes of both self and other depend in part on the values that we hold. In this sense justice is always to some extent in the eyes of the beholder, even though there are agreed-upon principles, codified laws, rules, and social norms that influence our beliefs and that help to regulate social conduct. Within this formal and informal system of prescriptions, however, people with different value systems will construe situations differently. In particular, they will evaluate actions and outcomes in different ways. For example, as my results showed, some may see an offense against authority as more or less serious than others, depending on the strength of values that are positively or negatively linked to right-wing authoritarianism.

That is not to say, however, that there are no commonalities in the value-based judgments that people make. People do not live in psychological worlds that are like islands in the sea of humanity. Individuals, groups, and societies may share common values, while differing from other individuals, groups, and societies in the importance that they assign to these values. Within a society, people may commit themselves to value priorities that are defined by a social or political ideology, and these priorities would be different from those who subscribe to a different ideology. Value systems also show similarities and differences in relation to gender, religion, political affiliation, and social class (Feather, 1975, 1987; Rokeach, 1973), as well as cross-culturally (Smith & Schwartz, 1997; Triandis, 1995). Thus, the social fabric presents us with both shared and disparate value systems and, within the constraints imposed by systems of laws, rules, and social norms, we would expect to find evidence for both similarity and difference in the way actions and outcomes are evaluated.

Values are therefore important variables to consider when we attempt to understand deservingness. They are the more distal general influences that affect our judgments via their effects on our evaluations of specific actions and outcomes. But, as I have tried to show throughout this book, they are not the only important variables. Our judgments of deservingness are also affected by the way we assess personal agency in terms of perceived responsibility, by perceptions of the positive or negative attributes of the person being judged, by interpersonal relations or self-reflexive relations of like or dislike, by variables that relate to social identity and self-categorization, and by knowledge structures that are based on more or less formalized codes of laws, regulations, and norms about which there is some degree of social consensus.

Taken together, these different variables affect our notions of justice both in situations where outcomes are positive and in situations where outcomes are negative and, via our judgments of deservingness, they influence the way we react to those outcomes both affectively and behaviorally.

References

Abelson, R. P. (1983). Whatever became of consistency theory? *Personality and Social Psychology Bulletin, 9*, 37–54.

Abelson, R. P., Aronson, E., McGuire, W. J., Newcomb, T. M., Rosenberg, M. J., & Tannenbaum, P. H. (Eds.) (1968). *Theories of cognitive consistency: A sourcebook.* Chicago: Rand McNally.

Abrams, D., & Hogg, M. A. (Eds.) (1990). *Social identity theory: Constructive and critical advances.* New York: Harvester Wheatsheaf.

Adams, J. A. (1965). Inequity in social exchange. In L. Berkowitz (Ed.), *Advances in experimental social psychology* (Vol. 2, pp. 267–299). New York: Academic Press.

Adorno, T. W., Frenkel-Brunswik, E., Levinson, D. J., & Sanford, R. N. (1950). *The authoritarian personality.* New York: Harper.

Ajzen, I. (1996). The social psychology of decision making. In E. T. Higgins & A. W. Kruglanski (Eds.), *Social psychology: Handbook of basic principles* (pp. 297–325). New York: Guilford.

Allport, G. W. (1937). *Personality: A psychological interpretation.* New York: Holt, Rinehart and Winston.

Altemeyer, B. (1981). *Right-wing authoritarianism.* Winnipeg: University of Manitoba Press.

Altemeyer, B. (1988). *Enemies of freedom: Understanding right-wing authoritarianism.* San Francisco: Jossey-Bass.

Altemeyer, B. (1996). *The authoritarian specter.* Cambridge, MA: Harvard University Press.

Altemeyer, B., & Hunsberger, B. (1992). Authoritarianism, religious fundamentalism, quest, and prejudice. *International Journal for the Psychology of Religion, 2*, 113–133.

Amato, P. R. (1979). Juror-defendant similarity and the assessment of guilt in politically motivated crimes. *Australian Journal of Psychology, 31*, 79–88.

Anderson, J. R. (1983). *The architecture of cognition.* Cambridge, MA: Harvard University Press.

Atkinson, J. W., & Feather, N. T. (Eds.) (1966). *A theory of achievement motivation.* New York: Wiley.

Bagby, R. M., Parker, J. D., Rector, N. A., & Kalemba, V. (1994). Racial prejudice in the Canadian legal system: Juror decisions in a simulated rape trial. *Law and Human Behavior, 18,* 339–350.

Baldwin, M. R., & Kleinke, C. L. (1994). Effects of severity of accident, intent, and "Alcoholism is a Disease" excuse on judgments of a drunk driver. *Journal of Applied Social Psychology, 24,* 2097–2109.

Ball-Rokeach, S. J., Rokeach, M., & Grube, J. (1984). *The great American values test: Influencing behavior and belief through television.* New York: Free Press.

Bargh, J. A. (1996). Automaticity in social psychology. In E. T. Higgins & A. W. Kruglanski (Eds.), *Social psychology: Handbook of basic principles* (pp. 169–183). New York: Guilford.

Baron, R. M., & Kenny, D. A. (1986). The moderator-mediator variable distinction in social psychological research: Conceptual, strategic, and statistical considerations. *Journal of Personality and Social Psychology, 51,* 1173–1182.

Berscheid, E., & Walster, E. H. (1978). *Interpersonal attraction* (2nd ed.). Reading, MA: Addison-Wesley.

Braithwaite, V. A. (1998). The value balance model of political evaluations. *British Journal of Psychology, 89,* 223–247.

Braithwaite, V. A., & Law, H. G. (1985). Structure of human values: Testing the adequacy of the Rokeach Value Survey. *Journal of Personality and Social Psychology, 49,* 250–263.

Braithwaite, V. A., & Scott, W. A. (1991). Values. In J. P. Robinson, P. R. Shaver, & L. S. Wrightsman (Eds.), *Measures of personality and social psychological attitudes* (Vol. 1, pp. 661–753). New York: Academic Press.

Branscombe, N. R. (1998). Thinking about one's gender group's privileges or disadvantages: Consequences for well-being in women and men. *British Journal of Social Psychology, 37,* 167–184.

Brendl, C. M., & Higgins, E. T. (1996). Principles of judging valence: What makes events positive or negative? In M. P. Zanna (Ed.), *Advances in experimental social psychology* (Vol. 28, pp. 95–160). Orlando, FL: Academic Press.

Brewer, M. B. (1977). An information-processing approach to attribution of responsibility. *Journal of Experimental Social Psychology, 13,* 58–69.

Brewer, M. B. (1979). In-group bias in the minimal intergroup situation: A cognitive-motivational analysis. *Psychological Bulletin, 86,* 307–324.

Brewer, M. B. (1991). The social self: On being the same and different at the same time. *Personality and Social Psychology Bulletin, 17,* 475–482.

Brewer, M. B. (1993). The role of distinctiveness in social identity and group behavior. In M. A. Hogg & D. Abrams (Eds.), *Group motivation: Social psychological perspectives* (pp. 1–16). New York: Harvester Wheatsheaf.

Brewer, M. B., & Brown, R. J. (1998). Intergroup relations. In D. T. Gilbert, S. T. Fiske, & G. Lindzey (Eds.), *The handbook of social psychology* (Vol. 2, pp. 554–594). Boston: McGraw-Hill.

Brewer, M. B., & Kramer, R. M. (1985). The psychology of intergroup attitudes and behavior. *Annual Review of Psychology, 36,* 219–243.

Brickman, P., Rabinowitz, V. C., Karuza, J., Coates, D., Cohn, E., & Kidder, L. (1982). Models of helping and coping. *American Psychologist, 37,* 368–384.

Brockner, J., & Wiesenfeld, B. M (1996). An integrative framework for explaining reactions to decisions: Interactive effects of outcomes and procedures. *Psychological Bulletin, 102*, 189–208.

Brown, R. (1965). *Social psychology.* New York: Free Press.

Brown, R., Hinkle, S., Ely, P.-G., Fox-Cardamone, L., Maras, P., & Taylor, L. A. (1992). Recognizing group diversity: Individualist-collectivist and autonomous-relational social orientations and their implications for intergroup processes. *British Journal of Social Psychology, 31*, 327–342.

Brunswik, E. (1952). The conceptual framework of psychology. In *International encyclopedia of unified science* (Vol. 1, No. 10). Chicago: University of Chicago Press.

Canter, D. (Ed.). (1985). *Facet theory: Approaches to social research.* New York: Springer-Verlag.

Carroll, J., Perkowitz, W., Lurigio, A., & Weaver, K. (1987). Sentencing goals, causal attributions, and personality. *Journal of Personality and Social Psychology, 52*, 107–118.

Cartwright, D., & Harary, F. (1956). Structural balance: A generalization of Heider's theory. *Psychological Review, 63*, 277–293.

Chaiken, S. (1987). The heuristic model of persuasion. In M. P. Zanna, J. M. Olson, & C. P. Herman (Eds.), *Social influence: The Ontario symposium,* Volume 5 (pp. 3–39). Hillsdale, NJ: Erlbaum.

Chaiken, S., Wood, W., & Eagly, A. H. (1996). Principles of persuasion. In E. T. Higgins & A. W. Kruglanski (Eds.), *Social psychology: Handbook of basic principles* (pp. 702–742). New York: Guilford.

Christie, R. (1991). Authoritarianism and related constructs. In J. P. Robinson, P. R. Shaver, & L. S. Wrightsman (Eds.), *Measures of personality and social psychological attitudes* (pp. 501–571). San Diego, CA: Academic Press.

Christie, R. (1993). Some experimental approaches to authoritarianism: II. Authoritarianism and punitiveness. In W. F. Stone, G. Lederer, & R. Christie, (Eds.), *Strength and weakness: The authoritarian personality today* (pp. 99–118). New York: Springer-Verlag.

Claes, J. A., & Rosenthal, D. M. (1990). Men who batter women: A study in power. *Journal of Family Violence, 5*, 215–224.

Cook, T. D., Crosby, F., & Hennigan, K. M. (1977). The construct validity of relative deprivation. In J. M. Suls & R. L. Miller (Eds.), *Social comparison processes: Theoretical and empirical perspectives* (pp. 307–333). Washington, DC: Hemisphere.

Costa, P. T. Jr., & McCrae, R. R. (1992). Four ways five factors are basic. *Personality and Individual Differences, 13*, 653–665.

Crick, N., & Dodge, K. A. (1994). A review and reformulation of social-information-processing mechanisms in children's social adjustment. *Psychological Bulletin, 115*, 74–101.

Crocker, J., Blaine, B., & Luhtanen, R. (1993). Prejudice, intergroup behaviour and self-esteem. Enhancement and protection motives. In M. A. Hogg & D. Abrams (Eds.), *Group motivation: Social psychological perspectives* (pp. 52–67). New York: Harvester Wheatsheaf.

Crosby, F. (1976). A model of egotistical relative deprivation. *Psychological Review*, *83*, 85–113.

Crosby, F. (1982). *Relative deprivation and working women*. New York: Oxford University Press.

Crosby, F. (1984). Relative deprivation in organizational settings. *Research in Organizational Behavior*, *6*, 51–93.

Crosby, F., & Gonzales-Intal, A. (1984). Relative deprivation and equity theories: Felt injustice and the undeserved benefits of others. In R. Folger (Ed.), *The sense of injustice: Social psychological perspectives* (pp. 141–166). New York: Plenum Press.

Crosby, F., Muehrer, P., & Loewenstein, G. (1986). Relative deprivation and explanation: Models and concepts. In J. M. Olson, C. P. Herman, & M. P. Zanna (Eds.), *Relative deprivation and social comparison: The Ontario symposium* (pp. 17–32). Hillsdale, NJ: Erlbaum.

Darby, B. W., & Schlenker, B. R. (1989). Children's reactions to transgressions: Effects of the actor's apology, reputation and remorse. *British Journal of Social Psychology*, *28*, 353–364.

D'Arcy, E. (1963). *Human acts: An essay on their moral evaluation*. Oxford: Clarendon.

Davis, J. A. (1959). A formal interpretation of the theory of relative deprivation. *Sociometry*, *22*, 280–296.

Deaux, K. (1972). To err is humanising: But sex makes a difference. *Representative Research in Social Psychology*, *3*, 20–28.

Deutsch, M. (1975). Equity, equality, and need: What determines which values will be used as the basis for distributive justice? *Journal of Social Issues*, *31*(3), 137–149.

Deutsch, M. (1985). *Distributive justice: A social-psychological perspective*. New Haven, CT: Yale University Press.

Doosje, B., Ellemers, N., & Spears, R. (1995). Perceived intragroup variability as a function of group status and identification. *Journal of Experimental Social Psychology*, *31*, 410–436.

Doty, R. M., Peterson, B. E., & Winter, D. G. (1991). Threat and authoritarianism in the United States. *Journal of Personality and Social Psychology*, *61*, 629–640.

Douglas, J. D. (1970). Deviance and respectability. In J. D. Douglas (Ed.), *Deviance and respectability: The social construction of moral meanings* (pp. 3–30). New York: Basic Books.

Dutton, D. G. (1992). Theoretical and empirical perspectives on the aetiology and prevention of wife assault. In R. De V. Peters, R. J. McMahon, & V. L. Quinsey (Eds.), *Aggression and violence throughout the life span* (pp. 192–221). Newbury Park, CA: Sage.

Dutton, D. G. (1995). *The domestic assault of women: Psychological and criminal justice perspectives*. Vancouver: University of British Columbia Press.

Eagly, A., & Chaikin, S. (1993). *The psychology of attitudes*. Fort Worth, TX: Harcourt Brace Jovanovich.

Eagly, A. H., & Chaikin, S. (1998). Attitude structure and function. In D. T. Gilbert,

S. T. Fiske, & G. Lindzey (Eds.), *The handbook of social psychology*, Vol. 1 (pp. 269–322). New York: Oxford University Press.

Eagly, A., & Steffen, V. J. (1986). Gender and aggressive behavior: A meta-analytic review of the social psychological literature. *Psychological Bulletin, 100*, 309–330.

Eckhardt, W. (1991). Authoritarianism. *Political Psychology, 12*, 97–124.

Ellemers, N., Van Rijswijk, W., Roefs, M., & Simons, C. (1997). Bias in intergroup perceptions: Balancing group identity with social reality. *Personality and Social Psychology Bulletin, 23*, 186–198.

Epstein, S., Lipson, A., Holstein, C., & Huh, E. (1992). Irrational reactions to negative outcomes: Evidence for two conceptual systems. *Journal of Personality and Social Psychology, 62*, 328–339.

Fairchild, H. H., & Cowan, G. (1997). The O. J. Simpson trial: Challenges to science and society. *Journal of Social Issues, 53*(3), 583–591.

Fazio, R. H. (1986). How do attitudes guide behavior? In R. M. Sorrentino & E. T. Higgins (Eds.), *Handbook of motivation and cognition: Foundations of social behavior* (Vol. 1, pp. 204–243). New York: Guilford.

Fazio, R. H. (1995). Attitudes as object-evaluation associations: Determinants, consequences, and correlates of attitude accessibility. In R. E. Petty & J. A. Krosnick (Eds.), *Attitude strength: Antecedents and consequences* (pp. 247–252). Mahwah, NJ: Erlbaum.

Feather, N. T. (1959a). Subjective probability and decision under uncertainty. *Psychological Review, 66*, 150–164.

Feather, N. T. (1959b). Success probability and choice behaviour. *Journal of Experimental Psychology, 58*, 257–266.

Feather, N. T. (1964). A structural balance model of communication effects. *Psychological Review, 71*, 291–313.

Feather, N. T. (1966). The prediction of interpersonal attraction: Effects of sign and strength of relations in different structures. *Human Relations, 19*, 213–237.

Feather, N. T. (1967a). An expectancy-value model of information-seeking behavior. *Psychological Review, 74*, 342–360.

Feather, N. T. (1967b). A structural balance approach to the analysis of communication effects. In L. Berkowitz (Ed.), *Advances in experimental social psychology* (Vol. 3, pp. 99–164). New York: Academic Press.

Feather, N. T. (1967c). Valence of outcome and expectation of success in relation to task difficulty and perceived locus of control. *Journal of Personality and Social Psychology, 7*, 372–386.

Feather, N. T. (1968). Valence of success and failure in relation to task difficulty: Past research and recent progress. *Australian Journal of Psychology, 20*, 111–122.

Feather, N. T. (1969a). Attitude and selective recall. *Journal of Personality and Social Psychology, 12*, 310–319.

Feather, N. T. (1969b). Attribution of responsibility and valence of success and failure in relation to initial confidence and task performance. *Journal of Personality and Social Psychology, 13*, 129–144.

Feather, N. T. (1969c). Preference for information in relation to consistency, novelty, intolerance of ambiguity, and dogmatism. *Australian Journal of Psychology, 21,* 235–249.

Feather, N. T. (1971a). Organization and discrepancy in cognitive structures. *Psychological Review, 78,* 355–379.

Feather, N. T. (1971b). Value differences in relation to ethnocentrism, intolerance of ambiguity, and dogmatism. *Personality: An International Journal, 2,* 349–366.

Feather, N. T. (1975). *Values in education and society.* New York: Free Press.

Feather, N. T. (1979). Value correlates of conservatism. *Journal of Personality and Social Psychology, 37,* 1617–1630.

Feather, N. T. (1980). Values in adolescence. In J. Adelson (Ed.), *Handbook of adolescent psychology* (pp. 247–294). New York: Wiley.

Feather, N. T. (1982a). Actions in relation to expected consequences: An overview of a research program. In N. T. Feather (Ed.), *Expectations and actions: Expectancy-value models in psychology* (pp. 53–95). Hillsdale, NJ: Erlbaum.

Feather, N. T. (Ed.). (1982b). *Expectations and actions: Expectancy-value models in psychology.* Hillsdale, NJ: Erlbaum.

Feather, N. T. (1984). Protestant ethic, conservatism, and values. *Journal of Personality and Social Psychology, 46,* 1132–1141.

Feather, N. T. (1985). Attitudes, values, and attributions: Explanations of unemployment. *Journal of Personality and Social Psychology, 48,* 876–889.

Feather, N. T. (1986). Cross-cultural studies with the Rokeach Value Survey: The Flinders program of research on values. *Australian Journal of Psychology, 38,* 269–283.

Feather, N. T. (1987). Gender differences in values: Implications of the expectancy-value model. In F. Halisch & J. Kuhl (Eds.), *Motivation, intention, and volition* (pp. 31–45). New York: Springer-Verlag.

Feather, N. T. (1989). Attitudes towards the high achiever: The fall of the tall poppy. *Australian Journal of Psychology, 41,* 239–267.

Feather, N. T. (1990a). Bridging the gap between values and actions. In E. T. Higgins & R. M. Sorrentino (Eds.), *Handbook of motivation and cognition: Foundations of social behavior* (Vol. 2, pp. 151–192). New York: Guilford.

Feather, N. T. (1990b). *The psychological impact of unemployment.* New York: Springer-Verlag.

Feather, N. T. (1990c). Reactions to equal reward allocations: Effects of situation, gender and values. *British Journal of Social Psychology, 29,* 315–329.

Feather, N. T. (1991). Variables relating to the allocation of pocket money to children: Parental reasons and values. *British Journal of Social Psychology, 30,* 221–234.

Feather, N. T. (1992a). An attributional and value analysis of deservingness in success and failure situations. *British Journal of Social Psychology, 31,* 125–145.

Feather, N. T. (1992b). Values, valences, expectations, and actions. *Journal of Social Issues, 48*(2), 109–124.

Feather, N. T. (1993a). Authoritarianism and attitudes toward high achievers. *Journal of Personality and Social Psychology, 65,* 152–164.

Feather, N. T. (1993b). The rise and fall of political leaders: Attributions, deservingness, personality, and affect. *Australian Journal of Psychology, 45,* 61–68.

Feather, N. T. (1994a). Attitudes toward high achievers and reactions to their fall. In M. P. Zanna (Ed.), *Advances in experimental social psychology* (Vol. 26, pp. 1–73). San Diego, CA: Academic Press.

Feather, N. T. (1994b). Human values and their relation to justice. *Journal of Social Issues, 50*(4), 129–151.

Feather, N. T. (1994c). Values, national identification and favouritism toward the ingroup. *British Journal of Social Psychology, 33,* 467–476.

Feather, N. T. (1995a). National identification and ingroup bias in majority and minority groups: A field study. *Australian Journal of Psychology, 47,* 129–136.

Feather, N. T. (1995b). Values, valences, and choice: The influence of values on the perceived attractiveness and choice of alternatives. *Journal of Personality and Social Psychology, 68,* 1135–1151.

Feather, N. T. (1996a). Domestic violence, gender, and perceptions of justice. *Sex Roles, 35,* 507–519.

Feather, N. T. (1996b). Extending the search for order in social motivation. *Psychological Inquiry, 7,* 223–229.

Feather, N. T. (1996c). Reactions to penalties for an offense in relation to authoritarianism, values, perceived responsibility, perceived seriousness, and deservingness. *Journal of Personality and Social Psychology, 71,* 571–587.

Feather, N. T. (1996d). Social comparisons across nations: Variables relating to the subjective evaluation of national achievement and to personal and collective self-esteem. *Australian Journal of Psychology, 48,* 53–63.

Feather, N. T. (1996e). Values, deservingness, and attitudes toward high achievers: Research on tall poppies. In C. Seligman, J. M. Olson, & M. P. Zanna (Eds.), *The psychology of values: The Ontario symposium,* Vol. 8 (pp. 215–251). Mahwah, NJ: Erlbaum.

Feather, N. T. (1998a). Attitudes toward high achievers, self-esteem, and value priorities for Australian, American, and Canadian students. *Journal of Cross-Cultural Psychology, 29,* 749–759.

Feather, N. T. (1998b). Reactions to penalties committed by the police and public citizens: Testing a social-cognitive process model of retributive justice. *Journal of Personality and Social Psychology, 75,* 528–544.

Feather, N. T., & Atchison, L. (1998). Reactions to an offence in relation to the status and perceived moral character of the offender. *Australian Journal of Psychology, 50,* 119–127.

Feather, N. T., & Dawson, S. (1998). Judging deservingness and affect in relation to another's employment or unemployment: A test of a justice model. *European Journal of Social Psychology, 28,* 361–381.

Feather, N. T., & Deverson, N. H. (in press). Reactions to a motor vehicle accident in relation to mitigating circumstances and the gender and moral worth of the driver. *Journal of Applied Social Psychology.*

Feather, N. T., & McKee, I. R. (1993). Global self-esteem and attitudes toward the high achiever for Australian and Japanese students. *Social Psychology Quarterly, 56,* 65–76.

Feather, N. T., Norman, M. A., & Worsley, A. (1998). Values and valences: Variables relating to the attractiveness and choice of food in different contexts. *Journal of Applied Social Psychology, 28,* 639–656.

Feather, N. T., & Oberdan, D. (in press). Reactions to penalties for an offence in relation to ethnic identity, responsibility, and authoritarianism. *Australian Journal of Psychology.*

Feather, N. T., & O'Brien, G. E. (1986a). A longitudinal analysis of the effects of different patterns of employment and unemployment on school-leavers. *British Journal of Psychology, 77,* 459–479.

Feather, N. T., & O'Brien, G. E. (1986b). A longitudinal study of the effects of employment and unemployment on school-leavers. *Journal of Occupational Psychology, 59,* 121–144.

Feather, N. T., & O'Brien, G. E. (1987). Looking for employment: An expectancy-valence analysis of job-seeking behaviour among young people. *Journal of Occupational Psychology, 78,* 251–272.

Feather, N. T., & O'Driscoll, M. P. (1980). Observers' reactions to an equal or equitable allocator in relation to allocator input, causal attributions, and value importance. *European Journal of Psychology, 10,* 107–129.

Feather, N. T., Volkmer, R. E., & McKee, I. R. (1991). Attitudes towards high achievers in public life: Attributions, deservingness, personality, and affect. *Australian Journal of Psychology, 43,* 85–91.

Feinberg, J. (1968). Action and responsibility. In A. R. White (Ed.), *The philosophy of action* (pp. 95–119). Oxford: Oxford University Press.

Feinberg, J. (1970). *Doing and deserving.* Princeton, NJ: Princeton University Press.

Ferguson, T., & Rule, B. (1983). An attributional perspective on anger and aggression. In R. Geen & E. Donnerstein (Eds.), *Aggression: Theoretical and empirical reviews* Vol. 1 (pp. 41–74). San Diego, CA: Academic Press.

Festinger, L. (1957). *A theory of cognitive dissonance.* Stanford, CA: Stanford University Press.

Festinger, L. (1964). *Conflict, decision, and dissonance.* London: Tavistock.

Festinger, L., & Carlsmith, J. M. (1959). Cognitive consequences of forced compliance. *Journal of Abnormal and Social Psychology, 58,* 203–210.

Fincham, F. D., & Jaspars, J. M. (1980). Attribution of responsibility: From man the scientist to man as lawyer. In L. Berkowitz (Ed.), *Advances in experimental social psychology* (Vol. 13, pp. 81–138). New York: Academic Press.

Fishbein, M., & Ajzen, I. (1973). Attribution of responsibility: A theoretical note. *Journal of Experimental Social Psychology, 9,* 148–153.

Folger, R. (Ed.). (1984). *The sense of injustice: Social psychological perspectives.* New York: Plenum Press.

Folger, R. (1986). A reference cognitions theory of relative deprivation. In J. M. Olson, C. P. Herman, & M. P. Zanna (Eds.), *Relative deprivation and social comparison: The Ontario symposium,* Vol. 4 (pp. 33–55). Hillsdale, NJ: Erlbaum.

Folger, R. (1987). Reformulating the preconditions of resentment: A referent cognitions model. In J. C. Masters & W. P. Smith (eds.), *Social comparison, social justice, and relative deprivation* (pp. 183–215). Hillsdale, NJ: Erlbaum.

Forgas, J. P. (1995). Mood and judgment: The affect infusion model (AIM). *Psychological Bulletin, 117*, 39–66.

Foster, G. M. (1972). The anatomy of envy: A study in symbolic behavior. *Current Anthropology, 13*, 165–186.

French, J. R. P., & Kahn, R. L. (1962). A programmatic approach to studying the industrial environment and mental health. *Journal of Social Issues, 18*(3), 1–47.

Frey, D. (1986). Recent research on selective exposure to information. In L. Berkowitz (Ed.), *Advances in experimental social psychology* (Vol. 19, pp. 41–80). New York: Academic Press.

Frieze, I. (1979). Perceptions of battered wives. In I. H. Frieze, D. Bar-Tal, & J. S. Carroll (Eds.), *New approaches to social problems: Applications of attribution theory* (pp. 79–108). San Francisco: Jossey-Bass.

Geen, R. G. (1998). Aggression and antisocial behavior. In D. T. Gilbert, S. T. Fiske, & G. Lindzey (Eds.), *The handbook of social psychology* (Vol. 2, pp. 317–356). New York: Oxford University Press.

Gerber, G. L. (1991). Gender stereotypes and power: Perceptions of roles in violent marriages. *Sex Roles, 24*, 439–458.

Gilligan, C. (1982). *In a different voice: Psychological theory and women's development.* Cambridge, MA: Harvard University Press.

Goffman, E. (1971). *Relations in public.* New York: Basic Books.

Graham, S., Weiner, B., & Zucker, G. S. (1997). An attributional analysis of punishment goals and public reactions to O. J. Simpson. *Personality and Social Psychology Bulletin, 23*, 331–346.

Greenberg, J., & Cohen, R. L. (Eds.). (1982). *Equity and justice in social behavior.* New York: Academic Press.

Greene, E. J., & Darley, J. M. (1998). Effects of necessary, sufficient, and indirect causation on judgments of criminal liability. *Law and Human Behavior, 22*, 429–451.

Greene, E., Raitz, A., & Lindblad, H. (1989). Jurors' knowledge of battered women. *Journal of Family Violence, 4*, 105–125.

Gurr, T. R. (1970). *Why men rebel.* Princeton, NJ: Princeton University Press.

Guttman, L. (1968). A general nonmetric technique for finding the smallest coordinate space for a configuration of points. *Psychometrika, 33*, 469–506.

Hamilton, V. L. (1978). Who is responsible? Toward a social psychology of responsibility attribution. *Social Psychology, 41*, 316–328.

Hamilton, V. L., & Hagiwara, S. (1992). Roles, responsibility, and accounts across cultures. *International Journal of Psychology, 7*, 157–179.

Hamilton, V. L., & Sanders, J. (1992). *Everyday justice: Responsibility and the individual in Japan and the United States.* New Haven, CT: Yale University Press.

Harary, F., Norman, R. Z., & Cartwright, D. (1965). *Structural models: An introduction to the theory of directed graphs.* New York: Wiley.

Harcum, E. R., Rosen, E. F., Pilkington, C. J., & Petty, L. C. (1995). External validation of laboratory evidence for earned dignity. *Journal of Applied Social Psychology, 25,* 1204–1213.

Hart, H. L. A. (1968). *Punishment and responsibility.* New York: Oxford University Press.

Hart, H. L. A., & Honoré, A. M. (1959). *Causation in the law.* London: Oxford University Press.

Hartshorne, H., & May, M. A. (1928). *Studies in the nature of character.* Vol. 1: *Studies in deceit.* New York: Macmillan.

Hartshorne, H., May, M. A., & Maller, J. B. (1929). *Studies in the nature of character.* Vol. II: *Studies in self-control.* New York: Macmillan.

Hartshorne, H., May, M. A., & Shuttleworth, F. K. (1930). *Studies in the nature of character.* Vol. III: *Studies in the organization of character.* New York: Macmillan.

Heath, A. (1976). *Rational choice and social exchange.* Cambridge: Cambridge University Press.

Heckhausen, H. (1977). Achievement motivation and its constructs: A cognitive model. *Motivation and Emotion, 1,* 283–329.

Heider, F. (1958). *The psychology of interpersonal relations.* New York: John Wiley.

Helmreich, R., Aronson, E., & Le Fan, J. (1970). To err is humanising—sometimes: Effects of self-esteem, competence, and a pratfall on interpersonal attraction. *Journal of Personality and Social Psychology, 16,* 259–264.

Heuer, L., Blumenthal, E., Douglas, A., & Weinblatt, T. (in press). The generality of procedural justice concerns: A deservedness model of group value and self-interest based fairness concerns. *Personality and Social Psychology Bulletin.*

Hewstone, M. (1989). *Causal attribution: From cognitive processes to collective beliefs.* Oxford: Basil Blackwell.

Higgins, E. T. (1996). Knowledge activation: Accessibility, applicability, and salience. In E. T. Higgins & A. W. Kruglanski (Eds.), *Social psychology: Handbook of basic principles* (pp. 133–168). New York: Guilford.

Hillier, L., & Foddy, M. (1993). The role of observer attitudes in judgments of blame in cases of wife assault. *Sex Roles, 29,* 629–644.

Hinkle, S., & Brown, R. (1990). Intergroup comparisons and social identity: some links and lacunae. In D. Abrams & M. A. Hogg (Eds.), *Social identity theory: Constructive and critical advances* (pp. 48–70). New York: Harvester Wheatsheaf.

Ho, R., & Venus, M. (1995). Reactions to a battered woman who kills her abused spouse: An attributional analysis. *Australian Journal of Psychology, 47,* 153–159.

Hogan, R. (1973). Moral conduct and moral character. *Psychological Bulletin, 32,* 644–657.

Hogan, R. (1975). Moral development and the structure of personality. In D. De Palma & J. Foley (Eds.), *Moral development: Current theory and research* (pp. 153–167). Hillsdale, NJ: Erlbaum.

Hogan, R., & Emler, N. P. (1981). Retributive justice. In M. J. Lerner & S. C. Lerner (Eds.), *The justice motive in social behavior* (pp. 125–143). New York: Plenum.

Hogg, M. A., & Abrams, D. (1988). *Social identification: A social psychology of intergroup relations and group processes.* London: Routledge.

Hogg, M. A., & Abrams, D. (1990). Social motivation, self-esteem, and social identity. In D. Abrams & M. A. Hogg (Eds.), *Group motivation: Constructive and critical approaches* (pp. 28–47). New York: Harvester Wheatsheaf.

Hogg, M. A., & Abrams, D. (1993). *Group motivation: Social psychological perspectives.* New York: Harvester Wheatsheaf.

Hogg, M. A., & Turner, J. C. (1987). Intergroup behaviour, self-stereotyping and the salience of social categories. *British Journal of Social Psychology, 26,* 325–340.

Hollander, E. P. (1958). Conformity, status, and idiosyncracy credit. *Psychological Review, 65,* 117–127.

Hollander, E. P. (1964). *Leaders, groups, and influence.* New York: Oxford University Press.

Holtzworth-Munroe, A. (1992). Attributions and maritally violent men: The role of cognitions in marital violence. In J. Harvey, T. Orbush, & A. L. Weber (Eds.), *Attributions, accounts, and close relationships* (pp. 165–175). New York: Springer-Verlag.

Insko, C. A. (1984). Balance theory, the Jordan paradigm, and the Wiest tetrahedron. In L. Berkowitz (Ed.), *Advances in experimental social psychology* (Vol. 18, pp. 89–140). New York: Academic Press.

Jetten, J., Spears, R., & Manstead, A. S. R. (1996). Intergroup norms and intergroup discrimination: Distinctive self-categorisation and social identity effects. *Journal of Personality and Social Psychology, 71,* 1222–1233.

Judd, C. M., & Krosnick, J. A. (1989). The structural bases of consistency among political attitudes: Effects of political expertise and attitude importance. In A. R. Pratkanis, S. J. Breckler, & A. G. Greenwald (Eds.), *Attitude structure and function* (pp. 99–128). Hillsdale, NJ: Erlbaum.

Kahneman, D., Slovic, P., & Tversky, A. (1982). *Judgment under uncertainty: Heuristics and biases.* Cambridge, U.K.: Cambridge University Press.

Kahneman, D., & Tversky, A. (1982). Availability and the simulation heuristic. In D. Kahneman, P. Slovic, and A. Tversky (Eds.), *Judgment under uncertainty: Heuristics and biases* (pp. 201–208). New York: Oxford University Press.

Karasawa, K. (1991). The effects of onset and offset responsibility and affects on helping judgments. *Journal of Applied Social Psychology, 1,* 482–499.

Kassin, S. M., & Wrightsman, L. S. (1988). *The American jury on trial: Psychological perspectives.* New York: Hemisphere.

Katz, D. (1960). The functional approach to the study of attitudes. *Public Opinion Quarterly, 24,* 163–204.

Kelman, H. C., & Hamilton, V. L. (1989). *Crimes of obedience: Toward a social psychology of authority and responsibility.* New Haven, CT: Yale University Press.

Kerr, N. L., Hymes, R. W., Anderson, A. B., & Weathers, J. E. (1995). Defendant-juror similarity and mock juror judgments. *Law and Human Behavior, 19,* 545–567.

Kirscht, J. P., & Dillehay, R. C. (1967). *Dimensions of authoritarianism.* Lexington: University of Kentucky Press.

Kleinke, C. L. (1975). *First impressions: The psychology of encountering others.* Englewood Cliffs, NJ: Prentice-Hall.

Kluckhohn, C. (1951). Values and value-orientations in the theory of action. In T. Parsons & E. Shils (Eds.), *Toward a general theory of action* (pp. 388–433). Cambridge, MA: Harvard University Press.

Kohlberg, L. (1984). *Psychology of moral development: The nature and validity of moral stages.* San Francisco: Harper & Row.

Kristiansen, C. M., & Giulietti, R. (1990). Perceptions of wife abuse: Effects of gender, attitudes toward women, and just-world beliefs among college students. *Psychology of Women Quarterly, 14,* 177–189.

Lagerspetz, K. M., Bjorkqvist, K., & Peltonen, T. (1988). Is indirect aggression typical of females? Gender differences in aggressiveness in 11 to 12 year old children. *Aggressive Behavior, 14,* 403–414.

Landy, D., & Aronson, E. (1969). The influence of the character of the criminal and his victim on the decisions of simulated jurors. *Journal of Experimental Social Psychology, 5,* 141–152.

Langer, E. (1975). The illusion of control. *Journal of Personality and Social Psychology, 32,* 311–328.

Langer, E. (1983). *The psychology of control.* Beverly Hills, CA: Sage.

Lerner, J. S., Goldberg, J. H., & Tetlock P. E. (1998). Sober second thought: The effects of accountability, anger, and authoritarianism on attributions of responsibility. *Personality and Social Psychology Bulletin, 24,* 563–574.

Lerner, M. J. (1965). Evaluation of performance as a function of performer's reward and attractiveness. *Journal of Personality and Social Psychology, 1,* 355–360.

Lerner, M. J. (1980). *The belief in the just world: A fundamental delusion.* New York: Plenum.

Lerner, M. J. (1987). Integrating societal and psychological rules of entitlement: The basic task of each social actor and fundamental problem for the social sciences. *Social Justice Research, 1,* 107–125.

Lerner, M. J. (1997). The justice motive: Where social psychologists found it, how they lost it, and where they may not find it again. Paper presented at the 6th International Conference on Social Justice Research, July 1–4, Potsdam, Germany.

Lerner, M. J. (1998). The two forms of belief in a just world: Some thoughts on why and how people care about justice. In L. Montada & M. J. Lerner (Eds.), *Responses to victimizations and belief in a just world* (pp. 247–269). New York: Plenum.

Lerner, M. J., & Miller, D. T. (1978). Just world research and the attribution process: Looking back and ahead. *Psychological Bulletin, 85,* 1030–1051.

Lerner, M. J., Miller, D. T., & Holmes, J. G. (1976). Deserving and the emergence of forms of justice. In L. Berkowitz & E. Walster (Eds.), *Advances in experimental social psychology* (Vol. 9, pp. 133–162). New York: Academic Press.

Leventhal, G. S. (1976). The distribution of rewards and resources in groups and organisations. In L. Berkowitz & E. Walster (Eds.), *Advances in experimental social psychology* (Vol. 9, pp. 91–131). New York: Academic Press.

Levine, J. M. (1989). Reaction to opinion deviance in small groups. In P. B. Paulus (Ed.), *Psychology of group influence* (2nd ed., pp. 187–231). Hillsdale, NJ: Erlbaum.

Lewin, K. (1935). *A dynamic theory of personality*. New York: McGraw-Hill.

Lewin, K. (1936). *Principles of topological psychology*. New York: McGraw-Hill.

Lewin, K. (1938). The conceptual representation and the measurement of psychological forces. *Contributions to psychological theory* (Vol. 1). (Reprinted in 1968 by Johnson Reprint Corporation, New York).

Lewin, K. (1951). *Field theory in social science: Selected theoretical papers* (D. Cartwright, Ed.). New York: Harper & Row.

Lewin, K., Dembo, T., Festinger, L., & Sears, P. S. (1944). Level of aspiration. In J. McV. Hunt (Ed.), *Personality and the behavior disorders* (Vol. 1, pp. 333–378). New York: Ronald.

Lind, E. A., & Tyler, T. R. (1988). *The social psychology of procedural justice*. New York: Plenum.

Lusk, C. M., & Judd, C. M. (1988). Political expertise and the structural mediators of candidate evaluations. *Journal of Experimental Social Psychology, 24,* 105–126.

McClelland, D. C. (1985). *Human motivation*. Glenview, IL: Scott, Foresman.

McClelland J. L., & Rumelhart, D. E. (1981). An interactive activation model of context effects in letter perception: Part I. An account of basic findings. *Psychological Review, 88,* 375–407.

McClelland, J. L., Rumelhart, D. E., & PDP Research Group (1986). *Parallel distributed processing explorations in the microstructure of cognition*: Vol. 1, *Foundations*. Cambridge, MA: MIT Press.

McConahay, J. G., Hardee, B. B., & Batts, V. (1981). Has racism declined? It depends on who's asking and what is asked. *Journal of Conflict Resolution, 25,* 563–579.

McCrae, R. R., & Costa, P. T. Jr. (1987). Validation of the five-factor model of personality. *Journal of Personality and Social Psychology, 52,* 81–90.

McGuire, W. J. (1960). A syllogistic analysis of cognitive relationships. In C. I. Hovland & M. J. Rosenberg (Eds.), *Attitude organization and change* (pp. 65–111). New Haven, CT: Yale University Press.

Maio, G. R., & Olson, J. M. (1994). Value-attitude-behaviour relations: The moderating effect of attitude functions. *British Journal of Social Psychology, 33,* 301–312.

Maio, G. R., & Olson, J. M. (1995). Relations between values, attitudes, and behavioral intentions: The moderating role of attitude function. *Journal of Experimental Social Psychology, 31,* 266–285.

Maio, G. R., & Olson, J. M. (in press a). Emergent themes and potential approaches to attitude function: The function-structure model of attitudes. In G. R. Maio

& J. M. Olson (Eds.), *Why we evaluate: Functions of attitudes*. Mahwah, NJ: Erlbaum.

Maio, G. R., & Olson, J. M. (in press b). What *is* a value expressive attitude? In G. R. Maio & J. M. Olson (Eds.), *Why we evaluate: Functions of attitudes*. Mahwah, NJ: Erlbaum.

Major, B. (1994). From social inequality to personal entitlement: The role of social comparisons, legitimacy appraisals, and group membership. In M. P. Zanna (Ed.), *Advances in experimental social psychology* (Vol. 26, pp. 293–355). New York: Academic Press,

Markus, H. R., & Kitayama, S. (1991). Culture and the self: Implications for cognition, emotion, and motivation. *Psychological Review, 98*, 224–253.

Marques, J. M. (1990). The black-sheep effect: Out-group homogeneity in social comparison settings. In D. Abrams & M. A. Hogg (Eds.), *Social identity theory: Constructive and critical advances* (pp. 131–151). Hemel Hempstead: Harvester Wheatsheaf.

Marques, J. M., & Paez, D. (1994). The "black-sheep effect": Social categorization, rejection of ingroup deviates, and perception of group variability. In W. Stroebe & M. Hewstone (Eds.), *European Review of Social Psychology* (Vol. 5, pp. 37–68). New York: Wiley.

Marques, J. M., & Yzerbyt, V. Y. (1988). The black-sheep effect: Judgmental extremity towards ingroup members in inter- and intragroup situations. *European Journal of Social Psychology, 18*, 287–292.

Marsh, H. W. (1990). A multidimensional, hierarchical model of self-concept: Theoretical and empirical justification. *Educational Psychology Review, 2*, 77–172.

Marsh, H. W., & Hattie, J. (1996). Theoretical perspectives on the structure of the self-concept. In B. A. Bracken (Ed.), *Handbook of self-concept: Developmental, social, and clinical considerations* (pp. 38–90). New York: Wiley.

Martin, J. (1981). Relative deprivation: A theory of distributive justice for an era of shrinking resources. *Research in Organizational Behavior, 3*, 53–107.

Martin, J. (1986). The tolerance of injustice. In J. M. Olson, C. P. Herman, & M. P. Zanna (Eds.), *Relative deprivation and social comparison: The Ontario symposium* (Vol. 4, pp. 217–242). Hillsdale, NJ: Erlbaum.

Masters, J. C., & Smith, W. P. (Eds.) (1987). *Social comparison, social justice, and relative deprivation: Theoretical, empirical, and policy perspectives*. Hillsdale, NJ: Erlbaum.

Mellers, B. A., & Baron, J. (Eds.) (1993). *Psychological perspectives on justice: Theory and applications*. Cambridge: Cambridge University Press.

Messick, D. M., & Cook, K. S. (Eds.) (1983). *Equity theory: Psychological and sociological perspectives*. New York: Praeger.

Messick, D. M., & Mackie, D. (1989). Intergroup relations. *Annual Review of Psychology, 40*, 45–81.

Mikula, G. (1980). On the role of justice in allocation decisions. In G. Mikula (Ed.), *Justice and social interaction* (pp. 127–166). New York: Springer-Verlag.

Mikula, G. (1993). On the experience of injustice. *European Review of Social Psychology, 4*, 223–244.

Miller, A. G., Collins, B. E., & Brief, D. E. (1995). Perspectives on obedience to authority: The legacy of the Milgram experiments. *Journal of Social Issues, 51*(3), 1–19.

Miller, D. L. (1974). Social justice. Unpublished D.Phil. thesis, Oxford University.

Miller, D. T. (1977). Personal deserving and justice for others: An exploration of the justice motive. *Journal of Experimental Social Psychology, 13*, 1–13.

Miller, D. T., & Vidmar, N. (1981). The social psychology of punishment reactions. In M. J. Lerner & S. C. Lerner (Eds.), *The justice motive in social behavior* (pp. 145–172). New York: Plenum.

Mirels, H., & Garrett, J. B. (1971). The Protestant ethic as a personality variable. *Journal of Consulting and Clinical Psychology, 36*, 40–44.

Mitchell, H. E., & Byrne, D. (1973). The defendant's dilemma: Effects of jurors' attitudes and authoritarianism on judicial decisions. *Journal of Personality and Social Psychology, 25*, 123–129.

Mitchell, T. R. (1982). Expectancy-value models in organizational psychology. In N.T. Feather (Ed.), *Expectations and actions: Expectancy-value models in psychology* (pp. 293–312). Hillsdale, NJ: Erlbaum.

Montada, L., & Lerner, M. J. (Eds.) (1998). *Responses to victimizations and belief in a just world.* New York: Plenum.

Nisbett, R. E., & Ross, L. (1980). *Human inference: Strategies and shortcomings of social judgment.* Englewood Cliffs, NJ: Prentice-Hall.

Oakes, P. J., Haslam, S. A., & Turner, J. C. (1994). *Stereotyping and social reality.* Oxford: Blackwell.

O'Driscoll, M. P., & Feather, N. T. (1985). Positive prejudice in ethnic attitudes: Australian data. *International Journal of Psychology, 20*, 95–107.

Olson, J. M., & Hafer, C. L. (1996). Affect, motivation, and cognition in relative deprivation research. In R. M. Sorrentino & E. T. Higgins (Eds.), *Handbook of motivation and cognition* (Vol. 3, pp. 85–117). New York: Guilford.

Parkinson, B. (1997). Untangling the appraisal-emotion connection. *Personality and Social Psychology Review, 1*, 62–79.

Parkinson, B., & Manstead, A. S. R. (1992). Appraisal as a cause of emotion. In M. S. Clark (Ed.), *Review of personality and social psychology: Vol. 13. Emotion* (pp. 122–149). Newbury Park, CA: Sage.

Pepitone, A., & L'Armand, K. (1996). The justice and injustice of life events. *European Journal of Social Psychology, 26*, 581–597.

Peterson, B. E., Doty, R. B., & Winter, D. G. (1993). Authoritarianism and attitudes toward contemporary social issues. *Personality and Social Psychology Bulletin, 19*, 174–184.

Pettigrew, T. F., & Meertens, R. W. (1995). Subtle and blatant prejudice in Western Europe. *European Journal of Social Psychology, 25*, 57–75.

Petty, R. E., & Cacioppo, J. T. (1986). The elaboration likelihood model of persuasion. In L. Berkowitz (Ed.), *Advances in experimental social psychology* (Vol. 19, pp. 123–205). San Diego, CA: Academic Press.

Piaget, J. (1932). *The moral judgment of the child.* New York: Harcourt Brace.

Pierce, M. C., & Harris, R. J. (1993). The effect of provocation, race, and injury description on men's and women's perception of a wife-battering incident. *Journal of Applied Social Psychology, 23,* 767–790.

Pierce, M. C., & Harris, R. J. (1994). Attributions about spouse abuse: It matters who the batterers and victims are. *Sex Roles, 30,* 553–565.

Prentice, D. A., & Crosby, F. (1987). The importance of context for assessing deservingness. In J. C. Masters & W. P. Smith (Eds.), *Social comparison, social justice, and relative deprivation* (pp. 151–182). Hillsdale, NJ: Erlbaum.

Read, S. J., & Miller, L. C. (1994). Dissonance and balance in belief systems: The promise of parallel constraint satisfaction processes and connectionist modeling approaches. In R. C. Schank & E. Langer (Eds.), *Beliefs, reasoning, and decision making: Psycho-logic in honor of Bob Abelson* (pp. 209–235). Hillsdale, NJ: Erlbaum.

Rector, N. A., & Bagby, R. M. (1997). Minority juridic decision making. *British Journal of Social Psychology, 36,* 69–81.

Ridgeway, C. L. (1978). Conformity, group-oriented motivation, and status attainment in small groups. *Social Psychology, 41,* 175–188.

Rim, Y. (1970). Valences and attitudes. *Personality: An International Journal, 1,* 243–250.

Robinson, P. H., & Darley, J. M. (1995). *Justice, liability, and blame.* Boulder, CO: Westview.

Robinson, P. H., & Darley, J. M. (1997). The utility of desert. *Northwestern University Law Review, 91,* 453–499.

Rohan, M. J., & Zanna, M. P. (1996). Value transmission in families. In C. Seligman, J. M. Olson, & M. P. Zanna (Eds.), *The psychology of values: The Ontario symposium* (Vol. 8, pp. 253–276). Mahwah, NJ: Erlbaum.

Rokeach, M. (1960). *The open and closed mind.* New York: Basic Books.

Rokeach, M. (1973). *The psychology of human values.* New York: Free Press.

Rokeach, M. (1979) (Ed.). *Understanding human values: Individual and societal.* New York: Free Press.

Rosenberg, M. (1965). *Society and the adolescent self-image.* Princeton, NJ: Princeton University Press.

Rosoff, S. M. (1989). Physicians as criminal defendants: Specialty, sanctions, and status liability. *Law and Human Behavior, 13,* 231–236.

Rotter, J. B. (1954). *Social learning and clinical psychology.* New York: Prentice-Hall.

Rotter, J. B. (1982). Social learning theory. In N. T. Feather (Ed.), *Expectations and actions: Expectancy-value models in psychology* (pp. 241–260). Hillsdale, NJ: Erlbaum.

Rubin, Z., & Peplau, L. A. (1973). Belief in a just world and reactions to another's lot: A study of participants in the national draft lottery. *Journal of Social Issues, 29*(4), 73–93.

Runkel, P. J., & Peizer, D. B. (1968). The two-valued orientation of current equilibrium theory. *Behavioral Science, 13,* 56–65.

Runciman, W. G. (1966). *Relative deprivation and social justice: A study of attitudes to social inequality in twentieth-century England.* Berkeley, CA: University of California Press.

Sagiv, L., & Schwartz, S. H. (1995). Value priorities and readiness for outgroup social contact. *Journal of Personality and Social Psychology, 69,* 437–448.

Sanford, R. N. (1973). Authoritarian personality in contemporary perspective. In J. N. Knutson (Ed.), *Handbook of political psychology* (pp. 139–170). San Francisco: Jossey-Bass.

Saunders, D. G. (1988). Wife abuse, husband abuse, or mutual combat? A feminist perspective on the empirical findings. In K. Ylloe & M. Bograd (Eds.), *Feminist perspectives on wife abuse* (pp. 90–113). Newbury Park, CA: Sage.

Saunders, D. G., Lynch, A. B., Grayson, M., & Linz, D. (1987). The inventory of beliefs about wife beating: The construction and initial validation of a measure of beliefs and attitudes. *Violence and Victims, 3,* 39–57.

Schank, R. C., & Abelson, R. P. (1977). *Scripts, plans, goals and understanding.* Hillsdale, NJ: Erlbaum.

Schleifer, M. (1973). Psychological explanations and personal relations. In A. Montefiore (Ed.), *Philosophy and personal relations* (pp. 170–190). London: Routledge.

Schlenker, B. R., Britt, T. W., Pennington, J., Murphy, R., & Doherty, K. (1994). The triangle model of responsibility. *Psychological Review, 101,* 632–652.

Schwartz, S. H. (1992). Universals in the content and structure of values: Theoretical advances and empirical tests in 20 countries. In M. P. Zanna (Ed.), *Advances in experimental social psychology* (Vol. 25, pp. 1–65). Orlando, FL: Academic Press.

Schwartz, S. H. (1994a). Are there universal aspects in the structure and contents of human values? *Journal of Social Issues, 50*(4), 19–45.

Schwartz, S. H. (1994b). Beyond individualism/collectivism: New cultural dimensions of values. In U. Kim, H. C. Triandis, C. Kagitcibasi, S.-C. Choi, & G. Yoon (Eds.), *Individualism and collectivism: Theory, method, and applications* (pp. 85–119). Thousand Oaks, CA: Sage.

Schwartz, S. H. (1996). Value priorities and behavior: Applying a theory of integrated value systems. In C. Seligman, J. M. Olson, & M. P. Zanna (Eds.), *The psychology of values: The Ontario symposium* (Vol. 8, pp. 1–24). Mahway, NJ: Erlbaum.

Schwartz, S. H., & Bilsky, W. (1987). Toward a psychological structure of human values. *Journal of Personality and Social Psychology, 53,* 550–562.

Schwartz, S. H., & Bilsky, W. (1990). Toward a theory of the universal content and structure of human values: Extensions and cross-cultural replications. *Journal of Personality and Social Psychology, 58,* 878–891.

Schwarz, N. (1990). Feelings as information: Informational and motivational functions of affective states. In E. T. Higgins & R. M. Sorrentino (Eds.), *Handbook of motivation and cognition: Foundations of social behavior* (Vol. 2, pp. 527–561). New York: Guilford.

Schwarz, N., & Clore, G. T. (1996). Feelings and phenomenal experience. In E. T. Higgins or A. W. Kruglanski (Eds.), *Social psychology: Handbook of basic principles* (pp. 433–463). New York: Guilford.

Schweder, R. A., & Haidt, J. (1993). The future of moral psychology. *Psychological Science, 4,* 360–365.

Seligman, M. E. P. (1975). *Helplessness: On depression, development, and death.* San Francisco: Freeman.

Shaver, K. G. (1970). Defensive attribution: Effects of severity and relevance on the responsibility assigned for an accident. *Journal of Personality and Social Psychology, 14,* 101–113.

Shaver, K. G. (1985). *The attribution of blame: Causality, responsibility, and blameworthiness.* New York: Springer-Verlag.

Shultz, T. R., & Darley, J. M. (1991). An information processing model of retributive justice based on "legal reasoning." In W. M. Kurtines & J. L. Gewirtz (Eds.), *Handbook of moral behavior and development: Research* (Vol. 2, pp. 247–278). Hillsdale NJ: Erlbaum.

Shultz, T. R., & Lepper, M. R. (1996). Cognitive dissonance reduction as constraint satisfaction. *Psychological Review, 103,* 219–240.

Shultz, T. R., & Schleifer, M. (1983). Towards a refinement of attribution concepts. In J. Jaspars, F. D. Fincham, & M. Hewstone (Eds.), *Attribution theory and research: Conceptual, developmental and social dimensions* (pp. 37–62). London: Academic Press.

Shultz, T. R., Schleifer, M., & Altman, I. (1981). Judgments of causation, responsibility, and punishment in cases of wrong-doing. *Canadian Journal of Behavioral Science, 13,* 238–253.

Sigall, H., & Ostrove, N. (1975). Beautiful but dangerous: Effects of offender attractiveness and nature of the crime on juridic judgment. *Journal of Personality and Social Psychology, 31,* 410–414.

Simons, C., & Piliavin, J. (1972). The effect of deception on reactions to a victim. *Journal of Personality and Social Psychology, 21,* 56–60.

Skinner, E. A. (1996). A guide to constructs of control. *Journal of Personality and Social Psychology, 71,* 549–570.

Skitka, L. J., & Tetlock, P. E. (1992). Allocating scarce resources: A contingency model of distributive justice. *Journal of Experimental Social Psychology, 28,* 491–522.

Skitka, L. J., & Tetlock, P. E. (1993). Providing public assistance: Cognitive and motivational processes underlying liberal and conservative policy preferences. *Journal of Personality and Social Psychology, 65,* 1205–1223.

Skolnick, P., & Shaw, J. I. (1994). Is defendant status a liability or a shield? *Journal of Applied Social Psychology, 24,* 1827–1836.

Skolnick, P., & Shaw, J. I. (1997). The O. J. Simpson criminal trial verdict: Racism or status shield. *Journal of Social Issues, 53*(3), 503–516.

Smith, E. R. (1998). Mental representations and memory. In D. T. Gilbert, S. T. Fiske, & G. Lindzey (Eds.), *The handbook of social psychology* (Vol. 1, pp. 391–445). New York: Oxford University Press.

Smith, M. B., Bruner, J. S., & White, R. W. (1956). *Opinions and personality.* New York: Wiley.

Smith, P. B., & Schwartz, S. H. (1997). Values. In J. W. Berry, M. H. Segall, & C. Kagitcibasi (Eds.), *Handbook of cross-cultural psychology*, 2nd ed. (Vol. 3, pp. 77–118). Boston: Allyn & Bacon.

Spears, R., Doosje, B., & Ellemers, N. (1997). Self-stereotyping in the face of threats to group status and distinctiveness: The role of group identification. *Personality and Social Psychology Bulletin, 23,* 538–553.

Spellman, B. A., Ullman, J. B., & Holyoake, K. J. (1993). A coherence model of cognitive consistency: Dynamics of attitude change during the Persian Gulf War. *Journal of Social Issues, 49*(4), 147–165.

Spence, J. T. (Ed.) (1983). *Achievement and achievement motives: Psychological and sociological approaches.* San Francisco: Freeman.

Steffensmeier, D. J., & Terry, R. M. (1973). Deviance and respectability: An observational study of reactions to shoplifting. *Social Forces, 51,* 417–426.

Steiger, J. H. (1980). Tests for comparing elements of a correlation matrix. *Psychological Bulletin, 87,* 245–251.

Steil, J. M. (1994). Equality and fairness in marriage. In M. J. Lerner & G. Mikula (Eds.), *Entitlement and the affectional bond: Justice in close relationships* (pp. 229–258). New York: Plenum.

Stewart, J. E. (1980). Defendant's attractiveness as a factor in the outcome of criminal trials: An observational study. *Journal of Applied Social Psychology, 10,* 348–361.

Stone, W. F., Lederer, G., & Christie, R. (Eds.) (1993). *Strength and weakness: The authoritarian personality today.* New York: Springer-Verlag.

Summers, G., & Feldman, N. S. (1984). Blaming the victim versus blaming the perpetrator: An attributional analysis of spouse abuse. *Journal of Social and Clinical Psychology, 2,* 339–347.

Tajfel, H. (1978). *Differentiation between social groups.* San Diego, CA: Academic Press.

Tajfel, H., & Turner, J. C. (1986). An integrative theory of intergroup conflict. In W. G. Austin & S. Worchel (Eds.), *The social psychology of intergroup relations* (pp. 33–47). Monterey, CA: Brooks-Cole.

Tesser, A., & Leone, C. (1977). Cognitive schemas and thought as determinants of attitude change. *Journal of Experimental Social Psychology, 13,* 340–356.

Tesser, A., & Martin, L. (1996). The psychology of evaluation. In E. T. Higgins & A. W. Kruglanski (Eds.), *Social psychology: Handbook of basic principles* (pp. 400–432). New York: Guilford.

Tetlock, P. E. (1986). A value pluralism model of ideological reasoning. *Journal of Personality and Social Psychology, 50,* 365–375.

Tetlock, P. E., Peterson, R. S., & Lerner, J. S. (1996). Revising the value pluralism model: Incorporating social content and context variables. In C. Seligman, J. M. Olson, & M. P. Zanna (Eds.), *The psychology of values: The Ontario symposium* (Vol. 8, pp. 25–51). Mahwah, NJ: Erlbaum.

Thagard, P. (1989). Explanatory coherence. *Behavioral and Brain Sciences, 12,* 435–467.

Thagard, P. (1992). *Conceptual revolutions.* Princeton, NJ: Princeton University Press.

Thibaut, J., & Walker, L. (1975). *Procedural justice: A psychological analysis.* Hillsdale, NJ: Erlbaum.

Tolman, E. C. (1932). *Purposive behavior in animals and men.* New York: Century.

Tolman, E. C. (1955). Principles of performance. *Psychological Review, 62*, 315–326.

Triandis, H. C. (1995). *Individualism and collectivism*. Boulder, CO: Westview.

Turiel, E. (1983). *The development of moral knowledge: Morality and convention*. New York: Cambridge University Press.

Turner, J. C., Hogg, M. A., Oakes, P. J., Reicher, S. D., & Wetherell, M. S. (1987). *Rediscovering the social group: A self-categorization theory*. Oxford: Basil Blackwell.

Tyler, T. R., Boeckmann, R. J., Smith, H. J., & Huo, Y. J. (1997). *Social justice in a diverse society*. Boulder, CO: Westview.

Tyler, T. R., & Kramer, R. (1996). *Trust in organizations*. Thousand Oaks, CA: Sage.

Tyler, T. R., & Lind, E. A. (1992). A relational model of authority in groups. In M. P. Zanna (Ed.), *Advances in experimental social psychology* (Vol. 25, pp. 115–191). New York: Academic Press.

Tyler, T. R., & Smith, H. J. (1998). Social justice and social movements. In D. Gilbert, S.T. Fiske, & G. Lindzey (Eds.), *The handbook of social psychology* (Vol. 2, pp. 595–629). New York: Oxford University Press.

Uleman, J. S., & Bargh, J. A. (Eds.) (1989). *Unintended thought*. New York: Guilford.

Van den Bos, K., Lind, E. A., Vermunt, R., & Wilke, H. A. M. (1997). How do I judge my outcome when I do not know the outcome of others? The psychology of the fair process effect. *Journal of Personality and Social Psychology, 72*, 1034–1046.

Van den Bos, K., Vermunt, R., & Wilke, H. A. M. (1997). Procedural and distributive justice: What is fair depends more on what comes first than on what comes next. *Journal of Personality and Social Psychology, 72*, 95–104.

Van den Bos, K., Lind, E. A., & Wilke, H. A. M. (in press). The psychology of procedural and distributive justice viewed from the perspective of fairness heuristic theory. In R. Cropanzano (Ed.), *Justice in the workplace: Volume II—From theory to practice*. Mahwah, NJ: Erlbaum.

van Knippenberg, A., & Ellemers, N. (1993). Strategies in inter-group relations. In M. A. Hogg & D. Abrams (Eds.), *Group motivation: Social psychological perspectives* (pp. 17–32). New York: Harvester Wheatsheaf.

Vermunt, R., & Steensma, H. (Eds.) (1991). *Social justice in human relations* (Vols. 1 and 2). New York: Plenum.

von Hirsch, A. (1986). *Doing justice: The choice of punishments*. Boston: Northeastern University Press.

von Hirsch, A., & Jareborg, N. (1991). Gauging criminal harm: A living-standard analysis. *Oxford Journal of Legal Studies, 11*, 1–38.

Vroom, V. H. (1964). *Work and motivation*. New York: Wiley.

Walker, I., & Pettigrew, T. F. (1984). Relative deprivation theory: An overview and conceptual critique. *British Journal of Social Psychology, 23*, 301–310.

Walker, L. E. (1984). *The battered woman syndrome*. New York: Springer.

Walster, E., Berscheid, E., & Walster, G. W. (1976). New directions in equity research. In L. Berkowitz (Ed.), *Advances in experimental social psychology* (Vol. 9, pp. 1–42). New York: Academic Press.

Walster, E., Walster, G. W., & Berscheid, E. (1978). *Equity: Theory and research.* Boston: Allyn & Bacon.

Weber, M. (1976). *The Protestant ethic and the spirit of capitalism,* T. Parsons (Trans.). London: George Allen & Unwin. (Original work published 1904–1905).

Weinberger, J., & McClelland, D. C. (1990). Cognitive versus traditional motivational models: Irreconcilable or complementary? In E. T. Higgins & R. M. Sorrentino (Eds.). *Handbook of motivation and cognition: Foundations of social behavior* (Vol. 2, pp. 562–597). New York: Guilford.

Weiner, B. (1986). *An attributional theory of motivation and emotion.* New York: Springer-Verlag.

Weiner, B. (1992). *Human motivation: Metaphors, theories, and research.* Newbury Park, CA: Sage.

Weiner, B. (1995). *Judgments of responsibility: A foundation for a theory of social conduct.* New York: Guilford.

Weiner, B. (1996). Searching for order in social motivation. *Psychological Inquiry, 7,* 199–216.

Weiten, W. (1980). The attraction-leniency effect in jury research: An examination of external validity. *Journal of Applied Social Psychology, 10,* 340–347.

Wellens, A. R., & Thistlethwaite, D. L. (1971a). An analysis of two quantitative theories of cognitive balance. *Psychological Review, 78,* 141–150.

Wellens, A. R., & Thistlethwaite, D. L. (1971b). Comparison of three theories of cognitive balance. *Journal of Personality and Social Psychology, 20,* 89–92.

White, G. F. (1975). Public responses to hypothetical crimes: Effect of offender and victim status and seriousness of the offence on punitive reactions. *Social Forces, 53,* 411–419.

Wiest, N. M. (1965). A quantitative extension of Heider's theory of cognitive balance applied to interpersonal perception and self-esteem. *Psychological Monographs, 79*(14) (Whole No. 607).

Wiggins, J. A., Dill, F., & Schwartz, R. D. (1965). On "status liability." *Sociometry, 28,* 197–209.

Wiggins, J. S., & Trapnell, P. D. (1997). Personality structure: The return of the big five. In R. Hogan, J. Johnson, & S. Briggs (Eds.), *Handbook of personality psychology* (pp. 737–765). San Diego: Academic Press.

Williams, R. M. (1968). Values. In D. L. Sills (Ed.), *International encyclopedia of the social sciences.* New York: Crowell Collier and Macmillan.

Wilson, G. D., & Patterson, J. R. (1968). A new measure of conservatism. *British Journal of Social and Clinical Psychology, 1,* 264–269.

Winter, D. G. (1973). *The power motive.* New York: Free Press.

Winter, D. G., John, O. P., Stewart, A. J., Klohnen, E. C., & Duncan, L. E. (1998). Traits and motives: Toward an integration of two traditions in personality research. *Psychological Review, 105,* 230–250.

Wright, R. A., Contrada, R. J., & Patane, M. J.(1986). Task difficulty, cardiovascular response, and the magnitude of goal valence. *Journal of Personality and Social Psychology, 51,* 837–843.

Wyer, R. S. (1974). *Cognitive organization and change: An information-processing approach.* Hillsdale, NJ: Erlbaum.

Wyer, R. S., & Goldberg, L. A. (1970). A probabilistic analysis of relationships between beliefs and attitudes. *Psychological Review, 77*, 100–120.

Zajonc, R. B. (1968). Cognitive theories in social psychology. In G. Lindzey & E. Aronson (Eds.), *The handbook of social psychology* (Vol. 1, pp. 320–411). Reading, MA: Addison-Wesley.

Zajonc, R. B. (1980). Feeling and thinking: Preferences need no inferences. *American Psychologist, 35*, 151–175.

Zajonc, R. B. (1998). Emotions. In D. T. Gilbert, S. T. Fiske, & G. Lindzey (Eds.), *The handbook of social psychology* (Vol. 1, pp. 591–634). New York: Oxford University Press.

Zwillenberg, D. F. (1983). Predicting biases in the punishment of criminals as a function of authoritarianism: The effects of severity of the crime, degree of mitigating circumstances, and status of the offender. Unpublished doctoral dissertation, Columbia University, University Microfilm No. 8311876.

Name Index

Subject Index